THE RETURN
OF THE
KING

The Intellectual Warfare Over Democratic Athens

Victorino Tejera

University Press of America,® Inc.
Lanham • New York • Oxford

Copyright © 1998 by
University Press of America,® Inc.
4720 Boston Way
Lanham, Maryland 20706

12 Hid's Copse Rd.
Cummor Hill, Oxford OX2 9JJ

Library of Congress Cataloging-in-Publication Data

Tejera, V. (Victorino)
The return of the king : the intellectual warfare over Democratic
Athens / Victorino Tejera.
p. cm.
Includes bibliographical references.
l. Democracy—Greece—Athens—History. 2. Plato—Views on
democracy. 3. Aristotle—Views on democracy. I. Title.
JC75.D36T45   1997   320.438'5—dc21   97—37555 CIP

ISBN 0-7618-0926-0 (cloth: alk. ppr.)
ISBN 0-7618-0927-9 (pbk: alk. ppr.)

Contents

Preface

It is a great irony of Western intellectual history that two inferior thinkers such as Speusippos of Athens (the pythagorizing idealist) and Demetrios of Phaleron (the grammarian and tyrannical governor of Macedonized Athens), were able—as the autocratic transmittors of Plato and Aristotle respectively—to impose their deliberate misrepresentations of the two greatest minds of the fourth century on their own generation and the posterity that followed. In the matter of the transmission of Aristotle, Demetrios was, of course, not more important than Theophrastos, together with whom he must have worked and whom he surely influenced deeply. Theophrastos was the botanist traditionally recognized as Aristotle's student and successor in the Lyceum. What such official recognition by 'the sources' is worth will emerge as we proceed with our study of the transmission of the texts to be taken up. But Demetrios has to be mentioned because the political practice of this member of the Lyceum was thoroughly oligarchal, and because it is probably his views that are behind the oligarchizing passages in the *Politics*. The success of the Academy and the Peripatos in refashioning the images of the two founders of the discipline of philosophy was a function of both their nature as schools and orthodoxies, and of the changes in the Athenian climate of opinion during the second half of the fourth century.

Here, still waiting to be properly understood *as dialogues* are the dialogues of the quick-witted, versatile Plato, an imposing figure according to the after-myths, who reaches his twenties in the intellectually brilliant, politically tragic last decade of the fifth century. He is steeped in the poetic lore of the culture (Homer, Hesiod, Pindar, Simonides), in the comic and adversarial compositions (Epicharmos, Sôphrôn, Aristophanes; Protagoras, Antiphon) of disputants and sociopolitical critics (Euripides and the semi-Socratics). He is aware of the antinomies about what-there-is propounded by Parmenides, and of Gorgias's echolalic counter to them; he is also aware of the cheapness of some of the Sophists (the *Euthydemus*) yet appreciative of their formidable (*deinos*) 'art of words' (*Sophistês, Politicus*). He is no doubt also well-read (or, better "well-versed") in both the poetic and the dogmatic "Presocratics" (as we call them, cf. the *Timaeus*). He is the first on record to use the terms 'philosophy' (*philosophia*) and 'philosophers' for the pursuit of knowledge and its seekers. And he is himself both verbally creative and anti–dogmatic, an admirer and exonerator of that authentic seeker and ethical disputant the historical Socrates (SocHp).

But he is presented to the public by Speusippos and the Academy as the author of a dogmatic system—suspiciously akin to views of the Pythagoreans—that (according to them and later idealists) is not fully consistent and in need of further development, *yet also* so brilliant and interesting as to earn for him the epithet of "divine," thus empowering him as a source of doctrine *no less credible than* the venerated Pythagoras. As any reader with literary sensibility will know, however, it is the beauty of the dialogues as *works-of-art in their* well-constructed wittily-tensioned *wholeness* that calls for their author to be apotheosized. Divinity cannot be attributed to not-fully-consistent doctrinal tractates that are not themselves a divine revelation. The compliment which this divinization pays to Plato's works is in fact a tacit revocation, in the assertive mode of unimplemented words, of their reduction, in the active mode of didactic practice, to the status of dogmatic tractates.

This Plato, puzzlingly, chose to present "his" doctrines in a form, the dialogue-form, from which they are difficult to extract with complete exactness (unless you already know what they are), in which they are never spoken by Plato himself, and in which they are surrounded by skeptical listeners: Thrasymachos in *Republic I*, Socrates in the *Sophistes* and *Politicus*. Or else, they are objected to by a disputant (*Protagoras*), or based on what is explicitly introduced as a myth, as is the doctrine of recollection in the *Meno*. Not only does Plato never speak in his own voice in the dialogues—a fact habitually overriden by such systematically misleading locutions as "Plato says" or "Plato believed that" or "according to Plato's theory of 'x';" it is also not at all clear that any speaker in the dialogues is his spokesman. If Socrates is not Plato's spokesman when he defends and praises the poets in the *Meno*, then why is he believed so literally when he banishes them in *Republic*? Why is a rhetorical Sophist from distant Elea, who both imitates and disparages Plato's Socrates, taken to be Plato's spokesman when Socrates is himself listening to his discourses with skeptical ears? Nor can *Timaeus* be taken to be Plato's spokesman in an oration which is explicitly admitted to be only "a likely story" (*ton eikota mython*, 29d2), but which is also listened to with polite and happy acceptance (29d4–6) by the Socrates who is to be poetically entertained by it in the fiction of the dialogue?

And if you are Aristotle, the Aristotle *who wrote dialogues* and authored a treatise on *literary forms* called the *Poetics*, and in your lecture notes you are treating some tenets of, or variants in, the dogmatic system of idealism about which there is (said to be) a course of lectures by Plato, why refer to his dialogues at all? And if it is the system that is in reference, how come *only* those doctrines are mentioned that happen to be echoed by speakers in the dialogues? Moreover, the fact that a few of the citations are not locatable in the dialogues at all would seem to show that they are quoted from notes of lectures *about* platonism as a doctrinal system—whether that system was put together by Speusippus or Xenocrates, orally expounded by Plato himself—the *ungeschriebene Lehre* thesis—or derived from a posthumous de-dramatization of Plato's dialogues. For it is in these cases that no need arises to cite any dialogue at all. Again if, as is likely, lectures were being given on platonism in the Academy, then why is there a refusal to mention as such *other* lecturers than Plato? Because—obviously—that would have identified platonism as the *Academic* production, which it is, rather than the invention of Plato's, which it is not.

Someone who is himself a composer of dialogues, would not have referred to the dialogues of the thinker from whom he is learning, in the simplistic *anti-dialogical* locutions that the Aristotelian corpus uses. This is why we will need to consider the possibility that, like the cross-references within the corpus, so-called Aristotelian allusions to "Plato" are mostly the work of the editors and transmitters of the corpus, given that they are so systematic, and that there are some cross-references to (what we think of as) later works in earlier works. Thus also, and for example, it has to be the editor of *Politics Book II* who, in alluding to the *Republic* doesn't know that Socrates is *not* a speaker in the *Laws*, or that the *Republic* is not, as we have it, "*mostly* a collection of statutes" (1265a2). In fact, all the references to "Plato" in the Aristotelian corpus consistently de-dramatize the dialogues.

The theory of ideas, as it is called and as if there were only one version of it, is not the inclusive matrix out of which the dialogues arose. It is, rather, something which, like the views and practices of the Sophists or the theory of one-man rule, Plato puts to dramatic use *within* the dialogues. In the *Republic*, for instance, the theory of ideas is knowingly rehearsed and put under observation for the reader by Plato's Socrates. But so also are militarism and élitism, as well as what we may call the Pythagorean curriculum all rehearsed, improved upon, and satirized with equal virtuosity and brought into exhibition for the scrutiny of the reader in the spirit of Plato's expressive needs and independent nature. Like the constitutional cycles of the city-state in *Republic* VIII or the practice of a rhapsode in the *Ion*, the theory of ideas is simply an important part of the thematic materials *to which* Plato applies his formative talents, both literary and conceptual. As I say in "The Hellenistic Obliteration of Plato's Dialogism,"

> The minimum of necessary collateral information required to understand an Athenian author should not be limited, as the dogmatists limit it in the case of Plato, to only what the pythagorizing Academy wanted to say about him in appropriating him to their own uses—especially where the information seems historically questionable, self-serving or *ex post facto*. The inclusive context should rather be, as with any author, all the socio-intellectual conditions and antecedents under which Plato's dialogues were produced [and to which they were a response].

If, furthermore, we consider the insurmountable objections that are raised in the *Parmenides* to the theory of ideas in conjunction with the (literary or compositional) fact that that dialogue must be taken as *first in the dramatic order* of recitation because it is the one in which Socrates is at his youngest, the probability imposes itself that one reason for its composition was to remind Plato's readers to always thereafter take the theory of ideas as something played with, or ironically alluded to, by Socrates in the dramatically subsequent dialogues.

Here also is the tampered-with, much-handled and long-unguarded *Nachlass* of Aristotle, with the evidence upon it of its hazardous history, and buried under layers of interpretations with disparate interests. While we cannot help approaching it with our own interests, we should not let the unphilosophical habit of wanting unambiguous doctrine and only doctrine (the doxographic fallacy) from a text, interfere with the effort to understand Aristotle's works in Aristotle's original terms so far as they can be recovered. These were Greek humanist and nature-inquirer's terms. They were also the terms of a didactic master who included rhetoric and poetics, as well as analytics, enthymeme and induction in the organon designed to equip knowledge-seekers for their reflective work. Neither should we expect his diversified investigations to satisfy the positivist demand for deductive consistency (the unity-of-science fallacy). This point must be mentioned because it coincides with the effort of late Antiquity to make Aristotle's findings compatible with, and deducible from, the Neoplatonist's One; in this, platonism and positivism are, in fact, "one."

This book, then, is a historiographic and interrogative reading of Plato and Aristotle that abstracts as much as the evidence allows from the "platonizing" and oligarchist patina of interpretations that discolor our understanding of them as intelligent thinkers. Perception of the very identity or shape of our texts has been distorted in the process—literarily as well as philosophically and philologically. Because this work is an interrogative presentation of alternatives to current readings of Plato and Aristotle, the suggestions advanced in it should not be taken as polemical but as hypothetical and corrigible.

The book has also tried to work with a conception of reflective activity that takes imagination and affectivity to be operative dimensions of rational practice as well as components ingredient in the human products that we as readers, auditors or viewers find ourselves responding to. If the alternative way of reading Plato and Aristotle suggested here is semiotically sound and historiographically valid, it should help unloose the Gordian-knot of philosophy's ties to the post-classical, anti-literary and anti-democratic schools that have interposed themselves between it and the original founders who practiced it as a discipline that is at once inventive and open-ended, analytic and co–ordinative, self-reflective and synoptic, in its scrutiny and explanation of whatever is of interest or problematic.

In a word, a satisfactory account of the period and texts covered by this book requires scholarship that is in good control not just of the philosophies, but also of the social history, the political or ideological motivations, and the historiographic gaps and omissions that have brought these works to the "interpretational" condition— the state of not-complete intelligibility—in which they now exist. It is hoped that the contextualizing combination of approaches taken by the book will serve to increase the intelligibility and enjoyability of Plato's dialogues, as well as serve to absolve Aristotle from the weaknesses and inconsistencies of his transmitters. It is also hoped that the response to it will be more dialogical than to previous works in which the advantages of the dialogical approach to Plato were also demonstrated.

Because the evidence upon which my findings depend is contextual, textual, and textural, and because these findings call for *a shift in the paradigm* according to which we are to read Plato's dialogues, a continuous prose discourse on the subject–matter of this book is not the form that would produce most conviction, at this point in the study of ancient Greek intellectual history. And I advert early to the matter of *form* because it is a working assumption of the investigation that Plato and Aristotle were themselves form-conscious thinkers, contrary to the belief—reflected in the practice of their modern readers that they were as oblivious to the form of what they wrote as their literalist (and platonist) readers have always been.

As thinkers, Plato and Aristotle were both of them non-alienated and dialogical in their different ways. The cultural matrix out of which their work arose, as a review of it will show, was itself commuitarian and interactional, namely, non-alienated and dialogical in the sense of *not* suppressive of one's other. That fifth–

and fourth-century Athenian polis-dwellers were form-conscious also, is evident from the attention they gave to drama, poetic song and recitals, to antilogistic rhetoric and refutationism, to comedy, drmatic sketches and satire. For these reasons the inquiry grew into a set of chapters related to each other by the common themes and aims purused in connection with the dialogues and treatises selected as the field of specific demonstration or instantiation of the overall themes and aims.

The aim, in fact, has been to get us to read Plato's dialogues non–doxographically and, therefore, as the literary master that he enjoyably is; and to read the Aristotelian corpus with a much greater awareness of its extremely unguarded beginnings and derivation, as well as of its interpolated, written-over, Peripatetic or post-Aristotelian nature.

The themes are the anti-oligarchic but timocratic character of the Athenian democracy, the high rational level of discourse in the Athenian public sphere, the pythagorization of the culture during the second half of the fourth century, with its conseuqent contamination of the sources by which we know it, the neglected literary abilities and perceptivity of Plato and Aristotle as factors *no less constitutive* of their work and greatness than their purely conceptual or "philosophic" sagacity. As this all–important point is made most explicitly in Chapter VI (after the requisite demonstration of the case), I venture to suggest that this chapter be read right after the ideo-historical Introduction. An earned conclusion can sometimes be the best gateway to an investigation that must begin *in medias res.*

1

Introduction

On the Intellectual History of Democratic Athens

The Pythagorean component of Greek intellectual activity is not a neglected aspect of Classical or post-Classical Greek thought. What is missing in connection with it, what we have not done explicitly enough, is to monitor its systematic denaturing of the extant sources of information about Classical antiquity and its ideological effect upon the literary and historical texts and their transmission. Nor are our reports of this activity yet free, either of anachronism or of the bias which the tainted sources themselves have created. As a historian Guthrie, for example, should not be so certain that what Pythagoras "inaugurated" was "a new tradition in philosophy," rather than a cultic mode of intellectual being and survival based on both a regulated rule of life and mathematico-numerological researches.[1] It is historiographically more accurate to say, rather, that Pythagoras inaugurated a new tradition of dogmatizing and research which sought to be identified with the whole of 'philosophy,' and came, some time in the fourth century, to be taken as such by large sectors of the climate of opinion. This at once changed 'philosophy' from being an open-ended search for intelligibility and explanation into the defense of developing or competing orthodoxies.

G.C. Field does draw attention, as I do in Chapters 4 and 5 below, to the totally school-centered and predatory nature of Pythagorean graphic activity from the fourth century on (PHC Ch. XIII). As W. Burkert says, in regretting that the principle of depending on a thinker's own words cannot be applied to Pythagoras and the Pythagoreans,

> whether an item of the tradition may be regarded as an authentic pronouncement of a Pythagorean must . . . be decided first on the basis of indirect testimony. For the mass of writing that was forged and attributed to Pythagoras and his pupils was so vast that, contrary to ordinary methodological principles, in the case of any text purportedly composed by an early Pythagorean, the burden of proof lies with anyone who wishes to maintain its authenticity. . . . In any case we are talking about writings which, in an unhistorical manner, attribute to Pythagoras and his school material from . . . Plato, Aristotle, and the Stoa, as well as popular philosophical thought (LSAP 218).

We will return to the problem of Pythagorean ideology and its influence as our inquiry proceeds. For the moment we need to note the historical coincidence according to which Pythagoreanism starts gaining public acceptance for itself at just about the time when communication in the culture of Athens and Greece was ceasing to be oral-aural and becoming visual-graphic enough for the culture to be called (in the technical terminology) fully literate rather than semi-literate, namely, unable to do without writing, having to depend on it for almost all communicative purposes. The coincidence suggests that it may have been the resort to writing that earned for the Pythagoreans the acceptance they came to have in the fourth century and after. It looks as if, by their sheer quantity, they pre-empted the non-poetic, less oral-aural fields of reflection in which prose and graphics would now have more scope.

Because of the non-literate, non-documented obscurity of the sixth to fifth centuries, and conveniently for its myth-making purposes, the first hundred years of the school are not recoverable. This is the period of transition from archaic to classical culture, and extends to the times of Philolaus and Archytas at the turn into the fourth century when Plato was in his late twenties. Athens had inherited the leadership of the Greek world in both economic development and culture as a result of its role in the defeat of the Persian empire in the 480's and 470's. The Acropolis, a fortress at the time of the Persian invasion, had been rebuilt by Perikles as the abode of Athena and the center of international power which Athens had now become. Both sides of the Sacred Way which divided the Acropolis, says Rostovtzeff, "were lined by a forest of votive offerings . . . and by the archives of the Athenian democracy—the most important decrees of the popular assembly engraved on stone" (HAW I. p.283).

But just because it was a democracy the wealthy, in this hegemonic city, were careful not to make themselves conspicuous with immoderate displays or palatial homes. An ominous exception to this rule was Perikles' ward Alkibiades, who publicly broke with such discretion by adorning the walls of his house with paintings (HAW 287). Is this exception the symptom of a decline-to-come in the fourth century of the non-polarizing good citizenship of the propertied classifications? The male citizens in any case, and as we know, spent little time at home. They met in the Agora or marketplace, or the Pnyx where the Assembly was held, at the Bouleterion or council-chambers and the law-courts. The lesser economic strata labored in their workshops or the docks and warehouses in the Piraeus. All classifications gave time to bodily exercise, and all young Athenians were taught their Homer and Hesiod along with music and, by the end of the century, how to calculate and at least to read, though not also to write with facility.[2]

The unenfranchised population-groups of resident aliens ('metics') and slaves grew greatly from 500–400 B.C. Because the citizens were too busy with public affairs and the defense of the *polis* to give time to trade or manufacture, the metics became dominant in commerce, banking and shipping. But they were not a class apart; "in society," says Rostovtzeff, "no distinction was made between an alien and a citizen" (p.289). About the slave-population, the oligarchist tract *The Constitution* of *the Athenians* complains that they are not distinguishable from the metics and citizens in the way they dress (CA I.11f.). The demes of the Attic country-side were more conservative, mindful of the past and still the majority; but, says Rostovtzeff, "they were devoted . . . to their country and came in their thousands, when they were needed, to the popular assembly" (HAW 291). The primacy of an Athenian citizen's duty to his community or polis was a matter of course, not felt to be oppressive. The moderate classical polis was, as the Aristotelian *Politics* will say, a dominant institution; but it was not dominationist in the modern sense, and did not becomes so until the introduction by the Macedonian conquest of a *heteronomous* sovereignty over it.

A natural accompaniment of democracy, in Athens at least, was freedom of thought and expression. By the middle of the century Athens rather than Ionia had become the focal point of intellectual activity in Greece. The greatest achievement of the Athenians, in the 160 years that go from Salamis to the death of Arisotle, was without a doubt the invention and development of Tragic drama by Aeschylus, Sophocles, and Euripides. This great art, astonishingly, was a *collective* possession of the polis-as-a-whole and not only gave *civic* secular form to religious dianoia but also, in raising the level of public self-reflection, became a favoring condition of the high rationality pervading both the documentary impulse of Thucydides' history and the critical impetus of Plato's dramatizations of the disputatious intellectual life of Athens. But we should not fail to note the effect of Greek drama upon *the level of rationality* available to discourse *in the public sphere*. There was of course a reciprocal causal relationship between drama (Aristophanes' comedies included) and the coeval changes from oral-aural to visual-graphic culture and from myth-sanctioned tribal morality to an explicitly reflective ethics trying to base itself on reason.

Noteworthy too was the development which Herodotus, the orators and the logographers, from Lysias and Isokrates to Demosthenes, gave to the art of words.[3] The 'antilogistic' turn within this larger movement which Protagoras (and his *dissoì lógoi*) and Antiphon (with his tetralogies) gave to the technique of disputation must not be overlooked because, combined with Epicharmos's and Sophron's art of the dramatic sketch, they became (structurally speaking) aesthetic ingredients of Plato's dialogue-form. The teaching of the art of words and disputation, as well as the knowing use-and-abuse of the art of speech-making, was the business of the Sophists and an important component of the public discourse within which Athenian public life was lived. So lively was the intellectual side of Athenian activity at the turn of the fifth into the fourth century, that torpidity becomes hard to find, and there is no countenancing of the practice of unqualified categorical assertion or dogmatism. Dogmatism would have been too easy to silence with Aristophanic wit or to refute with Zenonian dialectic or Socratic and semi-Socratic rationality.

With the increasing public acceptance of Pythagoreanism in the fourth century, however, all this was about to change. Now, it is the case that the prevalent cast of mind in Athens, civic and Tragic as it was, can be identified with Aristotle's humanism because of his expressions of it in the *Poetics* and *Ethics*, and because of the kind of genetic naturalism to be found in (for example) Book I of the *Politics*. This kind of humanism, at its best, transcends both élitist and levelling mentalities, for the reason that it is engendered by or is an implicit accompaniment of the experience of great art. It lives within what I call "a perspective of humanity" (MGT Ch. 3); it implicitly reaches out, beyond partisanship and ethnicity, to the party of humanity and the tragic core of human existence. This humanist mentality and the climate of opinion that made it possible were not, however, going to survive the social changes caused by endemic inter-city warfare, the violence of faction, the numerical diminution of the citizen-class in Athens,[4] and the rise of Philip of Macedon.

The public became unable to tolerate the enthusiastic practice of systematic interrogation, and was losing its taste for irony and refutationism. As communication became more graphic or visual, the need to give perceptible oral-aural form to expression also abated, as did the corresponding ability to perceive it. Individualism which, within the communitarian polis, had been competitive *but dialogical* begins to be alienated and monologous, *suppressive of one's other*. As the individual's responsiveness, his *thumos* becomes more defensive his allegiance to the city which nurtured him begins to cede its primacy to personal attachments and his circle of friends (as in the practice of oligarchism). As people became less community-centered, they wanted more answers not more questions. And, interestingly enough, eschatological or utopian answers got better hearings than the type of social-or natural-science answer to be found in the original Aristotle—the last of the Greek philosophers to be a knowledge-seeker rather than the *defender of an orthodoxy*.

Just such defenders, by mid-fourth century, were the Academic developers of the dogmatizing system of idealism which they seemed to have worked out in interaction and symbiosis with the Pythagoreans, now numerous in Athens and well-organized—even if they were also covered-up in their highest councils and principles of organization. This not-inimical relationship, as I point out in Chapter 4, was of the greatest benefit to the ideological interests of both parties although, unfortunately, not to philosophy as the critical search for, and comment upon, knowledge which it ought to be. In the precarious new times, charismatic revelations and pronouncements were more authoritative than knowledge-seeking observation or critical, non-ideological group-discussion.

But it is just group-discussion *as indoctrination*—as persuasive communicative interaction producing socially reinforced conviction—that Plato's Socrates finds it necessary to mention ironically in the *Republic* after his virtuoso diagrammatization, on the Divided Line, of the theory of ideas. And this was because in a climate of opinion that demanded and needed *certainty*, the Pythagoreans had to offer unconditional, or absolute, starting-points for reasoning, if they were to succeed with the public and themselves be a cohesive belief-community. And this is the socio-cultural meaning of what Socrates calls "the power of the dialectic" (*tou dialegesthai*) at *Republic* 533a7. Here, we must note, that all the later explanations of the nature of "dialectic" have been of its important derivative or subsequently developed meanings. Originally *dialegesthai* just meant "to dialogue or be in dialogue with," "to speak (*legein*) with or among (*dia*) others." I must therefore digress to explain both the form which Plato's Socrates gives to the idea of the absolute Good (whatever the way it might first have been proposed), and how he comes presciently (but not refutatively) to allude to the weakness in the postulation. The unemphasized weakness is that the starting-points of reasoning, in the Academy and among the Pythagoreans, were reached by group-induced acceptance of the sect's assumptions.

The theory of ideas, as rehearsed in the *Republic* desiderates an Absolute Good as the unconditional starting-point for knowledge, and gets to it as an extrapolation from the top end of the Divided Line in terms *that are themselves conditional*, as follows. Socrates had categorized the special knowledges or sciences as being all of them conditional, at 5110b5–511e. But in his exhibitive rehearsal of the theory of ideas he suggests that there is "a portion of the intelligible . . . which reasoning itself grasps by the power of dialectics, treating its hypotheses . . . as springboards to enable it to rise to that which requires no assumption and is the starting-point of all" (511 bff.).

This is Socrates's ironic answer to those who complain that the special sciences have starting-points that don't feel like terminuses to the inquirer. He is suggesting here (and at 532a) that *if* there is a knowledge that transcends the hypothetical nature of the special sciences, and it is achievable by the pure reasoning (*dia tou logou . . . aneu pasôn tôn aisthêseôn*) of a well-trained man with synoptic power, and it relates all the ideas of the arts-and-sciences to the idea of the good as their first principle, *then* it will provide a secure anchoring for the special knowledges and a terminal for the knowledge-seeker.

In avoiding *arbitrary* starting-points, and as the completion of the dialectic, it *would be* the goal of intelligence. We note that the demand for the unconditional arises within an unavoidably conditional situation. I am not just paraphrasing or interpreting as wistful the spirit in which Socrates speaks here; *outô kai hotan . . . epicheirê . . . dia logou ep'auto . . . kai mê apostêi, prin an ho estin agathon . . .* is conditional and entirely subjunctive: "In this way *whenever*-and-*if* someone by dialectic were to try, through pure reasoning apart from all sense-perception, to get to what each thing is in itself, and *were* not to give up *until* he *were* to grasp what the good in itself is, he [would] come to the end [and/or goal] of the intelligible."[5]

Besides relocating and recontextualiizing the search for knowledge within *a belief-community* whose basic premises were motivated by interests that were other than investigative, the Pythagoreans and their Academic emulators appear as encouraging the use of deduction (on the model of geometry) as an effective *persuasive* device, and as a mode of reasoning producing greater *certainty* than any other. And this sat only too well with an intellectual public tired of sophistry, at a time when there was too much else to be anxious about for it to be able to tolerate the anxiety of working from, or living on the basis of, revisable or uncertain premisses.

The cult of the charismatic Pythagoras, moreover, reinforced the popular tendency to prefer oracular revelations and pronouncements over the conditional hypotheses of the special knowledges. And it was from the alleged pronouncements of the mythified Pythagoras that the sect got *its most basic* premises; so that it becomes the unscientific habit of this would-be scientific school to derive the special knowledges deductively from first principles laid down by the Pythagorean cosmogonists and theologians. The special sciences will thus not have, as in Aristotle and the sciences later, their own distinct starting-points nor will their beginnings depend upon the specialized focus on their subject-matter that good induction and abstractive observation require. And this bad habit actually intrudes into the Peripatetic school after Aristotle's death, as we can see from the fragment on Metaphysics by the pseudo-Theophrastos. As far as the Academy is concerned we will see that, while it had to set up its image of a divinized Plato as *an authority* competitive with Pythagoras, this Plato—the Plato of Academic platonism—was not really inimical to the doctrines supposedly fathered by Pythagoras.

From early on Pythagorean doctrine associated geometrical figures and numbers both with the gods and the physical universe, according to a mention in the fragments of Eudoxus (early IV c. B.C.) and according to Neoplatonist reports about Philolaus (V c. B.C.).[6] For the early Pythagorean Alkmaeon, the soul is immortal because, like the stars which are immortal, it is in a state of eternal motion (LSAP 296). It is beliefs of this sort that favored the rise of astrology, the method of which is to start from unexamined assumptions about the stars, and then perform some instantiating *deductions* to reach conclusions about earthly events—care being taken to generalize the wording of conclusions enough to make them both defensibly vague and applicable to the client's self. In popular belief this of course overrode the clear implication in Aristotle that no legitimate inference is possible from the unchanging, *unconditional* laws of the eternal motion of the stars to events on earth, because these are all conditioned, so that generalizations about them must be hypothetical.

Returning to the political climate of the times, it is well to remember that if there were any *Athenian* Pythagoreans before the later decades of the fourth century, they would have been converts to the sect who, as such, must have been in sympathy with Pythagorean political views as well as desirous of the 'knowledge' they would get by initiation into this *foreign* sect. "*The Pythagoristai*," as de Vogel says, "make [an] appearance in Attic literature, which points to an invasion of Pythagoreans. . . . (shortly after 390)," 388 B.C. being the date of the conquest of southern Italy by Dionyisus I, the event which is believed to have precipitated the exodus. And these views, as we know, were dynasticist and pro-oligarchal. The contrast with the entrenched democratic, majority-view is so great that we have to conclude that the acceptance which Pythagoreanism came to have in the second half of the fourth century is intimately dependent upon changes that were taking hold in the political climate of opinion in Athens by mid-century.

These had to be changes that favored oligarchist minority views, until such views were swept into ascendancy by Philip's victory at Chaeronea in 338 B.C. But that this ascendancy did not wait until then to begin is shown, among other things and as I argue, by the successful imposition in the Academy of the literalist, monarchical-intellectualist interpretation of Plato's satirico-ironical *Republic*, an imposition which comes into the larger world in the decade-and-a-half between Aristotle's departure from the Academy (around the time of Plato's death in 348/7) and the aftermath of Philip's victory over the combined city-states of classical Greece.[7] And this interpretation becomes the orthodoxy of the Academy at the same time as the triumph within it of Speusippos's pythagorizing, counter-dialogical system of idealism. But in the fifty years between 380 and 330 it was not only Pythagoreanism that had its effects.

As J.K. Davies points out, the greater use of mercenaries and cavalry, and new relations with foreign *monarchs* were affecting the political and military scene. The formation of the Aetolian League in 367 re-signals the standing need or wish to federate among republics. The increased urge to participate politically is made visible by the appearance in *previously oligarchic* states of "primary decision-taking assemblies" (DCG 154). In a prize-speech of the '80's Lysias "sees Greece in so shameful a state, with much of her subject to the barbarian and many cities up-ended by tyrants" (xxxiii.3), referring to Persia and Dionysius I, while Isokrates, deploring the excesses of faction and revolution, also blames the hegemonic militarism of Sparta.

So far are cities from 'freedom' and 'autonomy' that some are under tyrants, others under Spartan governors, others are in ruins, others are under barbarian masters (iv.115–117).

We find Xenophon complaining, at the end of the *Hellenica* (VII.v.27) that, after the battle of Mantinea in 362 B.C.

> Each side claimed the victory, but neither appeared to have gained any advantage in land, city, or power than before the battle. There was even more confusion and chaos in Greece after the battle than before it.

Most interestingly, however, Greek technical and intellectual creativity continues unabated, but in different forms, into the first eighty years of the fourth century. Isokrates' school, Speusippos's Academy, Aristotle's Lyceum, the rise of Stoicism, Epicureanism and Pythagoreanism all reflect the increased interest in formal education. But the co-occurrence of these movements did create what C.J. de Vogel calls "the inextricable [intellectual] forest of the second half of the fourth century where Academic and Peripatetic concepts are inseparably mingled with Pythagoreanism" (p.14 PEP). Another symptom of the interest in education was the multiplication of instructional handbooks on the many arts and skills needed by citizens.

Though the historical work of most writers on the period has been lost, we have to note that this was when the new genre of Universal History was created by Ephoros.[8] Theopompos, on the other hand, created the kind of history that centers itself on the lives of forceful leaders, such as Dionysius and Philip. Capping this ferment, as Davies notes (DCG 153), "was the superhuman achievement of Aristotle in redefining an intellectual and moral world and in systematizing human knowledge in virtually every field." We must not forget however, and as we will see, that the organization of Aristotle's encyclopedic researches and output was in great part the work of Theophrastos, the Peripatetics and, later, of Andronikos of Rhodes his first-century editor. For this work of transmission was the opening by means of which non-Aristotelic reasonings and claims found their way into the collection of Aristotelian treatises.

While the democratic climate of opinion in Athens must have felt challenged by these new inputs, it does not seem to have weakened among Athenians themselves. It is rather (as later chapters will show) the pythagorist overwriting or destruction of sources, and the (also foreign) Peripatetic interpolations into Aristotle's lecture notes, along with the newly-enforced dorianizing (literalist and militarist) interpretation of Plato's dialogues, that have combined to give posterity the false impression that Plato and Aristotle, the two greatest intelligences of Athens in the century and its keenest observers and inquirers, were as oligarchist or as influenced by Pythagoreanism as Xenophon or the pythagorizers could have wished them to be, and as dull or uncritical as historians and commentators *who don't criticize the sources* claim them to be. A component or reinforcement of this falsification would of course have been the envy that blamed the Athenian democracy for the imperialism of Athens in politics, and for its innovativeness in the arts.

The tradition of Athenian democracy began, as we know, with the implementation of Solon's conception of *the state as mediator*. And this conception turns out, in historical retrospect, to be continuous with Aristotle's conception of the best practicable state as the balanced state: the state which balances the interests of the middle classes with those of the poor and the wealthy. This is the most stable state for Aristotle; it is not the Ideal State, a purely theoretical entity which, given Aristotle's definition of politics and *politikê* as a practical art-and-science, would *not* have gotten *from him* the insistent and extended, nay, the key strategic consideration that it gets from the Peripatetic users of (and adders to) Aristotle's lecture notes. The case for this conclusion is made in Chapter 4.

The other reason why the original Aristotle himself would not have appealed to the Ideal State is that to do so would have instantly identified him as an oligarchal *extremist*, which he was not, and thus nullified the quality and equanimity of the analyses and examples in his lectures. The Ideal State as I show, both in this book and elsewhere,[9] was a rhetorical device of the oligarchal interests in Athens that enabled them *to appeal*, with a semblance of rationality, *away from* the otherwise unassailable, entrenched Ancestral Constitution. The latter could only be reformed, not replaced as the Old Oligarch so-called regretfully notes (CA III.9).

One reform of the Athenian constitution that is not contemporaneous with the hypothetical dates of composition of an original *Politics* is that instituted by Antipater when he defeated the anti-Macedonian rebellion of 322 B.C.[10] He restricted the franchise to owners of 20 minae, who turned out to number 9000; this disenfranchised the remaining 22,000 citizens. Thus was implemented the oligarchic constitution which marked the end of even the nominal autonomy or internal democracy allowed to Athens since Chaeronea. The ensuing installation of a Macedonian-appointed governor over the Peloponnese completed this ending to the quasi-millenial freedom of the Greeks originally dominant in this part of the world.[11] But that both Philip and Alexander had envisaged what was to be a lasting combination of Greek city-states with Macedon as *hegemon*, is evidence of the strength of the institutions of self-governance which these states had devised for themselves.

One reason for the durability of the Athenian constitution was its inclusiveness. We find that the counter-revolutions of 411, 404, and 322 were engineered by small cliques of extremists and then overwhelmed by the citizenry-as-a-whole. For, it wasn't only the disadvantaged who were democrats. The notable statesmen and generals mostly came from wealthy families, many were aristocrats by birth; and the leaders of the majorities that threw out the oligarchic extremists were also well-to-do. We should therefore not neglect the good citizenship of the propertied classes which negates the picture of a polarized city-state that one is liable to get from the oligarchist sources. It also neglects the effects that rational—not only demagogic—persuasion may have had in the Assembly. To think of rhetoric as *only* a dangerous over-used instrument, as Hansen does in his book on Athenian democracy,[12] scants the level of rationality available to discourse in a public sphere that, in the mid-fourth century, could not yet have completely forgotten its Aeschylus and Sophocles, its Euripides, Aristophanes, its orators, antilogizers and semi-Socratics. It also side-steps the practical or moderate democratism of the élite in a tradition that goes from the charismatic Perikles and the impartial Thucydides to the majority of the propertied classifications that supported the Athenian democracy down to 322 B.C.

Naturally enough, convinced oligarchists were not going to desist from criticizing Athenian democracy, or from trying to subvert it because of anything the Old Oligarch may have said in his time. The trouble is that these criticisms are over-represented in the surviving literature and that, as A.H.M. Jones points out, while the contemporary, satisfied majority were mute (AD Ch.III), "our most valuable evidence comes from the criticisms of adversaries, which are . . . more fully reported than anything from the democratic side." So, for contemporary expressions of the basic ideals of democracy, he points out that we have to go to the panegyrics of public speakers on Athens: Perikles' Funeral Speech in Thucydides, an early fourth century Funeral Speech attributed to Lysias, the political principles appealed to in passing by other orators (who in IV c. Athens were mostly democrats), including some of the other political speeches in Thucydides' history, and the skit on a funeral speech in the *Menexenus*.[13]

Chapter 6, line 13 of *The Athenian Constitution* does say, with regard to Solon's administration "nevertheless the popular account is more trustworthy." Chapter xviii, line 30 also appeals to what "the populists (*dêmotikoi*) say," while Kleisthenes is introduced into the story as he promises the *dêmos* to *return* (*apododous*) *the polity* to the majority (*plêthei*). He doesn't promise "to turn or hand over" as careless or Tory translators say, but "to return" the government (*tên politeian*) to the *dêmos*, the "people" or majority in the constitutional

sense (not "the multitude" in some deprecatory sense). The translators notwithstanding, these and succeeding paragraphs speak sym-
pathetically of anyone—Kêdon or the Alkmaôinids—who opposed
the tyranny. And this is of a piece with the text's qualified praise of
Peisistratos's moderation in not being above the law, and as financ-
ing with loans the productivity of the disadvantaged (ch.xvi).

At Chapter xxvii.par.4 *The Athenian Constitution* quotes
Damonides' populist advice to Perikles ("to give the majority what
was theirs") without comment, but does mention *as critics* those
who claimed that payment for jury duty made the people worse.
Chapter xxviii (and passim) uses the locution "x was the leader of
the dêmos" while "y was the leader of the *others*" thus taking, it
would seem, the point of view of the people. The text, on the other
hand, is clearly hostile to Kleon for his demagoguery, and implicitly critical of the succeeding demagogues who were crowd-pleasers
and attended only to short-term advantages. It speaks of
Theramenes as controversial, but of Nikias and Thucydides as *kalos
k'agathos* (honorable gentlemen) without irony, where both
Thucydides the historian and Plato's Socrates use the term with
marked irony.[14]

CA knows that the proposed oligarchic "polity of Five Thousand"
was only a verbal device (*logôn monon êresthai*) of the counter-revo-
lutionists of 412/411, and it rightly describes their four-month government as *autocratic*. So, the comment (if it is by Aristotle) at
Ch.xxxii.2 that "It seems that during these crisis-times the administration of affairs (*politeuthênai*) went well (*kalôs*), the war both
going on and the men-under-arms governing (*ek tôn hoplôn tês
politeias ousês*)," is not offering praise to the Four Hundred, but rather
only to the fighting-men who resisted them and noting the luck of
Athens in the matter. As the next sentence says, "From them, indeed, the dêmos quickly took the government;" the antecedent of
"them" is still the Four Hundred in "*its* dissolution" (*tên tôn
tetrakosiôn katálusin*) as referred to in the next clause, not the resis-
tant seamen and hoplites.

The text then praises the Athenian people for their restraint in this case (xl), and goes on to say that "the dêmos, having become sovereign (*kyrios*)" and "having accomplished this return by itself, the dêmos showed itself just in its rule (*archontos dokountos de dikaiôs*)" (xli). This is followed by a summary history of eleven constitutional reforms, ending with the constitution which capped the success of the democratic revolution against the Thirty oligarchs. And this is where the text makes the remark that "a few (*oligoi*) are more easily corrupted by gain and influence than the many." What we have of CA then goes into its detailed description of "the existing constitution:" the offices, courts, and procedures of the city-state of Athens down to Aristotle's own time. The almost complete treatise can be dated to the years between 328 and 325 B.C. because the latest event mentioned in it is the archonship of Ktephisophon, 329 B.C., and because it assumes that envoys are being sent to Samos (lxii), a pratice which ceased in 322 B.C.

The historiographic point needs remarking, finally, that English or nineteenth-century editors and commentators call the constitution of the democracy which was restored in 403 B.C. and under which Aristotle lived, an "extreme democracy" (e.g. Sandys, ACA p.lxvi); but Aristotle himself does not. He, on the contrary, seems quite comfortable with what is "ancestral" (*patrios*) which he identifies with the present constitution and its genesis (ACA xxxiv.lines 18, 22). At xxix.17 he calls the laws with which Kleisthenes established the *democratic* constitution "ancestral laws;" and he does not fault the habit of falling back on ancestral practices in times of crisis, in places where he might have (such as at ACA xxi or xxxix). The tradition of English-language commentaries on Aristotle seems, in fact, to suffer from a Tory bias which disturbs the perceptions even of scholars of the democracy, such as A.H.M. Jones. But it is clear in any case that the text of CA is less in conflict with itself, and has not suffered from ideological interpolations to the degree that the Aristotelian *Politics* has; so that, in so far as it reflects Aristotle's attitude, it is more to be trusted than the latter work.

Given the date of CA, this also means that Aristotle's attitude as an *observer* of the democratic constitution remained *positive* until the end of his life. In this he will, thus, have been indistinguishable from the many educated and advantaged Athenians of his time. But he was also, most probably, discretely at variance with the *politically* élitist, spartanizing or macedonizing members of the Academy who had taken it over, redefined or founded it about the time of Plato's death, even though—or because—along with Plato himself, he was the superior intellect among them. When we come to the much-handled, unguarded Aristotelian treatises handed down to us by Theophrastos and the Peripatos, then, we must be ready to account for, or justify, non-equanimous, non-positive attitudes to the Athenian polity which are out of character with what we have found in Aristotle's "Constitution of Athens." In fact, and as we will see in the relevant chapters of this book, in so far as the difficult-to-date Aristotelian *Politics* reflects a contemporary climate of opinion, what it echoes are non-Athenian Hellenistic, or pythagorizing views not found in the "Constitution of Athens."

Notes

1. W.K.C. Guthrie *A History of Greek Philosophy I* (Cambridge U.P. 1962); Chapters IV and V. The historiographic hazard or anomaly in this book is that it wants "to understand as far as possible the spirit and doctrinal basis of [the Pythagorean] outlook" (p.146), an outlook which took its rise in the sixth century and was ignored in the fifth, on the basis of documents all of which—with a very few disputed exceptions—date from after the turn of the fourth century, so that it fails to disentangle neo-Pythgorean or Neo-Platonist doctrines from the undocumentable beliefs of the sect in the sixth to fifth centuries.

2. At *Protagoras* 326c–e, the Sophist uses the learning of writing and its

correction by the writing-master as a simile for the guidance and correction provided by good laws. This dialogue was composed in the early fourth century, but its dramatic date is around 430 just before the outbreak of the Peloponnesian war. See *Communication Arts in the Ancient World* Havelock & Hershbell (N.Y. Hastings House 1978); p.64–68). The possibility of anachronism—of referring to something familiar to the author but not familiar to the historical person behind his dramatic character—opens up a margin of error of forty-years or so. The *Lysis*, a skepticist imitation of Plato, mentions parents who ask their child to do their writing for them (cf. FAL).

3. Gorgias, who was not an Athenian, must in his long life-time have experienced the change from mainly oral-aural methods of communication to methods that used writing; but, if we go only by his extant remains, he too ends up as a logographer. More than that, as a well-paid famous foreigner in Athens, he seems to have practiced composition in writing for its own sake, as in his *On Not Being* and *Encomium on Helen*. The case of Gorgias also seems to show that in the early days of writing, it was used to enhance (rather than replace) the acoustic, or oral-aural, effectiveness of expression.

4. A diminution also suffered by Sparta, its rival for the hegemony. See F.W. Walbank "The Causes of the Greek Decline," *Journal of Hellenic Studies* LXIV (1944); cf. A.W. Gomme "The Law of Citizenship at Athens," *Essays in Greek History and Literature* (Blackwell 1937). Cf. also volume V of Curtius's *History of Greece.*

5. This understanding is also rehearsed in Chapter 4, not as a point in sociology of knowledge, but in connection with Aristotle's statement that the good is conditional and relative to the being whose good it is. The reader may remember as relevant that, earlier on, Socrates has avoided answering Glaucon's question about *the* Good.

6. For references to the sources, see LSAP 348f.

7. With exceptions, the most notable of which was Sparta.

8. As if in pre-figuration of the globalism, the *oikoumenê*, created by the success of Macedonian imperialism?

9. In PDOBO, CSFWPT, and "The Politics of a Sophistic Rhetorician," *Quaderni Urbinati di Cultura Classica* (Urbino 1992).

10. But because this kind of constitution is indifferently called by the

Politics either a moderate oligarchy or a moderate (*sic*) democracy, it is possible for it to have been contemporaneous with (or prior to) Peripatetic interpolations of the lecture-notes.

11. A detailed account of these events can be found in Bk.VI, Ch.6 of Hammond's *History of Ancient Greece* (Oxford U.P. 1959).

12. *Athenian Democracy in the Age of Demosthenes* (Oxford: Blackwell 1991); cf. my review of this aspect of his work, "Rhetoric *versus* Evidence" in *Philosophy and Rhetoric*, (1995).

13. But Jones is not accurate in his source-criticism when he takes Thucydides to be anti-democratic or anti-Periklean, or when he confidently asserts that "Plato's views on the subject are too well known to need stating," given that Plato nowhere speaks in his own voice in the dialogues and that Plato's Socrates is a *habitual ironist* and just *as critical* of the excesses of oligarchy as he is of those of demagogic democracy. As for Aristotle, Jones is right to worry about possible bias in the historical sources of the Aristotelian "Constitution of Athens," but he begs the question (which the present book is devoted to investigating) of the too-easy equation of the Peripatetic editing and overwriting of the *Politics* with the lecture-notes of the original Aristotle. The probability that the pages about the Drakonian constitution are interpolated, does not invalidate CA's greater reliability (as a basically pre-Peripatetic text) over the Peripatetic *Politics* as a reflection of Aristotle's attitude.

14. See my CSFWP Chapter 3 on Thucydides, and Chapter 2 below.

2

A Modern Defense of Xenophon's Oligarchic Socrates

Strauss's Composite

Where to Find the Thematic Raw Materials of the Composite

Decades ago the liberal scholar Alban Winspear asked a question we are all interested in but which, because it did not generate a feasible program of research, has to be reformulated before it can be answered. That question was and is: "Who is 'Socrates'?" Twenty-seven years later the conservative scholar Leo Strauss answered the question to his own, and his students,' satisfaction but without having reformulated it into an operational or source-critical way, namely in a way that distinguishes strictly between what is interpretation and what is validatable as a sociohistorical datum.

The diverse documentary worth of the extant sources has not been weighed sufficiently by recent scholarship, nor has it sufficiently noticed the big differences in *literary nature* among the various sorts of sources.[1] A deliberate comic dramatization by the historical Socrates' contemporary, Aristophanes, is not the same kind of *caricature* as that resulting from the credulous amalgam of sec-

21

ond-and *third-hand reports* patched together by Diogenes Laertius centuries later. Nor should it remain unquestioned that Aristophanes' caricature was at first *only* of the historical Socrates. The *literary vitality* of the 'Sckrates' so carefully—if economically— characterized in the dialogues which Plato devoted to the exoneration and augmentation of his image, has to be weighed against the *rhetorical plausibility* of the character named 'Socrates' in Xenophon's demonstrably propagandistic and less well-constructed, less dialogical discourses.[2]

It is not the historical Socrates only whom Aristophanes originally caricatured in the *Clouds*, because it was also (and more vividly) the figures behind the the new stereotypes of the speculative or sophistical nature-philosopher and of the Pythagorean refugee from western Greece looking for disputants and pupils in Athens, the city of talkers (*Kratylos* 398D–E.). Aristophanes is not satirizing well-paid men-of-knowledge such as Protagoras or Gorgias—*whose unpaid peer Socrates could already be seen to be*—but the unsuccessful nature-philosophers, and the displaced Pythagoreans who sought to make a virtue out of their poverty. Aristophanes blends these two types into the laughable and debased composite required by his comedy.[3] Given the phenomenon of Sophism in late fifth-century Athens, another component of the caricature had to be the equivocating and pedantic use of words. But this too is something which we don't find attributed to the historical Socrates by nondramatic sources; nor is it a characteristic of Plato's Socrates in the undoubted dialogues.

Originally Aristophanes would perhaps have given the name 'Socrates' to the meteorosophist (*Clouds* 360) in his comedy because the historical Socrates fit the caricature in the one respect that he was poor, but more problably because he was so well-known—much as we today call any solemn, reform-minded legislator a "Solon." It is doubtful, at the dates of the comedy's first two performances in 423 and 421 B.C. when he was in his middle forties, that the historical Socrates came anywhere nearer than this to Aristophanes' caricature. Little as we know about the historical Socrates, he is not known to have grubbed for fees, kept school, or inquired about cosmic phenomena beyond the time of his youth.

What has to be done to make the question 'who was Socrates' operational is to disambiguate the term 'Socrates.' To whom are we referring when we say 'Socrates'? Are we referring to the historical Socrates (SocH), to the 'Socrates' in Xenophon's works (SocX), to the Socrates of Diogenes Laertius's gossipy *Lives of the Philosophers* (SocL), to the dramatic character in Aristophanes' comedy *The Clouds* who is called Socrates (SocA), to the Socrates in Plato's dialogues when these are read *dialogically* or dramatically (SocP), or to a Socrates derived from a *literalistic* reading of the dialogues as advancing a system of doctrine? This last 'Socrates' will have to be symbolized as SocD because he is taken to have doctrines—contrary to what Cicero tells us about him in *Academica* I.iv.17f. to the effect that he never in his discussions acceded to "the admission of any positive statement," and that he was "in the habit of *reprobating entirely* a definite science of philosophy with a regular arrangement of subjects and a formulated system of doctrine."

Because this 'Socrates' is found to hold different doctrines by different expositors, an additional subscript is required to identify him, as in Nietzsche's case. In this context we might call him SocDn; but because Nietzsche also discusses character-traits of 'Socrates' as a person, even though he is not reading the dialogues dialogically, he can also be called SocN: not SocPn, because it is *not* Nietzsche's version of *Plato's* Socrates read dialogically.[4]

More, when we say "Plato's Socrates in the dialogues read dialogically," we find that we need to limit "the dialogues" to "the undoubted dialogues," because the locutions and behavior of 'Socrates' in some or most of the doubtful and spurious dialogues can differ markedly from that of the 'Socrates' in the undoubted dialogues. Finally, given the way people talk about 'him,' there is need for one more label, namely, SocU an undistributed (in the logical sense) 'Socrates' whose composite nature *cannot* be disambiguated clearly because the users themselves of the term are not able, *without a critical analysis* of the source they got 'him' from, to keep track of their complex references—references, e.g., to a conflation *of* the historical Socrates (itself an interpretive or hypothetical construction) *with* Plato's Socrates literalistically abstracted *and/or with* Xenophon's *or* Laertius's 'Socrates.'

Just as the association between 'Socrates' and Alkibiades is a fourth-century media-effect that cannot be proved historical without more evidence than the dramatic fictions in Plato's dialogues, so the attribution to the historical Socrates of traits from the caricature in *Clouds* is an after-effect of that play's farcical success.[5] Falling into the trap, Strauss speaks confidently of "the Aristophanean Socrates" (e.g. XS 21), and gives him a pivotal importance such that "he" decisively influenced, by reaction, the doctrinal characterization of *their* Socrates in both Xenophon's discourses and Plato's dialogues (SPPP, esp. 38–88 and passim). Strauss does not tell us, however, how he can be so certain that the reference of Aristophanes' Socrates in *Clouds* (423 and 421 B.C.) is to either the knowledge-seeker (*philosophos*, Plato's term)[6] or the questioner that the historical Socrates can safely be allowed to be. It is tautologous that the reference is to the *image the play created* in the public mind, an image which in the two decades before his death became exclusively attached to the well-known dialectician with the same name, rather than to the stereotypes alluded to by means of the character in *Clouds*.

To anticipate, it is certain that, had 'Socrates' in fact been the garrulous charlatan of the *Clouds* or the mediocre pedagogue given us by Xenophon, we can be sure that he would never have made the impact he did on Athenian life. Nor would he have made the entry into Western history that he has made. By way of orientation to what follows, we have to say that at first blush and on a dialogical reading of Plato's dialogues it seems unlikely that the qualities of Plato's memorable character can be made compatible with those of the rural, militarist, chauvinist, oligarchist character in Xenophon's discourses. Here, in any case, is the leading question generative of the present inquiry: Is Strauss's Socrates more Xenophontic than Platonic in Strauss's doctrinal sense, and more oligarchal than either the dialogical Plato or doctrinal Plato of other readers of the dialogues?

I will make explicit what is implicit in the above twofold question. My questions imply, first, that what Strauss calls "the Platonic–Xenophontic" (SA IV) is an ad-hoc amalgam of incompatible elements whose derivation must be made explicit and examined before it can be accepted or rejected.[7] Second, both the dialogical approach to the dialogues and my use of the term 'platonist' require that we reexamine *the decision-procedures* by which doctrines are ascribed either to the historical Socrates or to Plato's Socrates, or even to Xenophon's Socrates when the ascription invokes something called "the tradition" or appeals, tacitly or overtly, to *counter-dialogical* readings of Plato's dialogues and *non-rhetorical* readings of Xenophon's.

By 'ad-hoc' I mean a characterization which is a function of the system of political philosophy which Strauss derives from the literature of classical and—taking account of his view of the *Laws*—Hellenistic Greece. By 'platonist' I mean the response to Plato's dialogues that takes them to be advancing a system of doctrine, something which is precluded by any *consistently* dialogical reading carried through *with literary competence*. It is not that Strauss does not often appeal to the dialogue-form for purposes of understanding what the speakers in the dialogues are saying. The complication is that he does so for purposes of deciding not merely what doctrines *the speakers* might really be holding, but also for the purpose of deciding what doctrines Plato *himself* or the *historical* Socrates believed or was advancing.

Now, to say that Strauss's data-base for classical political philosophy extends (contradictorily) to the literature of *Hellenistic* Greece is also to draw attention to his too-easy granting of authenticity to spurious dialogues such as *Theages, Hipparchus, Amatores,* and his unquestioning appeal to doubtful dialogues such as the *Lysis, Alcibiades I,* and the *Menexenus.*[8] The importance of this is that the locutions and characteristics of the Socrates in dialogues that are not by Plato conflict with those of Plato's Socrates in the undoubted dialogues. This irremediably denatures the picture we get of Plato's Socrates, whether this picture is derived from a dialogical or dogmatic reading of the dialogues or a mixture of both such as Strauss's. If, for instance, we decide to treat the *Lysis* as authentic, then we are forced to grant that Plato's Socrates can be *a total eristic.* And this is an unlikely proposition, given the nature of Plato's project in his dialogue–series as a whole, and the ethical and intellectual characteristics of Plato's Socrates in the *Phaedrus, Gorgias, Protagoras, Meno* and other undoubted dialogues.

The radical change in the Greek language and the climate of opinion which followed upon the Macedonian conquest becomes relevant: monarchy and oligarchy will now be favored over democracy, not to mention neo-spartanism, militarism, and pythagorism over the old Athenian love of poetry and drama, participant civilism, and anti-elitism. The Hellenistic literature not only bristles with reflections of the change, but eagerly seeks to legitimate ideas of tyranny, slavery, and pythagorizing elitism. And it makes an enormous difference to our understanding of "classical political philosophy," divided as it is between pro-democratic and pro-oligarchic thought, whether we include the Academic *Laws* or not in the canon. As the founding document which I believe it to be of the Hellenistic age, *Laws* calls for one kind of understanding and appreciation; but if it is taken to be Plato's own authentic work, we have to postulate a second Plato (i) who could no longer write good Greek, (ii) who was not dialogical, (iii) who was no longer *equally critical* (in his exhibitive way) of both democracy and oligarchy as in the *Republic,* (iv) who could no longer allow *any* praise for the poets, as in the *Meno,* and (v) who has *abandoned his life-project* of exonerating the image of Socrates by dramatizing the high points of his intellectual life-cycle as represented in the communicative encounters that constitute the dialogues.[9]

In pursuing our two questions we restrict the focus to Strauss's political philosophy and its constitutive core, namely, his selection and view of Plato's works and his interpretive reconstruction of the thought and character of 'Socrates.' We have to remember that at the time Strauss (b. 1899) was a university student, Xenophon's Socrates was still equated by some scholars with the historical Socrates. The tendency of this now rejected, indemonstrable equation is one determinant of what Strauss calls 'Socrates' *simpliciter*. The reference of this term in Strauss, then, is to the hard-to-get-at existent we call 'the historical Socrates' (SocH). 'He' is hard to get at because of the absence of reliable archaeological or literary evidence.[10] The evidence which Strauss goes by, he derives mainly from Aristophanes, Xenophon, and Plato. So we must now re-examine, from the point of view of source-criticism, the nature and derivation of (i) Strauss's 'Aristophanean Socrates' and (ii) his "Xenophon's Socrates" in order to get clarity about the "Platonic-Xenophontic Socrates" of which they are the components.

Strauss's Aristophanean Socrates

Aristophanes' caricature has to be taken up first, given Strauss's view that it was in response to it that Xenophon and Plato have given us their—to Strauss—mergeable or interchangeable or mutually reinforcing Sckrates's.

Strauss's conception of Aristophanes' Socrates is a function of the location he assigns to it in ancient Greek intellectual history. Subject as *Clouds* was both to the conventions of the genre Attic Comedy and to Aristophanes' unpredictable inventiveness, Strauss nonetheless takes it to be

the most important document available . . . on the ancient . . . opposition between poetry and philosophy as such—between the two
forms of wisdom, each of which claims supremacy—as this feud appears from the side of poetry (SA 311).

Given that Strauss nowhere documents *the history of* the feud, we
have to guess at where he gets it from. We have to wonder too at
the anachronism involved in calling it "ancient," since the earlier
Presocratics all seem to have composed in verse down to the time
of Empedocles (d. post. 444 B.C.), and since the term "philosophy"
in Strauss's meaning first occurs in Plato's dialogues themselves.
Actually, as a matter of historical reality, the dispute is only as ancient as *Hellenistic* antiquity and the anti-dialogical failure which
takes what Plato's Socrates says about poetry in *Republic* as literal
doctrine, rather than as part of what is *dialogically called for* in his
extended satire of a militarist state guided by pythagorean intellectuality. In the *Meno*, Socrates *praises* the poets and puts them, as
similarly inspired, on a par (in point of knowledge) with the great
statesmen who have been saviors of their country.[11] Pythagorean
intellectuality was, of course, anti-poetic.

Strauss also states in the first of his books on the problem of Socrates (*Socrates and Aristophanes*)[12] that Aristophanes must have pon-
dered over "Socrates' *teaching,* and in particular on his teaching regarding the gods" (*ibid.*). Strauss concludes that Aristophanes felt
required by his comedic vocation to choose for his protagonist "an
Athenian sophist–philosopher, and among the Athenian sophist-
philosophers Socrates was the most outstanding."

There are several problems here. The assumption that the historical Socrates had "a teaching" in the doctrinal sense can remain only
an assumption. To make it at the outset of a study of Socrates is to
beg the question. Secondly, there is no evidence for such a teaching
independently of what can be ascribed to Socrates (SocP) by either
a *literalist* reading of Plato's dialogues or an uncritical acceptance of

the doctrines which Xenophon puts in Socrates' mouth (SocX). Thirdly, mustn't an honest inquirer who isn't a sophist object to the hyphenation of sophist with philosopher, both in itself and as inaccurate when *imputed* by Aristophanes to the historical Socrates (SocH), given that if Aristophanes *was* picking Socrates (SocH) as his subject from among notable real sophists, then Strauss is allowing that the historical Socrates was at the time the unsurpassed peer of such sophists as Gorgias or Protagoras. Since both Socrates' behavior in the dialogues and that of the historical Socrates in subsequent opinion, is seen and said to be *anti-sophistic*, he must be granted to have surpassed the sophists by *not* being one, namely, by having been interrogative rather than equivocal and a seeker rather than a persuader. Given the derogatory connotations of the term "sophist," it is revealing that *Xenophon himself* equates "philosophers," among whom he includes Socrates, with what can only be "sophists" at *Mem*.I.ii.31. This would seem to indicate that Strauss's hyphenation of the philosopher with the sophist is justified by Xenophon's acceptance of the popular equation between them in this passage.[13]

But if SocH surpassed the greatest sophists, i.e., was at least their match in argument, doesn't Strauss have to grant (contradictorily) the greater verisimilitude of Plato's Socrates over Aristophanes' caricature and Xenophon's portrait, since (i) Plato's dramatization gives sufficient reason for the superiority of his Socrates over the sophists, namely, that he emerges from the dialogues as a consistent, non-equivocating ethical inquirer in contrast to the pedestrian propagator of oligarchal precepts in Xenophon's discourses, and (ii) if this is the case, SocH (as already noted) cannot be the *whole* inspiration or *only* model for Aristophanes' caricature? Does a caricaturist, moreover, need to know any more about what his subject believes than what the general public thinks it knows? After all, *Clouds* is not a *philosophical* characterization of its own protagonist, but only a farcical synthesis of the vices imputable to a set of *inferior* and *disparate pedagogues*—unsuccessful sophists and nature-philosophers, or down-and-out pythagoreans. In other words, if the thesis is true that the *original* denotation of SocA was the historical Socrates, it has consequences that falsify it.

Strauss's other thesis to the effect that Plato's dialogues and Xenophon's discourses were intellectual responses to *Aristophanes'* "characterization" of the historical Socrates must be expanded, consequently, to include as a negative determinant of their work *the effect* of the caricature *on Athenian public opinion* in the two decades that remained of SocH's life. In an allegory of what Plato himself was doing in his dialogue-series as a whole, Plato's Socrates in the *Apology* is dramatized as addressing not only his detractors and the jury but *also* as correcting Athenian public opinion *more than* Aristophanes' comedy. While Xenophon's Socratic discourses appear to be doing the same thing, it is clearer in their case that they are preaching to the converted, namely, that they are designed to teach an oligarchist audience (and its children) how to take advantage of the great interest that posterity had in the figure of Socrates. And this explains why Xenophon's bland Socrates is so unobjectionable to readers like Strauss who draw sociopolitical inspiration from Xenophon. It also explains why Strauss has to come, circularly, to Xenophon's defense when the latter is taken as a political philosopher, and why he fits so well with Strauss's own pedagogy and political theory.

Strauss's Aristophanean Socrates (SocAs), in other words, is an interpretive construction responding to an intellectual-historical artefact or positum—the "ancient quarrel between poetry and philosophy"—derived from an anti-dialogical reading of an ironizing and satirical dialogical work, the *Republic*. The construction not only misses the irony, and "propositionalizes" or de-dramatizes the communicative interactions in that dialogue, it also misses the comedy in the *Clouds* while mis-taking a broad caricature for a well-pondered portrait. We see that, in the case of Aristophanes, Strauss is involved in a confusion of genres as well as committed to a self-refuting thesis.

Strauss's Appreciation of Xenophon's Socrates

The two books devoted entirely to Xenophon's Socrates leave no doubt that, to Strauss, this Socrates (SocX) is the acceptable and exemplary 'Socrates'.[14] Startlingly, however, he starts his interpretation of XSD with the unSocratic remark (not SocP) that "[Xenophon's] Socrates could have taught the art of generalship as well as the art of managing the household. . ." It is not Xenophon's words that claim this, but Strauss's in taking the latter to imply it. I call the claim unSocratic with Plato's *Ion* in mind, where Socrates (SocP) ridicules the rhapsode's claim to possess a superlative art of generalship because he has a thorough knowledge of generalship in Homer. Since Strauss speaks like a rhetorician here, we see why there is *no rhetorical analysis* of Xenophon's prose in his reading of it. He tends throughout to take Xenophon at his word: namely, because Strauss shares Xenophon's ideological premises he does not see that the latter's reconstruction of Socrates is ideological and, therefore, in need of critique.[15]

The concluding passage of *Memorabilia* (IV.iii.11) in which he lists the attributes of his Socrates, tells us what one of the basic premises of Xenophon was. As in other Xenophontic *loci*, we find, in the penultimate sentence of the work, that the way in which he uses the words *aretê* (human excellence) and *kalokagathían* (gentlemanliness) equates them with each other. And this equation is everywhere accepted by Strauss. The traits which Xenophon here assigns to his Socrates as the best and happiest of men are: piety (*eusebês*), justness (*dikaios*), self-control (*enkratês*), good judgment (*phronimos*), successful self-sufficiency (*autarkês*), and persuasive competence.

More than agreeing with Xenophon, Strauss's words, at XS p.106, seem to be a defense of him against accusations by Athenian democrats of having gone over to Sparta: "as we have learned from the elenctic conversation with Euthydemos, *harming the enemies of the city is part of justice.*" The allusion is to *Memorabilia* IV.ii.14-15. Are we supposed to remember here the all-or-none nature of Greek par-

ty politics according to which both oligarchs and democrats felt free
to appeal for outside aid, against their fellow-citizens, to oligarchs
and democrats (respectively) in other cities? If "enemies of the city"
includes "unjust" factions, this would exonerate all partisans who
sought or wished for outside aid against the party in their own city
from which they claimed to suffer unjustly. This could be called
Strauss's Xenophontic defense of Xenophon.

And if this is making too much out of very few words, consider
the oligarchic sophism, so to call it, ventured by Strauss (at XS 100)
to the effect that

> if the tyrant belongs to the *demos*, is the rule of the tyrants not democ-
> racy? Or is democracy tyrannical? Does this . . . follow . . . from the
> difficulties regarding justice, regarding law of which we hear earlier
> (I.ii.40-45)?

True, this is based on *Euthydemos's* "admi[ssion] that tyrants belong to the *demos*," an admission which—he concedes (IV.ii.39)—
may be due to his feeble understanding. But all that Xenophon was
reporting at IV.ii.37ff. was the elenchus by which Euthydemos was
brought to begin the study of prudence under Socrates, in the course
of which elenchus despots are included (unexpectedly) among the
dêmos and small but thrifty property-holders are included among
the plutocrats. Xenophon's tone here does not seem be one in which
an anti-democratic point is being made.

Picking up on the attributes of Xenophon's Socrates as they are
registered by Strauss, the most important thing to add to the list
above is SocXs's assertion to Antisthenes that "virtue is teachable"
(Strauss's words, XS 147) because *an* excellence, courage, seems to
have been taught to an acrobatic dancing girl (*Symp.*II.vii.13). Secondly, this Socrates is in possession of a "teaching" (e.g. XS 101ff.,
94ff., 58ff. and passim), and this teaching seems directed to producing gentlemanliness (*kalokagathia*) in Socrates' auditors. So the
Socrates Strauss gets from Xenophon not only possesses a teach-

ing, unlike the dialogical Socrates of Plato, but also believes, unlike Plato's Socrates in the *Meno* and *Protagoras*, that *aretê* (human excellence) *can* be taught.

What then is Socrates' teaching about, according to Xenophon; and what does Strauss make of it? Early in the *Memorabilia* Xenophon tells his reader that Socrates' "conversation was always of human matters (*anthrôpinôn*)," and that he used to examine (*skopôn*) "what was pious, or impious, what beautiful, what ugly, what just, what unjust, what was good judgment (*sôphrosynê*), what mania or madness, what courage was, what cowardice, what is a city, what is a politician, what is human government, what is a good ruler (*archikos*) and other such things, *the knowledge of which led to being a gentleman* (*kalouskagathous*, I.i.16). But in Plato's dialogues *literalistically read*, this concern is said to lead to the theory of ideas!

When Chaerecrates tells Socrates that he doesn't know how to convert Chaerophon into a friend, the response is that he must apply the kindness proper to a gentleman (*kalouskagathous*, II.iii.16). Speaking of friendship to Critobolus, Xenophon's Socrates, at II.vi.22, equates human excellence with gentlemanliness. It is thanks to their *aretê* he goes on to say that *gentlemanly* office-holders can exercise their power beneficially and ungreedily. At I.ii.7 Socrates is reported to believe that to a gentleman a good friend is the greatest gift, and that he never could see how anyone could accept money as a reward for his *aretê*. At I.ii.29 Socrates deems Kritias to be ungentlemanly (*ou prepon . . . kalôikagathoi*) in begging like a suppliant for improper favors from his beloved. At I.ii.48 Socrates' true associates are said to consort with him, not for political benefit like Alcibiades, but for the sake of becoming gentlemen (*ina kaloi te kagathoi genomenos*). At I. vi.13 the gifted person who teaches another is a gentlemanly citizen (*kalos kagathos politês*), in contrast to the sophists who, by *selling knowledge*, prostitute it. In fine, Socrates, to the author of the *Memorabilia*, was not only happy or blessed (*makarios*) as a man, but blessed in leading his auditors into gentlemanliness (*epi kalokagathia agein*, I.vi.14). In the coda to his work

(IV.viii.11), which lists all his excellences—piety, justness, self-control, intelligence, self-sufficiency—and which describes SocratesX as "so religious as to have done nothing without the advice of the gods, so just as never to have hurt anybody," Xenophon, in a triumphalist rhetorical flourish, again equates human excellence (*aretê*) with gentlemanliness.

In the conversation about farming as the *noblest and best* way of life which he narrates to Critobolus in the *Oeconomicus*, SocX calls his model interlocutor Ischomachus a true gentleman (*kalos te kagathos anêr*, vi.12; also vi.16; vii.2,3; xii.2; xiv.9). Now "Ischomachus" has the connotation of being "strong in battle;" so, we feel that when this gentleman par excellence (*ten epônymían . . . keklêsthai*, xii.2) digresses to talk about strategy and leadership, he is qualified to do so. Thus, when Ischomachus has concluded his discourse about the art of farming and its nobility, we are convinced of his knowledge and seriousness. Then in the digression on leadership that ends the book, he earnestly tells SocratesX that not only must a good leader be possessed of an education and natural gifts, he must also be *theion*, "able to rule with consent" (*ethelontôn archein*, xxi.12). *Theion* means "divine;" but in this context, the modern equivalent would be "charismatic," "enthusing." Ischomachus had been saying (sub-paragr. 8) that he is "well-minded" (*megalognômonas*) "who has many knowing followers; he whose judgment (*gnômê*) many wish to serve can be said to proceed with a mighty arm;" for it is not strength but judgment, adds Ischomachus, that achieves great deeds. In a way, he tells SocratesX, are not these the qualities that constitute the *kingly* character (*êthous basilikou*)?

While these theses are not advanced by SocratesX himself, Socrates has, for the sake of Critobolus, made himself a student of Ischomachus and can be seen to be very accepting of this gentleman's views. Xenophon thus gets the stamp of Socrates' approval for the views advanced by his Ischomachus. My reading of Xenophon is not congruent with Strauss's; for it is calculated to highlight phases of Xenophon's thought which Strauss doesn't emphasize albeit he does not disagree with them. Since I am critical of Xenophon's Socrates, where Strauss applauds him, SocXt cannot be exactly the same as SocXs. But the quality, for instance, of flatness in some Matisse paintings perceived and *disapproved* by one art critic, remains the quality of flatness perceived and *approved* by another— even while the differing critics will have contextualized the quality in different ways. If, however, the second critic goes on to say that in Matisse "flatness is all," and the most "painterly" thing about his work, we must now grant that there is a radical difference between the two critics.

So, in the analogy, does Strauss, in finding that Isomachus has established the high rank of perfect gentlemanship in farming, political economy, and war, feel (i) that Ischomachus has also established the *intellectual importance* of gentlemanship as well as the importance of "intellectual *differences* among men" for purposes of rulership, and (ii) that SocratesXs has agreed with the result. If "gentlemanliness is all," for Strauss, and quality of intellect is what qualifies individuals for rulership, then only the most intelligent gentlemen will rule. This naturally excludes non-gentlemen from rule, even if their intellectual quality is greater than the gentlemen's.

Another problem with Strauss's Xenophontic conclusion is the uncritical, and unhistorical acceptance of a term *kalok'agathía* which, when used by Thucydides for example, is used without the honorific connotations it has in Xenophon. In Thucydides, the *kaloik'agathoi* are simply the oligarchs—headed by Antiphon and Kritias—who delivered the anti-democratic coup d'état of 411 B.C. (Thucyd.VIII.-63-77). Among the connotations which the term has in Xenophon, there is naturally a political agenda with programmatic anticipations and uncrystallized operational references. However, since Strauss's Socrates is not only Xenophontic, but is also said to be "Platonic-Xenophontic" we will comment further only when we have clarified the reference and connotations of Plato's Socrates according to Strauss (SocPs), and have reviewed the way in which *kalosk'agathós* is used by Plato's Socrates. We will then also be in a

position to appreciate the differences, which I've insisted on elsewhere, between Xenophon's *Defense* of Socrates and Plato's *Apology*. In the former he is damned with faint praise, and not really
allowed to rise beyond being an exemplary schoolmaster somewhat
carried away by his own words. In the latter, as in the *Crito* and the
Phaedo, he is validated as a true culture-hero deserving of the entry
he has made into history.[16]

In Xenophon's *Symposium*, the only non-comic reference to
kalok'agathía is non-ideological.[17] It is made by Kallias in response to
a question of Antisthenes. There, they both equate it with justness
(*dikaiosynê*). We won't examine this composition of Xenophon's in
detail, as the Socrates in it is not edifying and we have already noted
that he believes virtues can be taught. But it does leave a puzzle.
The comic reference to *kalok'agathía* (at ii.4) rather laughs at the notion: unlike *young* men who come out of their gymnastic exercise
with pleasant odors upon them, older citizens (*eleutherioi*) should
take care to be redolent of *kalokagathía*. And they can acquire this
aroma, SocratesX says, by preaching nobility as Theognis enjoins,
and shunning all low-life. Does Xenophon—whom Strauss (like the
Hellenistic grammarians) believes to be a great stylist—not realize
that he has rather realistically satirized the sociopolitical class he is
dedicated to upholding? Or is the whole of his *Symposium* to be
understood as an instance of the Greek practice of deeply respecting the gods and heroes three–fourths of the time, then turning
around and satirizing them in a satyr-play for a change at the end?
The picture, in this discourse, of SocratesX as demotic not only risks
underming the exemplary role usually reserved for him; but his
would-be ironic self-presentation to the auditors as a *procurer* fails
both as didacticism and as irony. We come away rather with a picture of the would-be ruling class at play as unSocratically (not SocP)
sensuous (if not licentious), and narcissistic rather than witty.
Strauss's chapter on this *Symposium*, for its part, is quite uncritical
of the goings-on in it.[18]

Finally, the passing reference (by the Syracusan) to Aristophanes' *Clouds* (vi.8) has Xenophon poking second-hand fun at a Socrates whom the reference demotes back to his vulgar public image—a Socrates suddenly not, for the moment, Xenophon's (SocX) but Aristophanes'! The lapse would seem to show that the author's class-prejudices are capable of contradicting in the details his over-all ideological project. The passing reference to "the two Aphrodite's," at viii.9–10, would of course seem to show that Xenophon's *Symposium* is later than Plato's. Noticeably inferior as the former is to the latter as a literary work and as a characterization of Socrates, is it to be expected or not that Strauss does not discuss the matter?

Is there a Plato's Socrates, According to Strauss?

Strauss's understanding of "classical political philosophy" equates the science of politics with "the kingly art" (SPPP 87). Xenophon uses this term as we have seen, but Strauss also gets it from the Elean visitor in Plato's *Politicus*. Strauss notes, on the same page, that for SocratesP in the *Euthydemus* they are not the same because, says Strauss, Plato's Socrates distinguishes between philosophy *as dialectic* and the kingly art. Strauss' has assumed here that in the *Republic* the two studies are identical. The kingly art in Xenophon's discourses and the kingly art "in" Plato's dialogues have something in common for Strauss, except that in Xenophon's conception the kingly art is lacking in "the dialectic art." We must point out, however, that it is not SocratesP but *the Elean visitor* who shows how the kingly art may be provided with the dialectic. But, discounting for the moment SocratesP's irony in *Republic*, his conception of the dialectic is not the same as that of the rhetorical sophist in *Politicus*.

So it is strange to find Strauss saying, at the end of his discussion of the *Euthydemus*, that

Socrates was not the mortal enemy of the sophists nor were the soph-

ists the mortal enemies of Socrates. According to Socrates, the greatest enemy of philosophy, the greatest sophist, is the political multitude (*Rep*.492a5–e6).[19]

And this claim puts us in mind of Strauss's problematic hyphenation, earlier, of sophist with philosopher in his discussion of "the
Aristophanean Socrates." There he minimized the differences between them by speaking from the point of view of a public that
didn't keep them apart; here he has gone on to join them in an
alliance against the mass of citizens. I say it is strange because Plato's
Euthydemus puts on exhibit an abrasive interaction between SocratesP and two mediocre sophists at their outrageous worst. But Plato's
Politicus puts on exhibit for our unaided inspection—I mean, unaided by any words from Socrates—a most qualified sophist doing
his brilliant best to present the case for one-man rule.[20] The latter is
courteous but not particularly friendly to SocratesP *at whom he aims
several verbal barbs.*

Does Strauss then mean by "Platonic political philosophy" a philosophy that can overlook, in Plato's name, the difference between
his Socrates (SocP) and the Sophists in the dialogues? The reader of
the *Politicus* is assumed by its author to be listening to the Sophist
with Socrates's ears, so to say. In any case, it is not *dialogical* to take
the Elean Sophist's views to be "platonic," i.e., Plato's. There is no
evidence that SocratesP has accepted them. He simply, in the dramatic fiction of the dialogue, has not been allowed to question them
verbally; the visitor had insisted on having only *tractable* respon-
dents, and he and Theodorus his host are both against *disputation*.
The Elean visitor has in fact already derogated the *disputatious* sophist
by defining him negatively in the *Sophist*, the dialogue preceding
the *Politicus*.[21]

Wherever its title *Politikos* came from, the dialogue in which the
main speaker is the *rhetorical* sophist from Elea who has just put
down *eristic* sophists in the *Sophistês* by way of exempting himself
from the stereotype of the sophist, that title in Greek is *Politicus*.

And it is not best translated as "statesman," for the reason that the honorific connotations of the term in English beg a basic question that the dialogue raises. The meaning of *politikos* is "man of politics," as in *politikos anêr* (258b4). So *politikos* means here, as it is made to mean in the dialogue itself, "administrator of one of the six *imitations* of the true form of government." In addition, the visitor distinguishes the party pol (*stasiastikós*) from the politician at 303c2. In the thesis of the Elean visitor, it is the administrator of the best form of government, who is kingly or statesmanly; he is the *epistêmôn* man (301b5) who is possessed of "the kingly art or science," *basilikê*. It is this individual, or monarch, who should be called "the statesman" if we are to be faithful to the visitor's own usage and not beg the question of the Eleate's view of politics.

Strauss thinks (PP 214) that the *Politicus* "brings into the open what the *Republic* had left unsaid . . . the impossibility of the best regime presented in the *Republic*." But this impossibility *is* suggested by the text of the *Republic* when read rightly: "it is necessary to recall," says Socrates at 472b, "that we were seeking for *the sort of thing* justice is" (*hoion esti*); "a pattern (*paradeigma*) . . . of what the *perfectly* just man would be like" (*hoion an eiê*). In Shorey's translation of 472d2–3: "our purpose was not to demonstrate the possibility of the realization of these ideals." Socrates then likens what they've been doing—"trying to create in words the pattern of a good state" (472e1)—to a good painting of "the pattern of what the most beautiful man would be like" (*paradeigma hoion an eiê*) whose painter could then not prove that it was possible for such a man to exist; it would nonetheless be a good painting. And the supposedly affirmative passage on the possibility of implementation at 502b–502c does not go beyond this. Socrates says, "for, such a ruler having laid down the laws and customs that we have gone through . . . it is surely not impossible that the citizens will want to carry them out;" and, "that these things are best *if* (*eiper*) possible, has I believe already been shown;" and, "it would appear . . . that what we have said about legislation is best *if* it could come-to-be (*ei genoito*), and that though it is difficult for it to come-to-be, it is not however impossible."[22] In other words, the regime in *Republic* is not offered unconditionally, but *sardonically* and as necessary to the purification of the luxurious (*truphôsan*) and fevered (*phlegmainousan*) city (372d) which Glaucon has desiderated.

Strauss is not wrong in wanting "statesmanship, the art or knowledge peculiar to the statesman . . . [to be] . . . an ingredient of the vision of the idea of the good" (PP 210f.). He thinks that if it was, then "'politics' would be much more important according to the *Statesman* than it is according to the *Republic*." And this is not wrong either—only terribly incomplete. For, what we are getting in the *Politicus* is not the views of Plato's Socrates, but *the views of a pythagorizing, rhetorical sophist* from Phocaean Elea, the city of Xenophanes, Parmenides and Zeno, to which Leukippos also migrated. If these are views with which Strauss sympathizes, we grant them to him. But if he is suggesting that these are Plato's views, where is the evidence for it, and what is his decision-procedure for concluding that the Eleatic speaks for Plato himself?

Is Strauss not violating here the *dialogue-form* of Plato's work which he says he wants us to respect? Yes, such views *are* part of "classical political philosophy;" and Plato is our "evidence" for them, since his Elean visitor is made to rehearse them. But they are put on exhibit by Plato, in this dialogical way in all their equivocating persuasiveness, just so the Athenian reader who was likely to be a democrat, or a devotee of the ancestral constitution—could judge their validity *fairly and for himself*. Readers of Isocrates would have had their ideas clarified by the dialogue, in regard to his proposal for a pan-Hellenic military alliance *captained by a king*, as well as their ideas about the relation of this (and other kinds of) kingship to their home constitutions and laws. And oligarchal theorists are out-oligarched in explicitness by the dialogue: Plato knew, no less than we, that it is best in argument to confront the strongest version of a theory if we want to refute it. While the "explicitation" maximizes the strengths of the theory, it also uncovers its weaknesses with maximum effect. And this is what Plato has done for the theory of monarchy in the *Politicus*.

Strauss tells us in *Political Philosophy* (PP 160) that "the *Republic*, the *Statesman*" (as he calls it), "and the *Laws* . . . are devoted to political *philosophy*," and that "the political *teaching* of Plato is accessible to us chiefly through these three works" (my italics). It is true that *Laws* looks like a didactic work with a *teaching* in it, and we may grant that it is that; the problem is that this "posthumous" work is not by Plato himself, and that both the external and internal evidence point to its being an Academic production, issued under the auspices of Speusippos the pythagorizing head of the Academy after Plato's death. I have rehearsed the evidence elsewhere and can only recap it briefly here.[23] On just the external evidence *Laws* itself is a work datable, at best, to 346/345 B.C. two years after Plato's death, *if* we believe the Academic tradition about it; at worst, the text of *Laws* was in dispute down to the time of Poseidonius (fl. 100 B.C.). Cicero's *De Legibus* (ii.6) says that, with its prefaces and preambles, it is following the *Pythagorean* practice recommended by Zaleucus. Speusippos, scholarch of the Academy, was—not coincidentally—temporizing with the Pythagoreans.[24] The practice was one to which Poseidonius himself objected (Fr.178).[25] The author of the text of Book II of the Aristotelian *Politics* uncritically believes (1266 b6) both that *Laws* is "for the most part a collection of statutes," and that it is by Plato. He believes the main speaker in it to be Socrates (!): this latter is not a mistake Aristotle could have made. Since Aristotle had already left the Academy when *Laws* is said to have appeared, we have to question either Aristotle's intelligence or his access to the work. The former is impossible, the latter makes the passage unreliable. Only one third of the *Laws*, as we have it, consists of said statutes; so the Aristotelian *Politics* knows a *Laws* that is missing most of what our *Laws* contains.

The author of this passage has also referred to the work as a "Socratic discourse;" he thinks that something can be both a collection of statutes and a Socratic discourse! This cannot be Aristotle

who gives us, at *Poetics* vi.1450a19 his definition of a Socratic discourse. We recollect, also, that the text of our *Politics* goes back only
to its first century editors Andronicus and Tyrannion. R. Shute thinks
that Cicero did not know our *Politics*, which was being edited in his
lifetime; but Susemihl and Hicks think he knew it in an earlier form.[26]

Finally, the evidence in D.Laertius (iii.37) is not entirely unus-
able; he reports that "some say that" Plato left the work "in the
wax" (*en kêrôi*), and that Philip of Opus transcribed (*metêgrapsen*) it.
Since a physically impossible number of wax tablets would be required for our 600–page *Laws*, the phrase "in the wax" has to be
metaphorical, meaning a sketch or an outline. But an outline or
sketch is not a first draft; so that, whoever "transcribed" the *Laws*
from the sketch also wrote 90–99% of it. On top of all this is the
insurmountable double barrier of the bad quality of the much-
amended, much-edited prose of *Laws*, and its relentlessly
monologous nature, relieved only by a few ponderous attempts at
humor.

In going on to say that the task of setting forth the best possible
political order is left to the *Laws*, Strauss has quite misread the
Politicus by claiming that it "shows explicitly the necessity of the
rule of laws" (PP 223). The Eleatic visitor has, on the contrary, been
explicit in saying that the regime of the *epistêmôn* monarch is allowed to do without the laws because of his kingly art-or-science
(*basilikê*)! In any case, since there is no Socrates in *Laws*, Strauss's
view of the latter work belongs with consideration of his idea of
classical political philosophy, not with his view of Socrates. Finally,
as Strauss's interpretation of Xenophon's *Hiero* is also part of his
view of classical political philosophy, it is worth noting that Strauss
does not fail to pick up from the sophist in the *Politicus* the notion of
freedom that is advanced in the *Hiero*, namely, that freedom consists in the *willingness* of the ruled to be ruled. So it is the consent of
the ruled that turns a tyrant into a king, not only his knowledge of
the art-or-science of ruling, according to Xenophon and Strauss.

The Dialogical Socrates vis-a-vis Strauss's Socrates in the Dialogues

In the fifty pages devoted to Plato's *Republic* in the book *Political Philosophy* (159–209), Strauss sees that in Plato's dialogues "only his characters speak," and that "strictly, there is no Platonic teaching; at most there is the teaching of the men who are the chief characters in his dialogues "(PP 159).

Yet, knowing this, Strauss proceeds to de-dramatize the dialogical interactions in the *Republic* by purging the things said by the characters to each other of their interlocutory pregnancy, and propositionalizing the responses into categorical truth-claims *assertible in any context.* In facing this problem, let us look first at the several self-categorizations of his reading of *Republic* as-a-whole with which Strauss guides his readers.

He says, for instance, that in it "Socrates discusses the nature of justice with a fairly large number of people", or that in it "Socrates makes very radical proposals of 'reform' without encountering serious resistance." Again, he believes that "the scheme of the *Republic* stands or falls by the rule of the philosophers" (PP 162–3), and "finds indications in the *Republic* . . . that the only possible reformation is that of the individual man" PP 160). Strauss speaks of "the constructive assertions of the bulk of the *Republic*" (PP 161); he speaks of "the theses of the *Republic* summarized in the two preceding paragraphs," namely that "only men of exceptional wisdom" know what is good for others, and that it is this that creates "the necessity of the absolute rule of the philosophers." So, while (i) he does speak of points that the *Republic* as-a-whole might be said to be making, he also (ii) thinks of these points as *theses* about politics *asserted* by Plato himself. Point (i) is indeed the right first step to take in respecting the literary form or dialogical nature of Plato's dialogues, but the aesthetics and conceptualization of step (ii) are defective, as I will now explain.

The dialogical approach, or any approach which wishes to re-spect the constitutive form of the dialogues, requires that the un-derstanding or appreciation of these works be of them *as well-con-structed wholes*. The dialogical approach does not overlook the ar-chitectonic skill visible in each of Plato's compositions; but neither does it overlook the brilliance and imagistic aptness, or the topical and intellectual allusiveness of the verbal texture of his formative prose.[27] As in a play, whatever is said in a dialogue is said to an-other dramatic character; a speaker's statements are held in the sus-pension of the dramatic action as a whole, they are not addressed, over the heads of the *dramatis personae*, to the auditors of the work.[28] Just so, the communicative interactions in a dialogue are verbal ex-changes that have been put under observation by Plato for the reader-auditor's benefit and edification.

In other words, a dialogue of Plato's operates in the *exhibitive* mode of judgment just like poetry and drama. As distinct from con-trivances that show their meaning forth by having just the shape they do have, actions and conduct operate in the *active* mode of judgment by actively (often wordlessly) instituting new determina-cies in the environment. Categorical truth claims, on the other hand, operate in the *assertive* mode of judgment: the determinacies they institute are created by the truth or falsity of the assertion's claim. Assertive judgments can therefore be linear or serially analytic and additive, if their maker wishes. But active and exhibitive judgments, as the enactments which they are, tend to be complex and open-ended in the sense of modifiable by further action or interpretation, respectively. Exhibitive judgments often don't make *a* point at all, certainly not in the assertive sense; though they may constitute *an* experience. An exhibitive judgment or work can be exploratory, in-terrogative, or suggestive: either expressively suggestive of discon-tents and desiderata or suggestive of exemplarities. Nietzsche's *Kunstprosa* can be invoked to illustrate philosophic work in the ex-hibitive mode which is in an interrogative relation to its audience. The *Hippias Major* could be taken as an example of an aesthetic work—it is both artistic and about art—in the exhibitive mode which is overwhelmingly exploratory, as well as comic, anti-sophistic, and interrogative. But it is not *asserting* anything. It could no doubt be said to have *enacted* something about the equivocity of beauty, for instance, or the vanity of talented prima donnas like Hippias; but to claim that something like this is what it "says" as-a-whole is to impoverish it, *to miss the experience of it*, and to commit the heresy of paraphrase. So will it be with Plato's monumental dramatization of the extended conversation which his Socrates held with two of Plato's relatives and the Kephalides at their house in Peiraeus, on the evening of the festival-day of Bendis the Thracian Goddess.

I give one or two examples. For Strauss one of the lessons of *Republic* is that

Polemarchos no longer maintains that telling the truth is essential to justice. Without knowing it, he . . . lays down one of the principles of the *Republic*. . . . in a well-ordered society it is necessary that one tell untruths of a certain kind to children and even to the adult subjects[29].

This entirely misses both Socrates' *tone* of voice and the *irony* in the relevant passages (*Rep.* 377ff.,389b–c, 414b–415d, 459c–d) when it is he who speaks. So also does Strauss miss the laughability of and irony in the famous proposal (at 473d) that "the philosophers"—meaning Pythagorean men-of-knowledge—should be "the kings in their states," having found already that the "refutation of Kephalos' views of justice . . . contains the proof of the necessity of . . . the absolute rule of the philosophers" (PP 162).

He then says that "the [two] theses of the *Republic* summarized in the two preceding paragraphs show that Plato, or at any rate Socrates, was not a liberal democrat."

On the dialogical approach, of course, what Socrates says *ironically* about either pythagorean intellectuality or its ability to rule *proves* nothing substantive about his (SocP) beliefs except that he must know something about the history of Pythagorean politics in western Greece and the educational curriculum of the sect. And it proves nothing about Plato's own beliefs; only that, like Shakespeare, he was good at convincingly rehearsing other people's views on many subjects. Thus that Strauss's reading of the dialogues is after all non-dialogical is shown by his belief that Plato, through his Socrates, is laying down doctrines assertively, and by his failure to perceive that the doctrines of the visitor from Elea are *only* the visitors, not Plato's.

Nor is the Socrates in Plato's dialogues (SocP) as compatible with Xenophon's Socrates as Strauss thinks. On the dialogical approach Plato's Socrates only *tests* doctrines, or *parades them* with virtuoso brilliance—either to give pause to or entertain his interlocutors, as well as *Plato's* readers or auditors. I leave it to doctrinal readers to bring out the differences between Xenophon's and Plato's Socrates, when the latter is taken to have doctrines. But we may recall here that, according to Aulus Gellius (*Attic Nights* XIV.iii) Xenophon's *Cyropaedia* was the latter's monarchist answer to the appearance of the first two books of Plato's *Republic*. Gellius then adds that "Plato's" response to *that* was to say that "Cyrus . . . had by no means had a fitting education" at *Laws* III.694c. Gellius, we see, was both a doctrinal reader of the dialogues and believed that *Laws* was by Plato; yet if any echo of truth lingers in his story, it shows that *Xenophon himself* read the *Republic* as inimical to his own preference for militarism and monarchy or aristocracy. And this, in turn, has to mean that Xenophon did not see in the *Republic*—as Strauss sees in it—a defense of militarism or aristocracy.[30]

We can now note that Plato's Socrates does not use *kalosk'agathos* as a code-word for oligarchal gentility. At *Meno* 92e, the wealthy opportunist Anytus uses *kalosk'agathos* in response to SocP's ironic defense of Protagoras as a teacher. At *Protagoras* 315d–e, Socrates describes the handsome Pausanias as "well-born and well-bred"; and we remember how he is characterized in the *Symposium* as defending homosocial *erôs*, and as probably having distracted Phaedrus from remaining a philosophic follower of Socrates—as was to be hoped from the *Phaedrus*. At *Protagoras* 328b, the great sophist asserts that his distinction is to help people to become "good and competent." Crito describes Euthydemus as *kalos kai agathos* at *Crito* 271b, meaning that he looks physically "well-developed and handsome." Timaeus at *Timaeus* 88c thinks that cultivation of the arts and the love of knowledge (*philosophia*) make a person *kalos* and *agathos*.

At *Gorgias* 470e SocratesP asserts that men and women who are "honest and good" are happy. SocP gets Polus at *Gorgias* 474c, to agree that the "good and the fitting" are *not* the same thing as the "bad and the shameful." As part of his refutation of Kallicles Socrates distinguishes, at *Gorgias* 518a, exemplary citizens from exemplary tradesmen on the analogy of the difference between proper gymnastic trainers of the body and caterers to the appetites of the body. At *Apology* 21d SocP says he does not know what the "good and admirable" is any more than Meletus, but at least he knows that he doesn't know. At *Parmenides* 127b, Pythodorus is said to have described Parmenides as being "noble and handsome" in countenance. At *Theaetetus* 185e, Socrates tells Theaetetus that to reason beautifully is to be "good and beautiful," while in the frame-dialogue of the *Theatetus* (142b), Theaetetus is remembered by Eucleides as a "noble and competent" man. Plato the writer's uses of *kalosk'agathos*, in other words, are such as both befit the speaker using the expression and the object to which the expression is attached. The applications of the term in the dialogues are, thus, idiolectic rather than ideological. We conclude that neither Plato nor his Socrates, on a dialogical reading of the dialogues, is either teaching doctrine to his interlocutors or attempting—as their long-range literary strategy—to construct a tacitly acceptable defense of the oligarchal way of life. But these are just the two pedagogic and political aims that Xenophon demonstrably pursues in *his* political and "Socratic discourses."

The Hellenistic Drift of Strauss's Political Philosophy

We must now take account of *Laws*—a work in which there is no
"Socrates"—as it feeds into and is determinative of Strauss' conception of "classical political philosophy," my premise being that
Laws is properly a constitutive document of *Hellenistic* not classical
political thought. In one formulation of a distinction basic to his
political philosophy Strauss says,[31]

> Since philosophy consists in ascending from opinion to knowledge,
> and opinion is primarily political opinion, philosophy is essentially
> related to the city; as transcending the city, it presupposes the city;
> philosophy must therefore be concerned with the city to be politi-
> cally responsible.

And it is certainly right to desiderate that philosophic reflection
be politically conscious. But Strauss makes it clear, in saying this,
that he believes his distinction between "knowledge" and "opinion" to be a constitutive component of "classical political philosophy." He derives the dictum from Plato's *Republic*. But it is not
well derived; for, at the very start of the construction in discourse
which SocratesP undertakes in Book II of that work, his words are
"as it *seems* to me" (*hôs egôimai*, 369b4). And the cognate object required by "seems" is "opinion." It follows that Strauss is basing his
sharp distinction between "knowledge" and "opinion" on what is
only an opinion of Plato's Socrates at a certain juncture in the conversation he is holding with Polemarchos and his guests. But if the
distinctions made on the Divided Line—between conjecture-and-
opinion on the one hand and mathemorphic knowledge and the
idea-of-the-good on the other (Book VI)—are invoked as retroactively
justifying Strauss's between "knowledge" and "opinion," then it
must be said that this appeal is nothing other than a lapse into the
non-dialogical, doctrinal way of reading the *Republic*.

This is because when the dialogue is taken as the communicative interaction which it is and which it is dramatizing, we have to admit that Socrates' presentation of the theory of ideas (which the Divided Line diagrams) is a virtuoso turn performed for the benefit of his interlocutors, and staged by Plato to make visible to his readers both the strengths and weaknesses of the theory. The peformance is called for, dramatically speaking, because it gives the theory of reality appropriate to the improved pythagorism that is to characterize the archon-class in the remedial polity which Socrates has been fabling forth. The non-dialogical reading also fails to respond to *the change of tone* which mark Socrates' words when he is forced to give up on "the true and healthy city" (*alêthinê, hygiê polis*) by Glaucon's objections to its frugality (372b–373b). It should not be beyond the perception of good readers of ancient Greek that, in going on to construct the enlarged (373b1) and luxurious (*trufôsan*), feverish (*phlegmainousan*) city Socrates' tone has become sardonic. It has become sardonic *and ironic* because it is at once obvious that this new city will be in need of drastic remediation if it is to survive the perils of luxuriousness and lax defenses—in contrast to Sybaris of tragic precedent. Given Socrates' intellectual interests, furthermore, what else could the reader expect but for SocratesP to make the *intellectual* training—the education—of the warrior-class central to his new construction? The discussion of this, as it turns out, also becomes in Plato's formative hands an extended satire on, or implicit critique of, the pythagorizing curriculum and climate of opinion that was coming into vogue in the fourth century. What Socrates says in *Republic*, then, cannot be taken as either literal or programmatic assertion by him, or as a doctrinal principle of Plato himself.

Strauss's political philosophy, and his idea of "classical political philosophy," depend heavily on his interpretation of the Academic *Laws*.[32] As he says, "The character of classical political philosophy appears with the greatest clarity from Plato's *Laws*, which is his political work par excellence" (PP 26).

And his interpretation of *Laws* starts right out from a non-dialogical reading of Plato's *Crito*. Where Socrates was being *ironic* by addressing himself in the voice of the laws of Athens (50aff.), and the laws tell him that he "preferred neither Sparta nor Crete, which [he] is always *saying* are well governed," Strauss both misses the sarcasm and believes it to have been historically true that these states were better governed than democratic Athens. But we can confirm from *Hippias Major* 283e–285b that SocratesP did not believe this; for there the sarcasm, while also somewhat covered-up in consideration of Socrates' interlocutor, is extended enough to amount to a serious critique of the defects of Lacedaemonian legislation.[33]

On the other hand, on my hypothesis that the posthumous *Laws* is not by Plato but is rather an Academic production, the dialogical principle ceases to be mandatory. This principle is that if it's a *dialogue* and it's *by Plato*, then it must be read dialogically. The principle also lapses in the case of those spurious or doubtful dialogues that visibly try to enforce—like the *Laws*—a particular argument or doctrinal case. Some of the other doubtful or spurious works that Strauss invokes are: *Eighth Letter* (PP 62), *Minos* (PP 71, 134; WPP 88; SA 319), *Lovers* (SPPP 23), 2nd Letter (SPPP 13), *7th Letter* (SPPP 175), *Theages* (SPPP 9,20,46f.,112; XS 89), *Alcibiades II* (XS 19). Since these are all, by definition, post-Platonic or *Hellenistic*, Strauss is skewing his readers' understanding of "classical;" for, the classical century began with the end of the Persian Wars and ended somewhere in the first half of the fourth century. This much then of Strauss's data-base for what he calls "classical political philosophy," apart from the question of the *Laws*, is Hellenistic not classical.

As for the *Laws*, it is irrelevant that they can't be read dialogically, since Strauss in fact reads them in a doctrinal way. But on a dialogical reading of *Republic*, they are totally incompatible with the latter, at the same time that we have already seen Strauss saying that "strictly, there is no Platonic teaching" in *Republic* (PP 159). The literalist reading of *Republic*, into which Strauss frequently lapses, is in any case overriden by the doctrines of *Laws* which, for Strauss, are *the* statement of "Plato's political philosophy"—to use the standard misleading locution. So, if we may again abstract from the question of the *Laws*, then what is left of "Platonic political philosophy" (as Strauss calls it) is only the "teachings" in the *Republic* (as Strauss calls them) which are to be subordinated to those of *Laws*, and what Strauss gets from a literalist misreading of *Politicus* according to which the monarchist doctrines of a visiting rhetorical Sophist from Elea with pythagorist affiliations are attributed to Plato as his own, without a justified decision-procedure for doing so, and in spite of the presence of SocratesP throughout the dialogue.[34]

These doctrines are surely "classical" if "non-Athenian;" but they are not Plato's any more than Hamlet's or Hotspur's views of death are Shakespeare's own. They are and have been called "platonist," however, in the sense that Platonism and Neoplatonism are systems that owe and ascribe their doctrines to the literalist, anti-dialogical reading of Plato's dialogues. That what *Laws* recommends as the best regimes is that of a wise despot co-operating with a divine lawgiver, or else a system in which an oligarchal "Nocturnal Council" of knowlegeable men has the supreme power in the state, is not incompatible with the views Strauss takes to heart from the speeches of the monarchist Eleatic or from Xenophon's works. My counter-claim is that the latter are classical but not demonstrably Plato's, while the former occur in a Hellenistic document that, as an editorial construction, is not by Plato because it does not have the traits that characterize Plato's undoubted dialogues on a dialogical approach to the dialogues.

This in turn allows us to see that Strauss's Socrates is in the main Xenophon's Socrates, with some traits superadded of Plato's and pseudo-Plato's Socrates literalistically understood; and that in so far as SocratesXs has doctrines in addition to Xenophon's, these are derived from a literalist reading of both the undoubted and spurious dialogues as these are compatible with, or reinforce, the doctrines of the *Laws*.

The other respect in which "classical political philosophy" is not as unitary as Strauss makes out, is that in which some classical political writing is oligarchist or monarchist, some of it is visibly pro-democratic, some of it is about mixed constitutions and some of it is conservative in the sense of being a defense of the "the ancestral constitution," whether democratic or oligarchal, and whether the writing labelled itself as such or not. In short, Strauss's version of "classical political philosophy" is more unitary than it actually was historically, and makes it look more élitist and oligarchist than anything else—to the neglect of the anti-tyrannical, anti-factional, and anti-Sophistic nature of much of it. In the respect that Strauss's own political philosophy is élitist, and intellectualist in the sense that it claims to be a rigorous "knowledge" or science, it is no accident that it comes out as an extension of *his* view of "classical political philosophy."[35] Some instinct seems to have led Strauss to develop his own political message *in dissociation* from recognized oligarchist or pythagorizing-élitist sources, and *in association* with the overrated but defensible (because pedagogic) Xenophon and with the Plato literalistically understood who has also never lacked defenders.

Strauss's Place in the Warfare over Athens' Image

From the democratic or moderate Athenian point of view, then, this many-volumed study of "classical political philosophy" which assimilates political views wrongly said to be Plato's to Xenophon's oligarchism and militarism, and which anachronistically mixes Hellenistic attitudes inferred from such Hellenistic documents as the spurious and doubtful dialogues into those views—such a selective construction can be also seen to be a systematic *ex post facto* distortion of the actual climate of opinion of the West's first democracy in its hundred-and-ninety year history from Kleisthenes' constitutional reforms (512 B.C.) to Demades' acceptance of Antipater's imposition on Athens of an oligarchic constitution in 322 B.C. In the long history of *the warfare over the West's image of Athenian democracy*, Strauss's plausibility to his followers will count as a battle won for oligarchism by its Straussian variant. As a doctrinal interpretation of the texts of Plato and Aristophanes, however, it is one more defeat for the discipline of source-criticism in philology. As for the cause which seeks to reinstate *literary* sensibility or aesthetic responsiveness into our reading of ancient works, it is another denial (in a partisan interest) of the creative perceptions of two *great critics of their times*, one a witty dialectical dramatizer of the disputatious intellectual life of his city, the other a comedic caricaturist of its political and social attitudes.

Notes

1. A.D.Winspear *Who Was Socrates?* 1939 (N.Y. Russell & Russell 1960); L. Strauss *Socrates and Aristophanes* (Chicago U.P. 1966; Midway 1980); A.Bloom "Aristophanes and Socrates," in *Giants and Dwarfs* (N.Y. Simon & Schuster 1990) which contains a chapter on Leo Strauss.

2. Cf. V.Tejera "Ideology & Literature: Xenophon's *Defense* of Socrates and Plato's *Apology*," in E.Kelly ed. *New Essays on Socrates* (Lanham: U.P.A. 1984).

3. The historical evidence is summarized in A.Melero Bellido *Atenas y el Pitagorismo* (Universidad de Salamanca 1972).

4. Curiously enough, Nietzsche both liked and disliked the undisambiguated or *composite* Socrates (SocC) of 'the tradition;' and, as I have shown in *Nietzsche and Greek Thought*, what he loved about 'Socrates' corresponds to the traits given him by Plato in the dialogues when these are read dialogically. For this reason the symbol used in that book for Nietzsche's Socrates was SocCn rather than SocDn as above. The 'Socrates' Nietzsche disliked, however, corresponds to a composite of traits derived from Diogenes Laertius and Xenophon; so that, all in all, Nietzsche was referring to a *composite* Socrates who was both a culture-hero, and attached to *some rationalist dogmas*.

5. So, President Reagan, for example, will now never be rid of the image, foisted on him by the comics and the media, of the ever-napping unworried mumbler of soothing nothings. If it is claimed that there is a basis for the caricature in his actual conduct, the claim has to be tested against the historical record, not against other images in the pro-Reagan press or Nancy's memoirs. Many readers nonetheless take both the association between Alcibiades and 'Socrates' and that between Aristophanes' caricature and 'Socrates' as being historical. Sign that this is of their authors' literary success, it is also the opposite of historical proof for the associations: from the historiographic point of view in fact such success is what would *explain away* the associations in question.

6. See W.Burkert "Platon oder Pythagoras? Zum Ursprung des Wortes`Philosophie'," *Hermes* 88, No. 2 (1960), for the demonstration that the emergence and first uses of this term occurred in Plato's dialogues.

7. We key *Socrates and Aristophanes* as SA. Here are the other abbreviations that we will need. CM: *The City and Man* (Rand McNally 1962); XSD: *Xenophon's Socratic Discourse*: an Interpretation of the *Oeconomicus* (Cornell U.P. 1970); XS: *Xenophon's Socrates* (Cornell U.P. 1972); AAL: *The Argument and the Action of Plato's Laws* (Chicago U.P. 1975); SPPP: *Studies in Platonic Political Philosophy* (Chicago U.P. 1983). PP *Political Philosophy*, ed. H.Gildin (N.Y. Pegasus 1975).

8. For a recent attempt to bring up to date the dispute about the *Lysis*, see my "On the Form and Authenticity of the 'Lysis,'" *Ancient Philosophy* Vol.X, No.2 (1990). See also "Eco, Peirce, and Interpretationism," *The American Journal of Semiotics* Vol. 8, No.1–2 (1991), for the form which claims and counter-claims to authorial authenticity must take.

9. Cf. *Plato's Dialogues One By One*, Ch.10 "The Question of Form & the Problem of the *Laws*;" and Ch.II, *Nietzsche & Greek Thought*, "Nietzsche on the Greek Decline," for a discussion of the internal and external evidence for the non-authenticity of *Laws*, and for some comments on its place in Greek intellectual history.

10. See, for instance, K.E. Schwarzenberg "The Socrates of Demetrius of Phaleron," and his research on the extant archaeological portraitures of 'Socrates,' showing that the physical features attributed to Socrates by the sculptors and artists are all of literary or folk derivation. Proceedings of the 2nd Intl.Conf. on Greek Philosophy, in *The Philosophy of Socrates* ed. K. Boudouris, Samos 1990.

11. The alleged conflict stems from literalist readings of *Republic*, and from the pythagorist assumption that 'lógos' is opposed to 'poiêsis'. But Plato's dialogical practice is a tacit refutation of the necessity for such a conflict—given that his formative prose, his imagery, and his conceptualization combine to achieve a level of *great poetic art* in the well-formed dialogues which I have always described as "having literary closure while being intellectualy open-ended." Thus, it is not right to oppose Plato's *working* conception of 'lógos' to poetry as if reflectiveness or rationality were not a quality of poetry or as if imagination and affectivity were not aspects of 'lógos'. Nor was there any quarrel except in the minds of the pythagorizers and literalists between seekers after knowledge in imagistic-rhythmic prose (like Herakleitos) or in epic meters (like Parmenides, Thales, or Empedocles). And if the encyclopedic Pherecydes is adduced as having written prose, he cannot be invoked as either opposed to poetry (a signficant part of his subject-matter) or as exactly a "philosopher."

12. This work was published in 1966. It was followed by *Xenophon's Socratic Discourse*: an Interpretation of the Oeconomicus in 1970, *Xenophon's Socrates* in 1972, and *The Argument and the Action of Plato's Laws* in 1975.

13. SocratesX does, seemingly as a matter of course, casually call himself a *philosophos* at, e.g., *Oeconomicus* xvi.9.

14. *Xenophon's Socratic Discourse*: an Interpretation of the *Oeconomicus* (Cornell U.P. 1970); and *Xenophon's Socrates* (Cornell U.P. 1972).

15. Yet it would seem that Strauss knows very well that Xenophon had an ideology. In SPPP (p.106) he adduces the citation in *Hellenica* (III.1.1–2) of a certain "Themistogenes," *offspring of the Right*, as the pseudonymous author of the *Anabasis*. Is it not disingenuous of Strauss, knowing this, to have avoided discussion of the ideological element in the authors he appeals to? Cf. the discussion of ideology in Xenophon and Plato in my "Literature & Ideology: "Xenophon's *Defense* of Socrates & Plato's *Apology*," in *New Essays on Socrates* ed. E.Kelly (NES).

16. See "Ideology & Literature: Xenophon's *Defense* of Socrates & Plato's *Apology*," in E.Kelly ed. *op.cit.* p.1 above; and "Plato's Tragic Humor," Ch.2 of PDOBO.

17. It is made by Kallias in response to a question of Antisthenes; there, they both equate it with justness (*dikaiosynê*).

18. It is possible, speaking historiographically, that at this remove from the fourth century B.C., we fail to appreciate the ability of a classical Greek

to swing from the extreme of sobriety-and-restraint to an extreme of frivolity-and-sensuousness bordering on license.

19. This metaphor of SocratesP's is not the less effective because he is in
the middle of an ironic and extended fabulation about a city in the sky.
But notice the logically *undistributed* nature of the first two mentions of
'Socrates' in the quotation: it isn't clear whether the first two SocU's are
the historical Socrates, or SocP or SocX (since "kingly man" is an expression used by Xenophon's but not Plato's Socrates).

20. Cf. my "The Politics of a Rhetorical Sophist," *Quaderni Urbinati di
Cultura Classica* 1992; and "An Eleatic Sophist on Politics," Ch.14 of *Plato's
Dialogues One By One* (N.Y. Irvington 1984), for a fuller account of the
systematic nature of the equivocation instituted by the sophist between
politikê and *basilikê*, and of the pythagorizing and oligarchal imbrication of
his views.

21. The characterization of the Sophist in that dialogue is not entirely
negative: he was there called a *masterful* contriver or counterfeiter and a
knowing imitator of what is true and what is excellent. Being a *rhetorical*
Sophist himself, it was the disputatious or eristic Sophists (with whom he
tacitly classifies the elder Socrates) who are derogated by him. The visitor's
special severity with Sophists who "garrulously dispute" for "no pay,"
makes the allusion to Socrates explicit.

22. We note the use of the optative here, and the *conditional* force of the
participial construction in the first of the last three quotations.

23. "The Question of Form, and the Problem of the *Laws*," ch.10 of
PDOBO.

24. Aristotle *Nic.Ethics* I.vi.7: "The Pythagoreans seem to give a more
probable doctrine on the subject of the Good. . . and . . . Speusippus seems
to have followed them."

25. I take this occasion to correct a misprint in my PDOBO, p.140; what
Cicero says, at *De Leg*.ii.6, is that Charondas *and* (not *of*) Zaleucus wrote
preambles for *their* laws.

26. In *History of the . . . Aristotelian Writings* (Oxford: Clarendon 1888),
and *The Politics of Aristotle*, Rev.Text, Bks.1–5; Intro., Anal., Comm. (London: Macmillan 1894) respectively.

27. On the analogy of film, if the former is called the scenario, the latter
(the talking as "internal" to the situatedness of the conversation) would

be what screen-credits call the dialogue. Of course, there *is* nothing but 'dialogue' in this sense in a dialogue of Plato's. "Plato's prose" is, thus, *formative* in the fullest sense. The aptness with which the verbal micro-texture and the over-all structure of a dialogue resonate with, and reciprocally augment, each other must be credited to Plato's *artfulness*.

28. As happens once in the monologous *Laws*, at the beginning of Book V.

29. Note the slip involved in the reference to "citizens" (*politics*) as "subjects." While citizens are members of republics, one can only be a "subject" in a monarchy, tyranny or oligarchy. [*hupêkoos*, in the sense of "subject of a prince" does not occur in Plato's dialogues, according to Brandwood's *A Word-Index to Plato* (London: Maney 1976).]

30. For what it's worth, D.Laertius (iii.34) also reports that "Xenophon was not on good terms with [Plato]."

31. *Thoughts on Machiavelli* (Glencoe: Free Press 1958), p.291–2.

32. *The Argument and the Action of Plato's Laws* (Chicago U.P. 1975).

33. Similarly for the passage at *Protagoras* 342a–b, in which Socrates mockingly ironizes about the abundance of *sophistai*, men–of–knowledge, in Crete and Lacedaemon, given, he says sarcastically that there "the search for knowledge, *philosophía*, is older and fuller than anywhere else." Sophists, as Hippias complains to SocratesP, were not welcome in Sparta and, even when they spoke in public, were on principle not paid (*Hip.Maj.* 283e–284b9, 285b7).

34. As to "Why does [Plato] make his Socrates a silent listener to . . . his Eleatic stranger's speeches," Strauss admits (*The City and Man.* p.50) that "we do not know the reason." This simply means that Strauss has not grapsed what sort of a dialogue or work the *Politicus* is. It means, ironically, that Strauss has failed to implement his own principle of "logographic necessity," namely, the recognition that "every part of a written speech must be necessary for the whole; the place where each part occurs is the place where it is necessary that it should occur." Socrates is silent because he is *listening Socratically*, making us the readers his ironic co-listeners. Strauss is implicitly contradictory when he says both that Plato "does not *tell* us" why Socrates is silent and that Plato never *says* anything in his own voice in the dialogues (*ibid.*).

35. Some of the political works or documents overlooked by Strauss are listed in the Bibliography.

3

On the Prelude to the *Timaeus* and the *Atlantis*-Story

Revising the Foundation–Myth: An Oligarchal Appropriation of Solon

Is the *Kritias* an Unfinished Dialogue?

In turning our search-light onto the early intellectual history of the warfare over the image of the classical Athenian democracy, and given the state of the question, perhaps the best way in which to begin a reading of the *Kritias* is with a feeling for it as a *completed* whole. But since this already answers the question in my section-heading, I must say at once that I agree with Welliver in not finding the *Kritias* to be an unfinished dialogue.[1] Welliver, however, also concludes that the *Kritias* is of a piece and completely continuous with, the *Timaeus* so that the two are a unity. We will, therefore, need not only to judge whether and to what extent, each of these has dramatic coherence but also whether taken together they also do.

The problem is that while the signs of the *Timaeus'* being a platonist imitation seem to be explainable away, the signs that the *Kritias* is an oligarchist-platonist addition to Plato's work, tacked on for the purpose of enforcing a non-dramatic doctrinal interpretation of it, are much clearer and cannot be explained away. So, *if* the *Kritias* is not by Plato *and* it forms a unity with the *Timaeus, then* either the *Timaeus* or the standard interpretation of it must come under re-examination on the suspicion that it has been tampered with to allow for the attachment of the *Kritias* to it. We will pursue this two-fold leading question into the textural (literary) quality and textual (philological) nature of the dialogue in the interest of verifying or qualifying our overall understanding—so far as we can get one—of the responses to and warfare over the image of the Athenian democracy during the latter half of the fourth century.

One main reason for saying that, while it may be "unfinished" in some literary senses, it is *not* a fragment that breaks off before its ending is that, properly understood, the final words of the dialogue are indeed terminal: *kai ksynageiras eipen* means, "and having gathered them together, he spoke." or "having gathered them together, he addressed them." Not: "having assembled them, he spake thus . . ." (Bury); or: "having assembled them, he said . . ." (Davis). *eipe* does not only mean "say" or "say that." It could just as well mean "spoke up" or "spoke to" or "addressed [them]." And this meaning is quite compatible with the context, given that the proemium just preceding is so good that it obviates the need for any speech at all. Interestingly, this proemium is just *the speech with which* Shorey (who thought it's an unfinished dialogue) *ends* his 5-page essay on the *Kritias*, quoting in full Ruskin's elegant translation.[2] To make full sense, however, this translation should also have had a period six words from the end, and these six words should have been: "So (*kai*), having assembled them (*ksunageiras*), he addressed them (*eipen*)."

Does the 'Timaeus' Identify Itself as a Sequel to the 'Republic'?

Before we try to read either of our dialogues dialogically, we will first review the claims about the connection of the *Timaeus* to the

Republic. In the fiction of the former, Socrates has told his friends the day before about a previous conversation he once held on the subject of the constitution. The clauses "My yesterday's discourse was mainly about the sort of constitution and the kind of men which seemed to me to make it the best (*aristê*, 17c1–3)"; and "when you requested me yesterday to go over my views of the constitution (20b)," tell us that the Socrates in this dialogue discussed the constitution *thes* in summary form. Timaios adds that what he said about it was approved by all.

But it is a big leap from here to the assumption, unbridged by any text except 19a6–10, that this discourse was a summary of Socrates' extended construction in the *Republic*, given that all that these lines affirm is: "such indeed is what was said Socrates." For one thing, Timaios, from distant Lokri, was not present at Socrates' conversation about the constitution with the Kephalidai in Piraeus; so he cannot have been a witness to its accuracy as a summary of what it claimed to be a summary of. For another, if what is said between 17c6 to 19b is a rehearsal of that summary, it is neither to scale *in scope*, nor isomorphic *in content* with the discourse in Plato's *Republic*, even though Timaios confirms that 17c–19b has left nothing out. Still less is the summary consonant with *the tone* in which Socrates had developed his portrait of the Ideal State.[3] The differences in scope and content are enough to make it impossible for the summary to be of Socrates' extended fabulation in the *Republic* of the remedial constitution needed by the Ideal State.

Even more startling is the difference in tone, on a dialogical reading of *Republic*. As the luxurious and fevered (*truphôsa, phlegmainousa*) city which it becomes, if it is to be lived in by Glaucon, Socrates must build into it the remedies that will bring down the fever and protect it from external predations on its surpluses and luxuries. So, starting at *Republic* II.373a and because he is no longer dealing with the necessary, true and healthy city (*anankaiotate, alêthinê, hygiês, polis*), Socrates' tone becomes systematically sardonic. And it will remain implicitly sardonic throughout the rest of Socrates' extended fabulation—for all of its digressions, stories within stories, parables and allegories, for all of its diagrammatized theory of knowledge and reality and curriculum reform, throughout both its music criticism and political criticism, and behind its mathematical jesting (both in the clearly signalled case of the 'nuptial number' and the more covered-up case of the arithmetized disproportion between the satisfactions of 'the kingly man' and those of the tyrant).[4]

As a construction in the exhibitive mode that makes visible the un-Athenian consequences and human tensions inherent in the Ideal State, it cannot avoid being a satire of that conception. It is also a satire—gentle and witty as Plato makes it—of pythagorean intellectuality, because that is the mind-set most appropriate to a militarist-oligarchal state. Moderates and democrats had long been in the habit of appealing to the Ancestral Constitution. The oligarchists' counter to that was to appeal to the alternative high-sounding Ideal State (*malist' eiê kat' euchein polis*), the "most-to-be-wished-for state." It is this state that *Republic* puts under critical observation for us.

Incongruent as it is with the political content and entertaining intellectuality of Plato's *Republic*, the summary as given is nonetheless designed to be taken as a straight recapitulation of Socrates's discourse on the constitution in that work. Its purpose would seem to have been two-fold. It provides a dogmatic, Academic or platonizing interpretation of Plato's implicitly skeptical work: this is the interpretation, namely, that captures *Republic* for doctrinal-systematic use by platonizing idealists such as Speusippus, Xenocrates, and their successors. Secondly, it announces and prepares for the addition of sequels to the Timaeus, sequels that would further develop or reinforce the oligarchist-idealist components of the Ideal State taken literally. The experiment that makes the *Kritias* a sequel to the *Timaeus* is more successful than that which tries to make the Timaeus a sequel to the *Republic*. The first succeeds as much as it does because the Kritias is composed from its beginning as a continuation of the *Timaeus*.

But does the introductory conversation in the latter, from 17a to 19e, really succeed as an interlocking reference to Socrates' discourse on the state in *Republic*? The fiction here is that Socrates, on the day before today's meeting and Goddess-festival, has told his friends Timaios, Hermocrates and Kritias about a previous conversation he once held on the subject of the constitution. But even if we assume that the reference of these words is to the political discussion in *Republic*, this previous occasion—except for the detail that it was on the Bendidea—is itself undated and unlocatable in fictional-biographic or dramatic time. The situation is worse if we take the reference to be, not to the discourse within the *Republic*, but to "Republic" as the narrated dialogue which it is, and which is therefore already a report of what had happened to Socrates and the Kepahalidai on the Bendideia "the day before."

So, even if that previous conversation about the state was his discourse in the *Republic*, then the previous occasion mentioned yesterday is not this year's Bendideia. Today's rehearsal of it in *Timaeus*, then, is of yesterday's summary of an undatable discourse, even if the reference of that discourse was to a discussion that took place on a given Bendideia; so "today" is not fixable by any reference to the festival-day on which the discussion in *Republic* took place.

Kritias does note at 21a, as Socrates also does at 24e3, that today is a festival of the Athenian Goddess. The meeting-day of Timaios, Hermocrates and Kritias here in the *Timaeus* is indeed one day after this festival. But this festival is not the Bendideia, as Proclus mistakenly suggested. Bury's note to his translation of the Zurich text of *Timaeus* says that the festival is "the lesser Panathenaea, held early in June, just after (sic) the Bendideia." Archer-Hind also thinks the reference is to the Lesser Panathenaea; and they fell 2 months later, like the Greater Panathenaea, around the 26 to 28 of Hekatombaion. But the Bendideia fell on the 19th of Thargelion, while the üPanathenaea fell on the 28th of Hekatombaion. So Proclus is wrong in claiming that the *Timaeus* takes place on the day following the Bendideia. Festugière believes Proclus has confused the Lesser Panathenaea with the festival of Athena called the Plynterion which was on the 25th of Thargelion.[5] But all this does is to reduce the discrepancy to some three-or-four to nine days. So the claim that the conversation of the day before was the one that Socrates conducted with the Kephalidai in Piraeus at the Bendideia is not supported by the text after all.

To put all this in another way: the discourse in *Republic*—if it had been in reference—would have to be "yesterday's" story potentiated, raised to the square so to say, since it is a narrated dialogue about what happened 'yesterday.' So yesterday's discussion in dramatic real time could've been any discussion of the "Ideal State." If it was yesterday's discussion of the "Ideal State" discussed on the *Republic's* main speaker's "yesterday," wouldn't the wording have been 'yesterday's discussion' of the state discussed by you on "a yesterday," namely, on the eve of the Bendidea? In other words, the text of the *Timaeus* does not of itself connect it dramatically to the *Republic* as a sequel to it.

The 'Timaeus' Version of Kritias's *Atlantis*-Story

Kritias does not tell us what festival "today" is of the Goddess (*tên theon . . . en têi panêgyrei*, 21a). Because Socrates says that the story Kritias has told from 20e to 26e is "specially suited to the festival of the Goddess now going on" (24e3), we are left wondering to which Goddess (or festival) the myth of a war with Atlantis might be so suited. When the author has Kritias add that "it is all-important that it's not an invented fable, but a true account" (24e4f.), we wonder further whether he realizes that these words can't help functioning as a self-focusing device that emphasizes all the more the fabulous nature of the fable?

We note, accordingly, that the tale that Kritias tells more briefly here (20e–26e) and at greater length in the *Kritias* (108e–121c),[6] was told him by his eponymous grandfather on children's day (*koureteôsis*) of the three-day feast of Apatouria (*apatouriôn*). The relevant points are (i) that, as the festival was thought to commemorate a happy deception,[7] it was a kind of April Fool's day, and (ii) that Kritias the elder's friend, who brought him the story from Solon, was named Drôpides. The first, or supper, day of the festival was called the *dorpeia*; but the root verb-form *drô* ("make") in the first syllable of Drôpides surely determines most of the color, the connotational halo, of this name. "Makerson" is a suggestive English equivalent. *Drôpô* means "see through, cut through;" and is related to *drepô* "gather or cull;" while *drôpazein* is synonymous with *emblêpein* "to gaze at, look in the face," with *emblêma* meaning "insertion." All in all and in this context, Drôpides would seem to suggest a "perceptive maker-up or bringer-forward of stories."[8]

Given that the names of so many of the characters in the dialogues signal something about their owners, it is not too much to presume that Drôpides has this kind of aptness to it too. Like the self-focusing device mentioned above, it silently alerts the reader to the author's detachment about the story he is putting in the mouth of his speakers.[9] But that it is a practice of great authors like Shakespeare and Dickens, as well as Plato, does not of course preclude it from being imitatable.

The possible contradiction between the statedly oral-aural nature (at 21a7) of the story transmitted to, and by, Solon (in the Greek milieu) and the anomalous claim by the Egyptian priest (at 24a1) to have documents 9000 years old that certified it, is muted by the priest's explanation of it as a matter of Egyptian cultural and historical practices of long standing, which non-Nilotic peoples are unable to follow because of the illiteracy (23c3–4) and cycles of destruction that leave them without a recorded past from which to go on. Millenially-kept Egyptian records, however, allow the Egyptian priest to tell Solon of a prehistoric Golden Age of Athens among whose exploits was the defeat of a mighty host from the island empire of Atlantis in the west. This army was bent on extending its Afro-European conquests to both Athens and Egypt (25b). But Athenian valor and leadership defeated it, and liberated all who dwell on this side of the Pillars of Hercules. Unfortunately, however, cataclysmic quakes and floods then occurred which swallowed up not only the triumphant warriors of Athens but also the whole island territory of Atlantis, leaving the ocean impassable because of the mud shoals in which it came to rest.

The purpose of this telling is made clear in the next paragraphs, from 25d7 to 26e1, which pile more 'explanations' on the already 'explained' survival and transmisüsion of the extraordinary story.— Kritias says and marvels that while he cannot remember all the details of Socrates' yesterday's account, "not a single detail of [Kritias's account] has escaped [him] . . . even though it's so very long since I heard the tale . . . it is indelibly fixed in my mind like those encaustic designs which cannot be effaced" (26b–c). "Marvellous indeed," he says, "is the way in which the lessons of one's childhood 'grip the mind,' as the saying is" (26b2–4). More importantly, Solon's Kritias–transmitted description of prehistoric Athens' Golden Age turns out *by convenient coincidence* to be the very equivalent of Socrates' yesterday's description of the Best State

The Literalist Summary of Yesterday's State, and the Illusionism of "Xthes"

Kritias's says about his promised account that it will transport the city "fabled" yesterday (26c10) by Socrates into the realm of truth (*epi talêthes*) by imagining that these ancient Athenians of the elder Kritias are their ancestors and that the Best State will be, by deliberate selection (27b1), populated by them. But we notice that the promise is also an attempt to rake in Solon as an authority for, and supporter of, the Ideal Constitution (27b2): He "makes them citizens of this state of ours . . . according to the account and law of Solon" (*kata dê ton Solônos logon te kai nomon*). Kritias claims that the existence and Athenian citizenship of these forgotten mythical men is legitimated by "the declaration of the sacred writings" (27b5). Since citizenship was a jealously guarded status in classical Athens, adult readers could not have helped noticing that here it is granted on the basis of *foreign* Egyptian documents of impossible age.

Solon was, of course, the founder of the Ancestral Constitution (*hê patrios politeia*), and the legislator who "put an end to unlimited oligarchy (*oligarchian katalusai lian akraton*), emancipated the people, established the hereditary democracy (*dêmokratian. . . tên patrion*) and harmonized the different elements of the state" (*miksanta . . . kalôs*, Arist. *Politics* II.1273b35–74a21). It is clear that he is being co-opted here for oligarchism by Kritias, who will, in his own dialogue, be offering a mythicized defense of that political orientation and so, also but indirectly, will be enforcing an oligarchist interpretation of the *Republic* and a neoplatonist one of the *Timaeus*. Kritias naturally claims to have documents proving the Solonic nature of his version of the state, "these very writings" from my grandfather "are actually now mine" (*tauta ge dê ta grammata* 113b1).

Returning to the question of the putative linkages among the *Republic*, *Timaeus*, and *Kritias*, let us review the way in which the impression of connection among them arises. Kritias is saying in the last–mentioned dialogue how the *machimon*, the purely military class, lived apart from the other classes in the ancient God-governed territory that became Athens—seemingly because of the presence of divine heroes (*andrôn theiôn*, 110c) in it.[10] The members of this class had only shared property, "and from the other citizens they claimed to receive nothing (*ouden aksiountes . . . dechesthai*) but a sufficient sustenance. And they practiced all those practices mentioned yesterday (*ta xoes lechthenta*) for the proposed (*hypotethentôn*) guardians then described (*errêthê*)." So let us look again, from another angle, to see whether yesterday's summary model for Kritias's proposed state can really be pinned down in dramatic real time as a summary of the one described in Plato's *Republic*.

Here at *Kritias* 110d3 'yesterday' has to refer to Socrates' summary at the beginning of the *Timaeus*, from 17c6 to 19b—offered, he says at 20b3, "eagerly to gratify" (*prothumôs echarizomên*) Kritias the oligarch and Timaios the Pythagorean. To two such personages, naturally, only a pythagorizing oligarchy would be so gratifying; and this is what the summary gives them. "For," Socrates adds, "you alone among the living, after getting our city into a suitable (*preponta*) war, are able to confer on her all befitting qualities,"—war being, naturally, the rationale for militarization, and militarization the excuse for concentrating power in one or a few.

It will help the inquiry if we pause to register that the only occurrence of *xthes* in the *Kritias* is here at 110d3; it's important because it refers back to the uses of *xthes* at *Timaeus* 19a7 and 20b2 where Socrates first mentions and rehearses his speech of yesterday. Then, fifteen lines down Hermocrates interposes that, "also yesterday" at Kritias's house (20c7) "right after our return from you," Kritias had brought to their attention his story "from ancient tradition" (*ek palaias akoês*). So, these and the *xthes* at 110d3 are the places by reference to which the *Kritias* attaches itself to the *Timaeus*.

In the *Timaeus*, *xthes* had already been used three times in the first eighteen lines. Three of our entertainees (*daitumônes*) yesterday, Socrates implies, are our entertainers (*estiatôres*) today. Timaios' phrasing implies next that the entertainer or host yesterday was Socrates (*hypo sou ksenithentes*). The three were *with* Socrates, but were they *at* Socrates's? We are never quite told *where* that yesterday's conversation took place. In the phrase "as soon as I left from thence" (*enthende*) for—presumably—his own house, Kritias might be implying that it was at Socrates' place.

But just *where* today's *Timaeus* conversation is taking place we are not able to tell with certainty from the dialogue itself. At *Tim.* 20c8 it is specified that Hermocrates and his companion Timaios are lodging in Kritias's guest-suite (20c8), and Timaios is named as "the third of our trio" by Kritias (20d5). That the author is thinking of the place of today's *Timaeus* conversation as being Kritias's house, is implied by Hermocrates' being able to speak of a return (*aphikometha . . . kath' hodon*) to it at 20c8–9. However, if it *is* taking place at Kritias's house, wouldn't Kritias's scrupulous-sounding reference to the writings in his possession have said or implied something about having them at hand? The third *xthes* comes when, in response to Timaios' request, Socrates is refreshing his auditors' memories by recapitulating what he said yesterday "about the constitution, and the kind of principles and men which, for me, will make it come out the best" (17c1–3).

The other six occurrences of *xthes* all come between 25e2 and 26e8. The first at 25e2 (as already hypothesized), is part of Kritias's attempt to get Solon's blessing, so to say, for the citizens both of Socrates' summarized polity and his prehistoric proto-oligarchal Athenian archetypes. But this means that the author—and we are still in the *Timaeus*, not yet in the *Kritias*—either wants the reader to see that Kritias is a *tendentious* mythologizer or else he wants the reader to *accept* Kritias's mythopoeia. And these are incompatible alternatives, to which we will have to return.

The second and third occurences of *xthes*, at 26a5 and a8, are those which seem to locate the *Timaeus* conversation in Kritias's house. The fourth, at 26b4, is that in which Kritias says it is easier to remember some things heard in childhood than something heard yesterday. Kritias then states, at 26c9–d4,

The citizens and the city which you described to us yesterday as in a fable (*hôs en mythôi*), we will transfer into the realm or truth (*epi t'alêthes*) here, positing that one to be this one (*thêsomen hôs ekeinên tênde ousan*), and that the citizens you imagined are in truth those forefathers of ours of whom the priest spoke.

The sixth occurrence of *xthes* is in the context of Socrates' saying that the story is especially suited to today's festival of the Goddess, and that it is not invented but is a true account; and that, given his speech of yesterday, "it is his turn to keep silent" (26e9). Notice that it is Kritias's Atlantis story that Socrates has said is so appropriate, not the creation story into which Timaios then launches.

Now this, from the literary point of view, particularly from the point of view of dialogue-construction, creates an anomalous discontinuity. Given that most of the rest of the dialogue is going to consist of Timaios's cosmological discourse, it's puzzling that it is Kritias not Timaios that we find Socrates addressing. So much so that when Socrates goes right on to say "it is now necessary for you to discourse to us" (26e8–9), we notice (i) that Kritias has already said (a few lines up at 26c7–9) "I am ready to tell my tale *not just in outline but as heard in full detail*," and (ii) that *he has already given* us, *instead*, an *abbreviated* version of the Atlantis story. So what are these words an announcement of? Not of what Kritias *did do* back at 20e–262. It is, rather, an announcement appropriate to the longer story which he tells in the *Kritias*.

On the other hand, when Socrates had finished his summary of "yesterday's" description of the Ideal polis (at 20b), and reminded both Hermocrates and Kritias that it is now their turn to comply with his request—which was for a description of what that state would look like when "engaged in a suitable war"—Hermocrates adduces that Kritias is ready with a story he has been working to recollect since yesterday. And Kritias proceeds to tell it as we have it, from 20e to 26e. But there is no mention at this early stage (when it would not have been improper) of it's being preceded by, or having to be repeated after, the telling of a creation-story by the honorable (*timios*) Timaios.[11] That announcement doesn't come till 27a with an excuse about how, once Timaios has covered the generation of the cosmos he, Kritias, will take over from Timaios the humans about to be created in his discourse, and from Socrates' the selectively trained men mentioned in his polity.

The 'Kritias' Version of the First Part of the Atlantis–Story

Readers have no difficulty in granting that the purpose Timaios's prefatory prayer at the beginning of the Kritias, is to link up this dialogue with the *Timaeus*. At the end of it Timaios calls knowledge (*epistêmê*) the completest and best of medicines (*pharmakôn*), and turns the discourse over to Kritias. We notice two or three things about the indulgence he in turn asks for. First, that when Socrates grants it he extends it to Hermocrates' future address, thus bringing him too into the loop (so to say) which Hermocrates, however, never enters. Secondly, that 107b1–e1 is a long digression about the problems of representation (*mimêsis*), and that in the course of it he insults his auditors by speaking—with a clumsiness untypical of Plato's art of characterization—of their inexperience and ignorance in the matter of representing the Gods. At the end of the digression 107e2–3), thirdly Kritias claims that his "account is given on the spur of the moment."[12] And this is false; whoever the author is has forgotten that, in the *Timaeus*, both Hermocrates and Kritias have said that he had given a lot of thought to the matter since the day-before-yesterday's meeting with Socrates. And this is one difference between the Kritias in *Timaeus* and the one in his own dialogue.

Let us now look at some compositional differences between the stories as told in the *Timaeus* and in the *Kritias*. That "the [Atlantean] dwellers beyond the pillars of Hercules" and "*all* (*posin*) that dwelt *within* them" are the peoples at war (108e4), contradicts the fact that in the *Timaeus* account the empire of Atlantis was said to have conquered Libya and parts of Europe *within* the pillars of Hercules, as far as Etruria (*Tyrrênias*, 25b1–2).

While Kritias at 109a says that he must give precedence (*anankê kat'archas*) to the military and political situation of Athens, he only devotes 3 1/2 Stephanus pages to *it*. But to Atlantis he gives more than twice as many (113c–121c). He then narrates, at 109b, that the Gods piloted (*oiaki . . . ekybernôn*) the mortal herd with psychological rudders of persuasion instead of the rods and staffs of shepherds.

We note that this language tries to color over, with non-violent imagery, Kritias's actual historical image as the bloody tyrant that he was.[13] It, nonetheless, does not abandon the standard sophistical-pythagorean reference to the rulers as *herders*.

Sophist that he is (as, e.g., in Plato's *Charmides*), Kritias flatters the Athenians' love of knowledge and artfulness by putting them under the aegis of Athena and Hephaistos, the Gods of *philosophía* and *philotechnía*, and by making the Athenians autochthonous. He flatters Greek localism by twice insisting (109d3–4, 110a7–8) that the names of these first earth-born Athenians have been preserved, even while their works and writings were destroyed by intervening floods. He infers this because Solon stated that the Egyptian priests' narrative of the war mentioned most of the names of the heroes before Theseus, such as Kekrops, Erectheus, Erichthonius and Erysichthon.[14] Kritias says he returns to this point about the names at 113a because Solon got them from the priests in Egyptian, and had to translate their meaning back into Greek when beginning to draft his poem about all this, and "these very writings are . . . now in [his] possession, and [he] learnt them by heart when a child" (113b2–3). The other reason for this is to cover up the fact that Kritias's narrative is a purely Greek story. Note the assumption that proper nouns have meanings (connotations), not just denotation.

We take note also of the clumsy writing at 110c1–3, where all the species of herding animals of both sexes are said to be naturally able to attend (*prosakouein*) to their own species-excellence (*aretên*). Could this be an imitator's echo of *Republic* 397e, where Socrates ironically desiderates the principle that only if one man is allowed one job, only then will it be properly done . . .? Thus, two pages down the farmers are real (*alêthinôn*) farmers who practice *only* farming; though they are also men of good taste and noble nature (*philokalôn, euphyôn,* 111e4), namely, men who—in after-thought— would make "good oligarchist material," like Xenophon perhaps, the archetypical militarist oligarch and gentleman-farmer.

The military class, however, gets very brief mention within a contrastingly unhurried account of an idyllic ecology. They live quite separately from, though supported by, the productive classes whom the guardians protect. And they are mentioned, in just one reference at 110d4, as identical with the guardians "posited" in what Socrates said "yesterday" *xthes*. But shouldn't it be "the day before yesterday," given that yesterday was taken up with Timaios's cosmogonic discourse, and that just before it reference was made to Socrates' speech of 'yesterday'?

We're told where the military class lives two pages later, namely, atop the acropolis next to the temple of Athena and Hephaistos. We note that while it is repeated that they are allowed no gold or silver as in *Republic*, they are now said to live side by side with (or, in community with) the priests.[15] Different from the *Republic* also is the implication at 12c5–7 that their buildings, houses and profession were hereditary rather than occupied by selected, successfully trained warriors. And where in *Republic* there is only a general statement that reproduction must be controlled, here it is specified that their number must be forever limited to 20,000. No such figure is given in the *Timaeus* version of the Best State either.

Now Kritias's lines from 112e1–e10 sound like a peroration to the part of his discourse that deals with the proto-Athenians. So we notice that lines 113a1 to 113b7, already cited as explaining why we have the prehistoric names in Greek, are misplaced where they are— just before Kritias launches into his loving, much longer description of the Atlantis that wished to conquer ancient Athens and Egypt. The details of this description work subconsciously to expand the reference of Hermocrates' expectation that Kritias will "exhibit and celebrate the goodness of these ancient citizens" to include the Atlanteans (more than the proto-Athenians), in what Derrida would called a retroactive "supplementation." It is also clear that, like the *Timaeus* version, the Athenian part of *this* equally literalist account is quite alien in spirit to that of the brilliantly humor-filled, implicitly critical, and successfully entertaining *Republic*.

The Athenian part of the *Kritias* Atlantis story, then, does not coincide enough with either the Athenian part of the *Timaeus* version of the story, or with the content and spirit of the original *Republic* (of which the latter is *not* a good summary) for it to be believably by Plato himself. But this proves nothing about the authenticity of the *Timaeus*. It does suggest examination of the *Timaeus* for signs of tampering for the purpose of attaching the *Kritias* to it. [16] And this is perhaps a good place at which to note that the Socrates of the *Timaeus* as we have it, is discursive in an uncharacteristic way. He is neither interrogative, as in the undoubted elenchtic dialogues, nor is he inventively and wittily discursive as in the undoubted longer dialogues; nor, again, is he the complete and attentive listener of the *Politicus* and *Sophist*—until, that is—Timaios launches into his cosmologic paean. One valid literary response to the fussy introduction to this paean, is that, where Socrates ought to have little else to do than listen to Timaios's poetic creation-story, he is made to talk, with dogmatic brevity in a un-Socratic, assertive way. In addition, his interlocutors alternate with him and each other in a rather disjointed way.

Clumsy Prose in the Prelude to the Timaeus, and the Role of Hermocrates

Look now at the Athenian part of the Atlantis story as told in the *Timaeus*. It was Socrates statements about 'the best state' that caused Hermocrates to interpose that he, Timaios and Kritias were still considering just that subject when Kritias mentioned Solon's (alleged) story "from ancient tradition" (*ek palaîas akoês*, 20d1). At this point Kritias, without further ado or any talk of *reciprocating* verbal *favors*, proceeds immediately to tell his tale in an action that answers Hermocrates' question "whether it is not pertinent (*epitêdeios*) to our agreed prescription (*epitaksin*)."

Thus it is Hermocrates who is used to establish that an agreement was reached yesterday. It is Kritias, however, who at 27a., *after* his first delivery of the story commits himself to a *repetition* of it once Timaios has completed his account of the origin of the cosmos (*peri physeôs to pantos*), in accordance "with the arrangement your guests have made": Kritias promises at the end of his first account, disjointedly and with unsocial forwardness,

> Now, therefore,—and this is the purpose of all that I've been say-ing—I am ready to tell my tale, not in brief outline only but in full detail just as I heard it (26c6–8).

Actually it is the reader only, then, who first owes to Hermocrates the idea that Kritias's tale is pertinent to the summary of 'yesterday's *politeia*. For, it is later implied by Kritias's words at 26a5 that Socrates had on that day made a proposal to which Kritias quickly agreed, "thinking that for the most arduous part of all such undertakings, I mean supplying a story fitly corresponding to our intentions, we should be fairly well provided" (Archer-Hind). The implication also is that it was a group agreement. But again, this is very clumsy prose; and, as thinking, it is not very coherent.

Recollect, however, that on ending his summary, Socrates had said to "Kritias and Hermocrates" naming them (19c9), that he wasn't up to praising that Best City and its people sufficiently. And *we* think as we read this: "but that *is* what Socrates *did* do on a literalist reading of *Republic*, and what he appeared to do on a dia-logical, ironic reading of same. "But that is no marvel," he con-tinues—in words that are rambling and unskilfully indirect (from 19d1 to 20a)—considering that neither the poets ("not that I dispar-age them") nor the Sophists ("although I believe them to be prac-ticed in beautiful speech-making") are good at representing politi-cal men who are also men of knowledge and men of action (19e6–8). That leaves only you, and our honorable and philosophic Timaios from well–governed Locri, to do the job. Hermocrates, too of course—he adds in polite afterthought—is no novice in these matters and is reputed to be trustworthy about them.[17] The afterthought shows, incidentally, that Socrates must be addressing Kritias more than the others.

Here at 20b Socrates has also said: "This" [i.e. the thought about the political competence of those mentioned]" was in my mind yesterday when I eagerly satisfied your request to discourse on the polity" (*dio kai xthes egô dianooumenos* . . ., 20b2), for no one else is up to doing this job. This is too *ex post facto* to be as honest as it is polite. Socrates goes right on to claim (20b–c), using *xthes* once, that he did "in turn prescribe for you this theme . . . and you all . . . agreed to reciprocate (*antapodôsin*) with a feast of words."

Observe now the relationship between these words, from 26e2 to 27b7, between Socrates and Kritias and 25e–d where Kritias, on ending his "brief" (*hôs syntomôs eipein*) *Timaeus* account of grandfather Kritias's Solon story, uses *xthes* five times, prepares the way for bringing Socrates' summarized Best City into "the realm of truth" (26d1) in full detail, and equates *this* best city of Socrates's with his own storified, ancient city. Socrates here agrees that it is a story appropriate to the day's Goddess–festival, and *then and there* (27b8–10) abruptly gives the floor to Timaios—with an ungracious *command* to invoke the Gods—for his performance of the comogonic discourse that takes up the rest of the dialogue.

Let us compare the wording on either side of the first telling of Kritias's tale, with the wording which agrees that telling the tale *again later* will be appropriate to, and "in entire harmony and accord with" (*pantôs harmosousi kai ouk apaisometha*) the equation between Kritias's mythical Athens and Socrates's Best City.

At 20e–21a Kritias wants to tell the story both as payment of the group's debt to Socrates, and to praise and honor the Goddess whose festival–day it is. And here at 21a Socrates says he wants to hear the story. *But then* at 21e and 21b it's clear that the story is going to be a myth (as pointed out above), because it's based on 9000-year old documents,[18] is derived from an Egyptian priest who transmitted it to Solon who told it to Drôpides Makerson, who told it to grandfather Kritias—and because it is recited on Apatouria Deception Day. *And then again* at 26c9–10 Kritias lapses into calling Socrates' "yesterday's" account a "fable" which he will "now" turn into truth. But: which "yesterday's account"? Is the reader supposed to take this to refer to the one in *Republic*, or to Socrates yesterday's summary account at the beginning of *Timaeus*—a supererogatory summary, by the way, if `yesterday's account' was as superb as the group's indebtedness to Socrates makes it seem. And what about the contradictions embedded in (i) the interlocutors taking or summarizing `yesterday's discourse' literalistically, (ii) calling it a "fable" which will be made true, and (iii) the doctrinal reading of *Republic* and *Timaeus* which adduces the "likely story" (as the latter calls itself) in literal confirmation of the non–tabulational nature of the polis–discourse in *Republic*—a discourse which Socrates himself had called a fabulation about a city in the sky. Finally, the "now" in the wording under inspection is also out of place, since the longer, detailed account that Kritias says he's ready to give is not given in the *Timaeus* at all, and can be found only in the *Kritias*.

Now, while it is completely contradictory to find Kritias, the certified extreme oligarchist, trying to get away with co-opting the *foundationally democratic* Solon for his own view of the state, it is less odd to find Hermocrates the Sicilian general of whom we hear in Thucydides, making up a party with the tyrannic Athenian and the pythagorizing Locrian physiocrat. As a Syracusan exile who had once urged the destruction of imperialist Athens, he cannot be identified, any more than Kritias, as friendly to Athens.

Notice, then, what exactly the role of Hermocrates is in the *Timaeus-Kritias* sequence. He speaks once only in each of them, in the *Timaeus* at 20c4–d3, in the *Kritias* at 108b9–c5. He is also mentioned in the former at 19d1 and 20a8, and referred to as *hodê* (this one) at 26a8. The purpose of the first locus is to open up for Kritias the chance to address the group. The second locus is only a response to Socrates' saying that when it is Hermocrates' turn to speak he will be granted the same indulgences as Kritias; it also encourages Kritias, in a battle-metaphor, not to be faint of heart in competing with the poet Solon, whose alleged story he is retelling.

Note, however, that Socrates' reference to Hermocrates in the *Kritias* is compositionally non-functional. It is not followed up, and its only role is that, without it we wouldn't know that Kritias is a member of the party. And the opportunity is not taken to state what it is that Hermocrates is expected to discourse about. *That* is never mentioned, either in the *Kritias* or in the *Timaeus*. Thus neither the *Kritias* nor the *Timaeus* can really be said to promise a sequel to themselves called the *Hermocrates*. Hermocrates' only function, we see, is to have introduced Kritias to the chance to make his speech (in the *Timaeus*), and then encouraged him in making it a second time in the *Kritias*. But he's not really needed in the *Kritias*, if it is read apart from the *Timaeus*.

Scrutinizing the Ante-Cosmogonic Part of the Timaeus

Let us return, after all this, to look at how Kritias gets into the *Timaeus* in the first place. At its beginning (17a1) to 19c9 the conversation is exclusively between Timaios and Socrates, although we notice that Timaios answers in the first person plural at 18e5 *memnêmetha* (we remember), and that Socrates has been using the plural "you" all along. There is some equivocation on the part of the writer here about remembering and not remembering: at 17b7 Timaios does not quite remember "the extent and nature of what [Socrates] proposed for discussion." So (i) he conveniently wants Socrates to briefly tell what these were again, but (ii) he remembers enough to confirm that Socrates' retelling of yesterday's discourse is accurate—up to the just-mentioned *memnêmetha* at 18e5. I say "conveniently" because the response allows Socrates to go on recapitulating the polity that is supposed to reflect the political content of *Republic* literalistically understood, and because, after this *memnêsthai* the recapitulation becomes inaccurate on any reading of *Republic*.

Then at 19a8–10 Socrates is found to be prematurely asking "have we now said enough for a summary of yesterday's discourse" (Archer-Hind), and Timaios answers that this is just what was said. But Socrates goes on both to say more about it, and to complain that he would like to see this polis and its members brought to life in words (19c2), as when "on beholding beautiful creatures, whether made by a graphic artist or in truth alive but at rest, the desire overtakes one to see them moving into those actions of which their physique holds the promise." This is an interesting simile, but it creates difficulties for the platonist reading of *Republic*, if Socrates's summary is claimed to be of that work or its political content.[19]

We notice in Socrates' "Gladly would I listen to anyone who would depict in words [this state] . . . going into war," the tucked-in anticipation[20] of Kritias's war–story in the *Kritias*; while war, and the enmity of other states, are mentioned twice each in the rest of 19b–c. But the emphasis in the original *Republic*, on either a dialogical or literalist reading, was on the education of the guardians not on their preparedness for war. And wasn't it already "depicted in words" as a "city reposing in [a verbal] discourse" by Socrates himself (*Rep*.592a8–b1)? That the city will be "in action" does not obviate the pleonasm, but does insult Socrates' discursive city (on a literalist reading of it) as not revealing its war–potential immediately enough.

Next, this Socrates' "inability" (at 19d2–3) to enlarge sufficiently upon the merits of this city and its men is not ironic modesty, but uttered with literal intent. Here, he goes on—uncharacteristically, for both the Socrates who is either ironic about the poets or condescending to them when ironizing about other things—to put himself in the same boat with poets who aren't able to dramatize what they have not experienced. As if, we can only say, Socrates had never been described (in Plato's dialogues) as good in battle and stoical in war-endurance; and as if he hadn't already ironically banished poets from the Ideal State.

Again, the "esteem" (19e3) he claims to have for the class of Sophists—who are likewise unexpert in describing those who are *both* men-of-knowledge" (*philosóphôn*) *and* political men (*politikôn*)—makes this Socrates suspect. For, the Socrates of the undoubted dialogues has no good words to say about the Sophists except with appropriate irony.

Italian Locris, whether really "well-governed" or not, was (we note) an ally of anti-Athenian Syracuse. This makes Timaios and Hermocrates compatible guests, but it doesn't make Timaios pro-Athenian. Italian Locri was famous for an incredible victory of its 15,000 men over 120,000 Krotonites.[21] But about Timaios the speaker, what is relevant is not that no fifth-century Locrian physician-mathematician can be found who might serve as his model, but (i) that, assuming Plato to be the author of the cosmogonic discourse in the *Timaeus*, he puts pythagorizing or platonizing opinions in Timaios's mouth with such mytho-poeticism and iterated corrigibilism, and (ii) that Plato was being read so literalistically from the third century B.C. on, that the cosmological treatise[22] of an imitator calling himself Timaios Lokris was believed to have been the basis of Plato's original dialogue. So little was Plato's brilliantly formative prose understood after his death that an imitator could be believed to be his original or model. The last literary or compositional quirk to note about Socrates' diction, just before and just after Kritias's outlining of the Atlantis story, is that it gets flat and is repetitious about its point, at 20b–c and at 27e. Not to be told, finally, anywhere in the dialogue what Hermocrates was to speak about in his alleged turn—doesn't that make the *Timaeus* a dialogue with an obtrusive loose end, if it is really part of a trilogy?

And this loose end in *Timaeus* points us to the loose end in the *Kritias*, at 108c8: "but this [that I am doing] will soon show you what sort of thing [it should be]." How is Hermocrates to learn what he must discourse on from the telling of the Atlantis story? It's been told once, and he hasn't learned. He has just been tediously (but explicitly) told about the difficulties of representation in words. If he is to learn from the moral implicit in the Atlantis–story, that moral would be about how a mighty empire can be defeated by the valor and leadership—the Gods assisting—of a smaller force standing alone (25c2), or a tenth in size. Is he, then, as an anti-Athenian Sicilian and ally of Locrian Timaios, expected to pick up on this theme and call on *his* memory, or oral tradition, and retell, on behalf of Timaios, the story of the incredible victory by the Sagra, *epi Sargai*, in Archaic times?

The incredibility of that *historical* event would, to an author planning a sequel to his *Kritias*, lend plausibility to the *non-historical* Atlantis-story in it. In this case, the Locrain parallel would reinforce further the parallel between the defeat of Atlantis by the proto-Athenians and the defeat of imperialist Athens by the Syracusans. Historically, in classical Athens, it was the democrats who supported its expansionist policies; the oligarchists, naturally, not only opposed these policies but counted many Spartanizers (like Kritias) in their ranks. Actually, the story of the amazing victory at Marathon would have been much closer to Athenian memory: that it ensured the survival of Assembly democracy is probably what gets it replaced by the triumph at Sagra.

Signs that the Kritias is a Foundation Story for Children

The more than two-dozen points of varying importance covered in the six previous sections combine to cast doubt on the quality of the prose, the compositional or dialogical skill and ideology of *only* the *Kritias*, and *only the* ante-cosmogonic *prelude* of the *Timaeus*, not upon the body of the *Timaeus*. Outside of the group-members' lapses into clumsy prose, this interlocutory prelude taxes our ability to suspend disbelief both because of the Atlantis-story itself and the way it is introduced, and also because of its discernible but covered-up ideological purpose. It is not introduced by Kritias with irony or humor, or in anything like the skillful way in which Plato's Socrates introduces his stories in the undoubted dialogues. Yet it comes, as we have seen, with all the signs of being a made-up story with a veiled purpose. But it is clear that Kritias wants it to be believed (as Homer is believed) as mythistorically legitimate. So that where the self-focusing devices in the storytelling of Plato's Socrates alert us to his irony, in Kritias's discourse they only reinforce the artificiousness (the made-upness) of the story. Can it be that, like the oligarchist discourses of Xenophon, it was composed as a childrens' story, or for the edification of the young?

We remember that, during the first half of the fourth century in Athens, oligarchy was in total disrepute because of the bloody deeds of the Thirty tyrants (as they were called) under the leadership of Kritias.[23] So, it is difficult to believe that Plato, who died in 347 B.C., could have composed a dialogue like the *Kritias* with its anti-Athenian, oligarchist tendencies. Now these biases are all concentrated in the *Timaeus* prelude and the *Kritias*. So, even if Plato were the composer of this story, it is unlikely that he would have published it in his life-time. The *Kritias*, however, has never been said to be a posthumous work.

Also from the architectonic point of view, if the generative idea for these compositions—as in the claim that they form a sequence— was to speak first about the natural cosmos and next about human society, then the first telling of the Atlantis story is out of place in the *Timaeus*. But if it belongs there,[24] then its retelling in a separate dialogue by the same author is supererogatory, and we are warranted in examining the *Kritias* in separation from the *Timaeus*. We are also warranted in looking for connections it might have with other pedagogical and oligarchist literature of the times after Plato's death, and the adjustment of the Academy to the militarist, dorianizing rule of the Macedonians.

In contrast to the Athenian democracy which it had conquered, the Macedonian court was feudal, and included the corps of Royal Pages consisting of the children of the nobles, to whose education attention had of course to be given. In the case of Sparta, the practice was to leave the boys at home until age seven. From then on, until the end of their twenties, they were under continuous surveillance, training for war, eating in the *syssitia*, sleeping in barracks according to age groups, while their *education in words* was carried on by the *elder* citizens. We can tell what this mainly consisted of from the hint at *Hippias Major* 285d6–e1:

> They [the Spartans] like to hear about the genealogies of heroes and men, foundation of cities in ancient times and, in summary, all about antiquity . . .

Now notice what Kritias says at 107d about representing Gods and heroes: "we accept [in such cases] shadowy (*skiagraphia*), unclear (*asaphei*), and deceptive (*apatêlôi*) sketches." T.B.L. Webster calls it "illusionistic shading" in his book on fourth-century art and literature. An audience of docile youngsters would not want to make anything of the detail, for instance, in which the Athenian citizenship of the proto-Athenians is vouched for by *Egyptian* documents. It *is* a story about the Golden Age of the Greeks, a favored topic in the culture; but the ascription of an Egyptian origin to it is a favorite pythagorizing ploy. Egypt and the orient were, indeed, the source for many of the *Märchen* which we know in Hellenized form— just as Kritias's story is not only Hellenized but tells how it was Hellenized. And the child-targeted wit which quotes the Egyptian priest as calling *all* the Greeks children is not bad pedagogy, since it reinforces the child's solidarity with his culture as a whole. This is part of the apt artificiousness of the story which adults, however, would be seeing through. The story *was* told to Kritias in his childhood, by a very old man. And it is told today to its adult auditors on Apatouria Deception Day. The detail in the story which makes today's Athenians descendants of the *autochthonous* proto–Athenians is a typically oligarchal ploy also; for it reflects the claims to being an "aristocracy of original settlers."[25]

As a matter of intellectual history, finally, we should notice the kinship between this tale and the ideology of Hellenistic historiography according to which it is Fortune that guides human events. And fortune (*Tychê*), as in Polybius, can guide them to *astonishing* conclusions.[26] It does much to palliate the readers's initial inclination to take the *Kritias* as something other than a children's story— à propos the precedent of *Gulliver's Travels* cited earlier—that the transmitters of *this* story have always offered it as part of the platonizing core of the idealist system which they claim to find in Plato's dialogues. The unauthentic details to which doctrinal readers are blinded, however, are not doctrinal or neoplatonist. That which betrays the story for what it is, are its anti-democratic *counter-Athenian* biases and the details of the child-oriented aptness with which it is told by Kritias, the never-to-be-forgotten leader of the oligarchal party. It is also the case that, together with the passage of time, the frontal boldness that sets Kritias to tell it almost succeeds in obviating his inappropriateness as the teller of an Athenian foundation story. For, the story he tells glorifies Athens just enough to mask its would-be valorization of the oligarchism which it covertly favors.

It could only have been a time when oligarchism was riding high in post-classical Athens, that would have dared to put Kritias forward as having *anything* to do with the foundation of Athens, the city he had terrorized, bloodied, and lost his life to. And if it is not the "frontal boldness" of the oligarchist Plato-imitator that chose him, we have to hypothesize that enough time has gone by for people to have forgotten the horrors he perpetrated upon the Athenians. *In this case*, the words in Aristotle's *Rhetoric* (1416b26–28) would seem to apply: . . . "people don't need a story when you praise someone like Achilles; but if it's Kritias, then you must [narrate], for they don't know [what he did] . . ." In this case and *a fortiori, Plato could not have been the author* of the *Kritias*.

We also remember the case of *Gulliver's Travels* in which a book written as a political satire got read and reclassified as a children's story. Have I taken what could well have been composed as a children's story, and read and reclassified it as a literary-political manipulation? The *Kritias*, of course, comes to us from within a given tradition of transmission-and-interpretation, a tradition of interpretation which has never been monitored for the influence its ideology may have had on its interpretations of, and elaborations on, Plato's dialogues. That the interpreters were for decades and centuries the very people responsible for the material, documentary transmission and copying of the texts of the dialogues, only complicates the case and makes it more difficult.

In contrast to the Athenian democracy which it had conquered, the Macedonian court was feudal, and included the corps of Royal Pages consisting of the children of the nobles, to whose education attention had of course to be given. In the case of Sparta, the practice was to leave the boys at home until age seven. From then on, until the end of their twenties, they were under continuous suveillance, training for war, eating in the syssitia, sleeping in barracks according to age groups, while their education in words was carried on by the elder citizens. We can tell what this mainly consisted of from the hint at *Hippias Major* 285d6–e1:

> They [the Spartans] like to hear about the genealogies of heroes and men, the foundation of cities in ancient times and, in summary, all about antiquity . . .

Now notice what Kritias says at 107d about representing Gods and heroes: "we accept [in such cases] shadowy (*skiagraphia*), unclear (*asuphes*) and deceptive sketches"—T.B.L. Webster calls it "illusionistic shading" in his book on fourth-century art and literature. An audience of docile youngsters would not want to make anything of the detail, for instance, in which the Athenian citizenship of the proto-Athenians is vouched for by *Egyptian* documents.

Finally, as the celebratory discourse this Socrates said he wanted it to be (21a3), the aspect of the Goddess which it's recited to honor can remain unnamed, because the adult part of the audience to whom the story is addressed did not need to be told. She is the embodiment of their self-image as a conquering *aristokratía*. *Dêmokratía*, the Goddess of classical Athens, has now been overcome not only in deeds but also in words by the platonist imitator(s) who composed the *Kritias* and connected it to the *Timaeus*. Avoiding explicit use of the terms *demokratí* and *oligarchia* to both of which there were objections, the author's story has implicitly honored "temperate aristocracy" (*aristokratía sôphrôn*) as the oligarchs were pleased to call it.[27]

The festival of the Athenian Goddess that Kritias has been celebrating, we can now infer, is not just that of Athênê *poliás* (protector of cities) but rather, under her equivocal aspect as *apatouria*, that of warlike Athênê *aristeutikê* (promoter of valiant deeds). The *Kritias* creator has replaced the Athênê *isonomikê* of the classical polity—alien as she had to be to the Macedonian conquerors—with a Goddess more acceptable to himself and to the succesors of Philip and Alexander who saw themselves as the ruling class of Macedonian Athens.

Notes

1. W. Welliver *Character, Plot and Thought in Plato's Timaeus-Critias* (Leiden: Brill 1977).

2. P.Shorey *What Plato Said* (Chicago U.P. 1937). The device is a behavioral, though not conscious, judgment that the eloquent proemium *could* be an ending.

3. Cf. P.Friedländer "nobody any longer . . . believe[s] that Plato is here recapitulating an original version of the *Republic*. . . . the state sketched

here would have preserved the machinery of the ideal state without its soul." (*Plato* 3 vols. Tr. H. Meyerhoff, Princeton U.P.1969); v.3, p.356–7.

4. J. Adam's appendices to *Republic VIII* solve the problem of making intelligible and executable the operations portentously posited by Socrates at 546b–d. My essay on "Plato's Ironies: Textural, Structural, and Allusional: On the Mathematical Humor in Bks.VIII & IX of *Republic*," works out some of the humorous ramifications of the mythico-mathematical formulation: it operates, at the surface level, as both a challenge to pretentious mathematical amateurs, and as a numerological in-joke for Pythagoreans. Viewed architectonically, it is a reminder that Socrates and his Muses have shifted into a solemn jesting mode.

5. Respectively, Archer-Hind's *The Timaeus*, p.66 ad loc.; and *Proclus Commentaire su le Timée* Tr. & Notes A.J. Festugière (Vrin 1966); p.55.

6. Assuming that there is only one author to the two Kritias's.

7. An Athenian-Ionian admission-to-citizenship or socialization festival, it was also a celebration of the victory of the Athenian champion Melanthus over the Boetian king Xanthius. At the start of combat, and contrary to the rules, a man in a goat-skin came into view behind Xanthius. When Xanthius, deceived (*apataô*), turned to check this out, Melanthus slew him; and according to a scholium to Aristophanes' *Archanians* 146, the apparition was due to Dionysos. An alternative derivation supported by F. Welcker (*Griechische Götterlehre* 1863) is that "apatouria" comes from *a* for *hama*, and *patoria*, as suggested by Xenoph.'s *Hellenica* i.7.8, *hoi pateres kai hoi syngeneis*. . . . The first day of the festival was called *doropía* or *dorpeia* (Photius *Lexicon*, & Athenaeus *Deipnosophists* iv.171).

8. See E.Boisacq *Dictionnaire Étymologique del la Langue Grecque* (Heidelberg: Winter 1923), and P. Chantraine *Dictionnaire Étymologique del la Langue Grecque* (Paris: Klincksieck 1968). Applying the literary convention that exploits the consonance of name with character to Kritias, *his* name, for historical reasons, could only be a standing symbol of and synecdoche for oligarchism and political terror. The phonetic overtones of the word itself become sinister because of the cruel and arbitrary judgments—(*kritês* = judge)—of the tyranny of the Thirty.

9. It is another question whether speakers other than Socrates are always as detached from their stories as Plato's Socrates usually is from his. How detached, for instance, is the sophistic rhetorician from Elea, in the *Politicus-Sophistês*, from the myth he makes up in the course of his defense

of one-man rule? Notice that it is Socrates who *insists*, before the telling, that it is a reliable oral-aural report of Solon's (*Solônos akoên*, 21a4–8), and then again at the end of it (at 26e5) that it "is not an invented fable but a true history" (*mê plasthenta all' alêthinon* . . .). Are these interjections uttered in the same ironic tone as that which comes over in the quoted words of the Egyptian priest at 24a1, words about which even the literalist A.E. Taylor could not but say that they "could hardly be anything but satirical" (op.cit., p.54). Taylor is struck by the anomaly of the priest's claim to have in his possession manuscripts (*grammata*) nine-thousand years old.

10. The word *máchimon*, we note, is used twice in the *Timaeus* (24b1, 25d2), and twice in the *Kritias* (110c5, 112b3). It is used just once in the *Republic* (III. 386c1, in the dat.pl.), and only *before* the specifics about the warriors' education have been introduced. But where the two standard words for the military class in *Republic* were *phúlakes* for "guardians" and *epikouroi* for "auxiliaries," the former occurs only at *Krit.* 110d5 and 112d4, the latter not at all in the *Kritias*. "Guardians" is used at *Tim.* 18a3, 17d3 and, with a different meaning, at 40c1.

11. Cf. the pun at 20a1 and 20a4, between *timás* and *Timaîos*.

12. And, accordingly prays to Mnemosynê at 108d3.

13. The claim by Avery that Kritias was not always an oligarch does not hold up; the examination of it by Adeleye reconfirms not only his extreme oligarchism, but also his cleverness. Cf. G. Adeleye "Critias Member of the Four Hundred?", TAPA 104 (1974); p.1–10. Xenophon's *Hellenica* (quoting Theramenes) says that he was "the sharpest hater of the commons (*misódêmos*) during the democracy, and the most anti-bourgeois (*misochrêstos*) during the aristocracy" (II.iii.47).

14. In Greek the inseparable prefix *eri* is, of course, an intensifier; so the word-play is with *theos* (=divine) and *chthôn* (= earth): "very divine," "very earthy."

15. The Zurich text (XV, p.113), has *hieron* here, as does the Oxford text; but Bury, who is otherwise translating from the Zurich text, follows Hermann who prints (Vol.IV, p.428; Praef.xxx) *hiereis* "priests." The latter imports a difference with the *Timaeus* version of the Athenian part of the story in which it is said that "the priestly class is separated off from the rest" *Tim.*24a6.

16. This suggestion does, however, lead to the question, if the beginning of *Timaeus* was touched up to allow for attachment of the *Kritias*, how

come the beginning of *Republic* was not touched up by the inclusion of Kritias and Timaios in it among the other named auditors at *Rep*.328b? This would have made it indubitable that the 'yesterday's' discourse mentioned in *Timaeus* was indeed the *Republic*. What was the situation in the Academy, on this hypothesis, that protected the *Republic* but not the *Timaeus*—if the latter was touched up?

17. Thucydides *History* vi.72 characterizes Hermocrates as "a man who was in general second to none in point of intelligence, and [who] had shown himself in this war both competent by reason of experience and conspicuous for courage." The fact that he was exiled (Thucyd. viii.85), toward the end of his career, would explain his presence in Athens. He was *also*, however, *conspicuously anti-Athenian*—given the real threat to Syracuse presented by imperialist Athens.

18. Fourth-century B.C. Greeks wouldn't have to know about orality, literacy, and the change from traditional law and pre-literacy to transcribed law and written literature, to feel that a 9000-year old document is an impossibility.

19. Or, on a dialogical reading, if it is claimed that this is the same Socrates as speaks in the *Republic*.

20. Or—logically—if it is part of the untampered with *Timaeus*, is it only made to seem such by the later attachment of the *Kritias* to the *Timaeus*?

21. So much so, Dunbabin reminds us, that it passed into a proverb of events happening contrary to expectation: *alêthestera tôn epi Sarga*, "truer than at the Sagra," the river where, helped by the Dioskouroi and Locrian Ajax, they triumphed (like the proto-Athenians against Atlantis?). See T.J. Dunbabin *The Western Greeks* (Oxford U.P. 1948), p.357 ff.

22. Most safely datable as composed between 100 B.C. and 50 A.D. See T.H. Tobin *Timaios of Locri On the Nature of the World and the Soul* (Chico, Calif.: Scholars Press 1985), and H.Thesleff *The Pythagorean Texts of the Hellenistic Period* (AboAkademi 1965), and "On the Problem of the Doric Pseudo-Pythagorica," in *Pseudoepigrapha I* (Geneva: Fondation Hardt 1972); also, W. Burkert Review-Article of Thesleff's *The Pythagorean Texts of the Hellenistic Period*, in same.

23. See, for example, P. Krentz*The Thirty at Athens* (Cornell U.P. 1982).

24. As it well may, but without the frills that attach it to a projected repetition.

25. Cf. L.Whibley *Greek Oligarchies* 1896 (N.Y Haskell 1971); sect.31.

26. See, e.g., C.B. Welles *Alexander and the Hellenistic World* (Toronto: Hakkert 1970), p.201. Also *Athenian Myths & Institutions* W.B. Tyrrell and F. Brown (Oxford U.P. 1991). Cf. W. Fowler "Polybius' Concept of *tychê*," *Classical Review* 17 (1903), p.446ff.; and P.Shorey "*tychê* in Polybius," *Classical Philology* 16 (1921), p.281ff.

27. Originally Thucydides' term: in Book III, Chapter 82 of his history.

4

On the Ambivalence and Ideology of the Aristotelian *Politics*

The Return of the King in the Peripatetic *Politics*

If we call the *Kritias's* would-be replacement of fourth century ideas about the Solonian origins of the Athenian polity with a story about its foundation by some anti-Atlantean proto-Athenians—who had connections with Egypt and were visibly oligarchist in their behavior—*an attempt* to legitimate the military-oligarchal rulership of Athens by the Macedonians *in the* same *mythhistorical mode* that is found in great-family genealogies and city *Entstehungsgeschichten*, then the Peripatetic overwriting and rewriting, which we will next examine, of the Aristotelian lecture-notes and *hypomnêmata* that are *The Politics*, must be called an attempt to legitimate monarchy and oligarchy in the *epistêmôn* (the 'knowing' or 'scientific') *mode* aspired to equally by members of the Academy, the Peripatos, and the Pythagorean sect.

Ambivalence or Development, Revision or Interpolation

The editors who reprint H. Kelsen's essay on the Aristotelian *Politics* in their useful volume *Articles on Aristotle 2*, characterize it accurately enough as "examin[ing] [Aristotle's] ambivalent attitude to the rival charms of despotism and democracy" (*op.cit*.ix).[1] The constitutionalist himself, however, takes the evidence examined to point to a guarded case of a veering towards platonizing monarchism rather than to ambivalence. Kelsen concluded that the alternation, in the *Politics*, of a "disarming" apology for (moderate) polity as the best constitution with a rhetorically cautious defense of (competent) monarchy as the best constitution, was generated in response both to the actual situation under Macedonian rule and the entrenched climate of opinion in pro-democratic Athens.[2] He notes, too, that

> this dual structure of [the Aristotelian] politics, according to which on one hand hereditary monarchy is best, on the other moderate democracy, corresponds exactly to the dual morality of his ethics, which alongside the practical virtue of deeds sets up as an ideal theoretical contemplative knowledge (p.191).[3]

Kelsen is unemphatic about the ideological motivation of the change, because he found it natural that the *Politics* should reflect the sociopolitical situation of Athens in Aristotle's time. Yet he is also aware that the Athenian climate of opinion had continued to repudiate the idea of charismatic monarchy well after Chaeronea.

The hypothesis of the present essay is that this duality or change of views should not be taken as a *development*, not just because monarchy to a democrat is a *regressive* political form but because, if Aristotle is responsible for it, it would represent a regression towards the 'platonism' from which Kelsen (following Jaeger) believes Aristotle to have become progressively independent.

Verifiable as the story is of how Aristotle goes into the Middle Ages as a Byzantine logician so much in agreement with Academic 'platonism' that he is used as the best introduction to the doctrinal or pythagorizing interpretation of Plato's dialogues,[4] clear as it is that the reception-history of Aristotle's thought is a history of its *platonization* by his commentators, transmitters, editors and translators, is not the faith surprising that what we are reading in his texts are his very own dictated or written words?[5] Should we not be more ready to suspect, as we read the texts, that they have been tampered with, overwritten or interpolated? Shouldn't the unguarded state in which his treatises and *hypomnêmata* lay for centuries concern us?

Shouldn't we demand an explanation of the Peripatetic neglect and loss of his dialogues, before setting the problem aside and deciding that the fact that he was a *composer of readable dialogues* is irrelevant both to his own extant works, and irrelevant to 'his' criticisms of Plato's thought—*dialogically* embedded as this thought is in a score of differently designed literary masterpieces both big and little? Have we let the bad editorial habit of listing under his name works that are not by Aristotle influence us to the point that we give more credence than we should to *everything in* both pseudo-Aristotelian works and works that are either only partly by Aristotle or have been edited into existence by others than Aristotle? Are we so sure that we have successfully identified what is by Theophrastos rather than by Aristotle in the corpus?

Do we not also too easily forget, when trying to understand Aristotle, that the 'Aristotelism' (so to call it) of his Peripatetic successors was weak, not integrally polymathic, and much invaded by the stoicism and platonism of the intellectual climate of the Hellenistic (i.e., orientalized) *oikoumenê*, in which they now lived as unfree and alienated subjects of a dorianizing (and 'medizing') military empire? By "not genuinely polymathic" I mean that they became pursuers of only some special knowledges, not of all the knowledges as Aristotle had been. And this begins the separation—*in the Lyceum itself*—of literary studies from natural history.

The music theorist Aristoxenus, an early older member of the school, was not only a specialist but came to it as a Pythagorean. Not untypical of Theophrastos's important students, for example, was Demetrios of Phaleron (Cicero, *De Fin*.v.19,54; *Laws* iii. 6,14; *De Off*.i.1.3), about whom we forget to note that he was an *oligarchist* administrator of Athens, not just a knowledgeable librarian. So that, as someone with power who was a connoisseur of books, he was certainly more influential over the Peripatos, its library, political works—and whatever else it had to transmit—than the mere grammarian could have been that he is often listed as.[6]

The "disservice to history" which the historian Tarn ascribes to Theophrastos's school after 317 B.C.,[7] seems to have included any amount of tampering in favor of oligarchism with the political texts in the care of the school. Grote tells us that an Athenian reaction against "th[e] obnoxious Phalerean" seems to have been the cause of the legislation restricting philosophic activity which led to the departure of *all* the philosophers from Athens at the time.[8] And D.Laertius, after mentioning Theophrastos's friendship with Kasander the oligarchal ruler of Athens (Bk.V on Theophrastos and Demetrios), also quotes Theophrastos as saying, "Readings make ['do make' or 'make for', or 'cause'] revisions. Putting them all off and not caring, our young people will no longer tolerate" (*hai d'anagnôseis poiousin epanorthôseis to de anabállesthai panta kai amelein ouketi pherousin hai hêlikíai,*V.37)![9]

If these words of Theophratus reflect his practice, we cannot accept Zeller's statement that "It is not to be supposed that Theophrastos deviated in any respect from the principles of Aristotle's political doctrine."[10] We have to wonder, rather, how he could have made it given what we know about the literary practices of the Hellenistic age, about its competing dogmatisms, its alienated and unfree intellectuality, and the radical conceptual changes which it underwent.[11] Zeller himself takes note of the Stoic influence on Theophrastos's conception of human fellowship; while Cicero's *De Finibus* assigns to Theophrastos the introduction of the idea of Fortune into Peripatetic ethics and politics.

A measure of how weak the Peripatos was as a renewer or transmitter of the original Aristotle, can be inferred from the fact that Andronikos (I c. B.C.) did not attach enough importance to his dialogues to edit or include them in his ordering of the recovered works of Aristotle which Sulla had brought to Rome. Another measure is that from the time of Theophrastos's successor, Strato, down to the time of Andronikos's edition, the heads of the school don't seem to have the disciple's habit of quoting Aristotle's words or treatises themselves as such, even when in dispute and competition with Stoicism and Platonism. They, for instance, tacitly accept the elimination by the Stoics of poetics and rhetoric from Aristotle's organon, namely, from the set of disciplines presupposed in, or needed for, the pursuit of knowledge.[12] But about the use, respect for or lack of respect for, and availability of, the pragmateia, as we call the treatises, we can have only hypothetical and badly evidenced accounts. A recent study is P. Moreaux's *Der Aristotelismus bei den Griechen von Andronikos bis Alexander v. Aphrodisias*; but for important details the reader should consult L. Tarán's careful review of the question.[13]

H. Shute, in his history of the Aristotelian writings, proceeded on the working assumption that if we can't explain how it happened that there is "repetition of . . . nearly the whole of the Aristotelian titles in the works ascribed [by ancient cataloguers] to Eudemus, Theophrastos, and, later, Straton," we don't have a general grasp of the process by which the writings were transmitted.[14] Here is his suggestion about how Aristotle was used in the lectures provided by the school.

The notes on Aristotle's lecture, whether his own or those taken by his former pupils . . . were read out to the class who, as I believe, could not otherwise easily obtain access to copies of them. Occasional notes and criticisms were interpolated by the lecturer, who . . . did not always warn his hearers as to what was interpretation and what text.

"[T]he free way in which Aristotle's immediate successors . . . seem to have treated the master's works or lectures" is accounted for, says Shute, only if there never did exist autographs of them or if "merely . . . generally accurate notes" of them existed.

The information contained in Strabo's and Athenaeus's stories about "the books of Aristotle and Theophrastos," properly analyzed, can also help us to an idea of what was going on in the Peripatetic school.[15] In a list of notable large libraries, Athenaeus speaks of that (or those) of "Aristotle the philosopher, Theophrastos, and Neleus, who preserved the books of the two last named" (I.3a-b). "From Neleus king Ptolemy Philadelphus," Athenaeus says, "purchased them all and transferred them . . . to his capital . . . Alexandria." From this reference by Athenaeus, doesn't Shute infer too much, when he takes it to be simply to "the works . . . of Aristotle" (op.cit. p.20), since Theophrastos—if we are to believe the will cited by D.Laertius'(V.52)—bequeathed all the books in his estate to Neleus. Athenaeus also notes that in the time when he was a Peripatetic, the wealthy politico Apellikon had "bought up Aristotle's library and many other books" (V.214d–e).

Strabo's account is in Bk. xiii, section 54 of his Geography where Neleus is described as "an auditor of both Aristotle and Theophrastos, and the inheritor of the library of Theophrastos, which included that of Aristotle" (*tên bibliothêkên tou theophrastou, en hêi ên kai hê tou Aristotélous*). Strabo says here that Theophrastos was the first person to collect books, and teach the kings of Egypt how to arrange a library. Neleus's library was inherited by the private people who were his heirs in Skepsis. Knowing the Attalid king's avidity for books with which to equip his library in Pergamon, they kept theirs hidden underground and without much order. Later, they sold to Apellikon for a lot of money "both the books of Aristotle and those of Theophrastos," but only after they had suffered from moths and moisture. Strabo then says that "seeking to amend (*epanorthôsin*) what was moth-eaten (*diabrômátôn*), he transcribed (*metênegke*) the text into new copies, not filling it in well (*anaplêrôn ouk eû*), and issuing the books full of mistakes (*hamartadôn plêrê*)."[16]

Strabo continues, in the second half of his report:

So it befell that the earlier Peripatos after Theophrastos lacked books entirely except for a few mostly exoteric works, and was therefore not able to philosophize effectively, but only to talk inflatedly about their theses.[17]

So, not only did the Peripatetics after Theophrastos not know all of the works of Aristotle that became available with Andronikos, they deprecated Aristotle's dialogues. David the Armenian in his prologue to the Categories[18] quotes Alexander of Aphrodisias as having said that in these "exoteric" works one reads only opinions and lies, whereas the lecture-notes (*akroamatika*) covered both opinion and the truth. Shute also reminds us of the tendency among Peripatetic editors

to exalt the esoteric and unpublished works above the exoteric and published ones. We find, as we should expect, that references to esoteric works are much more common in treatises which were in vogue through the period of darkness than in those which . . . remained unpublished during that time. The Peripatetic philosophers, in giving their wares forth . . . took care to inform th[e] world that they had . . . more valuable goods in reserve which could only be obtained by direct initiation and oral instruction (op.cit.103).

These esoteric lecture-notes, however and as we are learning, were not safe from "revision" (*epanórthôsis*) and interpolation by their users and in-house copiers, nor were they safe from booksellers and their copiers—who, Strabo says, "never collated" (*ouk antibállontes*) their books (ib.XIII.i.54). Strabo concludes by saying that the later Peripatetics were uncertain in their "philosophizing and Aristotelianizing" because of the mass (*plêthos*) of errors in their material.

In any case, however many or few of Aristotle's own writings the successors may have had, we see that they felt quite free to "edit" or revise, rewrite or interpolate, them in the interest of "the truth" or their own views. This freedom of course disappears with the issuance of Andronikos's edition in the mid-first century B.C. But we can also see that so platonized or pythagorized, and stoicized, was the intellectual atmosphere of the time that commentaries were at once felt to be needed, both to save the assumptions with which the Academy, the Stoics, and the Pythagoreans had perfused the culture, and to make intelligible the newly constituted Aristotelian body of works. And this need would be felt most sharply at just those points where the original Aristotle's assumptions were different from theirs.

So dualistic, for instance, is the psychology of the Peripatos that where for Aristotle the psychê was the form or principle of the life-cycle of its body, it became in the Theophrastean school—for Clearchus, for example—an entity separable from the human organism (Wehrli Fr.7).[19] The pseudo-Theophrastean "metaphysical fragment," as it's called, may not be by Theophrastos himself,[20] but the dualistic way it separates 'objects of sense' from 'objects of reason' (I.i) is only one sign of how platonized the school was.[21] While as metaphysics it is naturally a theoretical book (in Aristotle's sense of first philosophy), it is also in contradiction with him in its pythagorizing theoreticism about the special knowledges: these are to be deduced from first principles provided by the kind of cosmotheology which the fragment itself is; the special sciences or knowledges will thus not have, as in Aristotle, their own distinct starting-points, nor will they depend upon observation. We hear of a dispute in the school about whether the earthquake of 373 in Helike and Bura was divine retribution or due to natural causes,[22] thus establishing the co-existence of supernaturalism in the school with whatever remnants of (Aristotle's) naturalism may have survived in some of its members.

This being the case, it is not far-fetched to hypothesize that the duality of views about monarchy and democracy in the Aristotelian *Politics* owes its existence not to ambivalence or 'development' on Aristotle's part, but to additions and changes that were made in it by its professorial users, transmitters and copiers. Knowing how drastically scholars at Alexandria could treat the text of Homer—a poet whose words were relatively fixed in the memories of the rhapsodes, the schoolmasters, and the culture—we cannot expect heads of the Lyceum, who were accountable to no one, not to have treated their esoteric inheritance with parallel aggressiveness. And Theophrastos, the most authoritative of the Peripatetics and the most downright about the relation of "reading" to "revising" that we know of, was in complete control of the Lyceum for more than 34 years after Aristotle's death.[23] Alarming also is the parallel with Plato, and the canonical set of his dialogues, into which and to which, dialogues not by Plato crept or were added.

It is intellectually paradoxical but historiographically most significant that Philip Merlan's account of "The Peripatetic School from Theophrastos to Andronikos and Boethus" brings out not how Aristotelian it was, but the ways in which it anticipated the Neoplatonists who were to adopt some of its terminology. Finally, that so many Peripatetics (beginning with Theophrastos) were not Athenian, namely, had no attachment to an ancestral constitution that was democratic, would also explain the absence of continuators of the moderate-Athenian tendency in Aristotle's notes on politics.

Hellenistic Assumptions about Politics, and the Pythagorization of the Climate of Opinion

Now, not only is political theory an essentially controversial subject-matter in itself, but political values must have been debated, changed or renewed with the greatest intensity after the Macedonian conquest of Athens and Greece at Chaeronea in 338 B.C. We can begin to get an idea of the state of Athenian opinion about politics in the earlier mid-fourth century from Plato's dialogical satire of one-man rule in the *Politicus*, and the intellectual context it presupposes.[24] So, granting the co-existence of democratic views side by side with monarchist views in the 'Aristotelian' *Politics*, let us note that the *polis* is a dominant (*kyrios*) institution in 'the democratic Aristotle' (as we will call this set of views) for reasons responding to the nature of non-alienated, participatory community, whereas in monarchist theory (and 'the monarchist Aristotle') it must be dominant (and dominationist) for reasons of security, since the post–barbarian or non-tribal monarchy does *not reproduce itself naturally*; for instance, the succession crucial to its continuation, is determined by arbitrary nomination, by the circumstances of the monarch's death, or by violent conflict. In contrast to the communitarian *polis*, it is only an alienated aggregate of non-participatory *subjects*. "Civic" institutions, as we would call them, do not prevail (*ischúein*) in this kind of state or are either nominal, manipulated or overrriden just as they are also overriden—but more noisily—under demagogic democracy.

Kingship, for Greeks in the fourth century, began to break out of its tribal Homeric past into Athenian reality as the neighboring Macedonian monarchy loomed ever larger over their affairs and as, with the spread of Pythagoreanism and the success of the Sophists, Athenians became familiar with the rationales for monarchy and oligarchy provided by the sect and by the professional non-Athenian arguers and speech-writers—by the former as a systematic doctrinal matter, by the latter on an ad hoc basis. At this time too, a specifically Athenian twist to the possible uses of monarchy was provided by the reasoning in Isokrates' *Panegyricus* speech (c.380 B.C.) and his Address to Philip (346 B.C.) whom he, nonetheless, reminds that "those among the Hellenes who have acquired such [monarchical] authority have not only been destroyed themselves but their kindred have been obliterated from mankind" (*To Philip* 108).[25] Isokrates' idea was that a war–leader[26] who could be entrusted with the supreme command over a Hellenic alliance—not with the governance of any cities but his own—would not only actualize the potential greatness of the Greeks vis-a-vis the rest of the world by subduing the Persian empire, but would prevent faction in the home states and avoid the chronic hegemonic disputes that were sapping the strength of the Greek states.

The point to note is that the ideologies of the proposed supreme generalship and the Homeric monarchy of Athenian memory are, both of them, radically different from those of the monarchies surrounding fourth-century democratic Athens down to 322/21 B.C. the year of Aristotle's death. Though Athens had been forced to become, in its constitution, a drastically limited timocracy (of 9000 citizens) as a condition of peace in that year, when Antipater put down its anti-Macedonian revolt, we can be sure that this did not immediately extinguish the democratic sentiment that had nurtured its political vitality for the 190 years since the constitution of Kleisthenes. This component of the climate of opinion in the city in which Aristotle matured and got his higher education is naturally not the only antecedent at work in fourth-century political discourse. In opposition to this hereditary background factor would be the more-difficult-to-perceive fact that Alexander's behavior *vis-a-vis* the localist Greeks, if examined in the light of the *Panegyricus*, actually seems to have taken this oration and Isokrates' *pan-Hellenic* advice to his father Philip, as a guide to his career.

But this, in turn, was not just an index of Alexander's desire to be fully a Hellene; it was also a political response to the strength of the city-states' attachment to their home-constitutions. The distracting factor here no doubt is the fervent, well-documented democratic (and *localist*) patriotism of Demosthenes. And there is a contrast to be made between the defensive localism of each and every Greek city-state, oligarchic or democratic, and the pan-Hellenism and phil–Hellenism of Alexander's political conduct.[27]

Following the groping but patchy lead of J.B. Bury who ventured some suggestions in his *A History of Greece* about Aristotle's "prejudices" because these translate into assumptions affecting his focus,[28] let us (in a spirit of corrigibility) review what can be uncovered *apriori* about his political stance from his personal circumstances. Growing up "in the narrow self-satisfied community of little remote Stagira, he had imbibed," Bury assumes, "the dislike which was openly or secretly felt towards Athens in all the Chalcidean regions. And," Bury assumes further, "he never overcame this distrust; he always remained a citizen of Stagira and lived in Athens as a stranger." These last three claims demand confirmation or falsification on the basis of the available evidence, as much as does the serious parallel claim that "he was also prejudiced against Macedonia." To back *this* claim Bury reminds us that,

> The Chalcidians looked upon their Macedonian neighbors as far below themselves in civilization; and Aristotle's experiences of Pella [as] a spectator of the scandalous quarrels between Philip and Olympias, did not create a favorable impression. He was thus disposed to hold . . . entirely aloof from the enterprises of Alexander.

So far, we are still within the realm of plausibility. But Bury's next suggestion is stronger: "not only did he not sympathize, he disapproved. For he was wedded to the idea of the small Greek republic, he condemned the large state" (p.835). The 'Aristotelian' *Politics* does say (VII.1326b27ff.), "the city must be in easy communication with all points in the country, and that "in extent and size the land should be such that it enables its inhabitants to live a life of free and sensible leisure"—but this is not necessarily to "condemn the large state." It is an exclusion of it only *in our retrospective view*. What it does show is that the *Politics* does not want to discuss the imperial states of its time.

Again, while autarchic self–satisfaction is plausibly imputable to Stagira, that does not preclude Aristotle the man-of-knowledge from desiderating something richer and more intellectual for his model state. Yes, as a governing-class Greek Aristotle may well have shared "the Hellenic conviction that Hellenes were superior by nature to peoples of other race;" but well-traveled as he was and kindly house-holder that the tradition believes him to have been, this only trans-lates into a matter of not giving, within a Greek city, equal political rights to metics and foreigners. Granting that Aristotle was neither Macedonian nor Athenian, it does not follow for this intellectual, who got his education in Athens, did his writing and started a school there, that "he lived [there] as a stranger." The case is rather like that of a Harvard-or Columbia-educated intellectual who is neither a New Englander nor European but is thoroughly at home working and teaching in Boston or New York, and equally at home in the American intellectual tradition. "Initial prejudice" would make him as much an "impartial" as a "partial judge" of American (or Athe-nian) institutions. On the evidence of the *Politics*, finally, we have to agree that Aristotle "took as the type of democracy . . . the Athenian institutions" (p.834). At the same time, we may doubt that the Stagi-rean constitution, whatever its differences from the Athenian, did much service as a model for Aristotle.

Considering the influence which Plato's dialogue the *Politicus* will be seen to have had, and the uses to which it *and* the *Republic* were put on a literalist understanding of their de-dramatized contents, and considering the ideological effort which the Academy, after Plato's death, put into constructing the *Laws*, we have now to ex-amine these works for what they imply or can tell us about the assumptions of the Hellenistic age. And, because of the way the first two have been denatured and misread and the way the last presents itself, we need to examine them not only as political phi-losophers, but also as literary critics or philologists and as source-critics or historians. We will then be in a position to consider the contrasts and coincidences that emerge between the assumptions of the *Politics* in its un-unified parts and the assumptions of its col-lateral, mostly alien, sociohistorical context.

Now, the passages which Stobaeus (5th c. A.D.) preserves on the Pythagorean doctrine of monarchy[29] are all later than the dialogue featuring the subject, and appear to have been influenced by the

Academic or literalist interpretation of it. Any development of the idea of monarchy—or of the legitimation of monarchy on the basis of its knowledge or "scientific" competence—among pre-Platonic Pythagoreans or Sophists is undocumentable apart from the dialogue. In any case, the visitor from Elea in the *Politicus* is obtrusively identifiable as a rhetorical Sophist with Pythagorean affiliations. That he has not been seen as such is due to the habitual de-dramatization of the dialogue by literalist readers interested only in its abstractible doctrinal content.[30]

As it happens, the Eleatic Sophist in the *Politicus* takes up (at 276d–e and 284c–285c) the very same topics that are treated by Xenophon, the spartanizing oligarchist, in both his *Hiero* and at the end of the *Oeconomicus* (Bk.xxi). These topics, kingship and despotism, are discussed by him with the same *obliviousness to the rule of law* as shown by the rhetorical Sophist's defense of monarchy (in spite of Socrates junior's weak or belated protests). But it was just the characteristic of the Macedonian kingship of Philip and Alexander that it was non-constitutional in the sense that there was *no legal basis* for its customary and ad hoc procedures.[31] For our intellectual-historical purpose, however, it does not matter whether Xenophon is reformulating (in his own unintellectual and understated way) views similar to those of the pythagorizing Sophist from Elea, or whether Plato is using the Eleatic rhetorician in order to put on exhibit for our inspection the rationale provided for these views by the Pythagoreans. Whatever the chronological priorities between Plato and Xenophon, it is the conception of the ruling-class farmer—a conception not exclusive to Xenophon's Ischomachus—that is being played with by the Eleatic Sophist in the *Politicus*. The tip-off to this is the idea of the ruler as man-herd in the Sophist's discourse. But, while Xenophon and the Eleate are both antidemocratic, it is clear that the latter—with his pythagorizing claims to knowledge or "science"—is intellectualizing *the common oligarchal idea*. Secondly, Xenophon held *his* views in the context of a laid-back paternalist *paideia,* where the Eleate as a paid professional must operate by re-sults-getting, covered-up persuasion.

The Eleate's discourse, in point of literary fact, is so covered-up that it escapes readers not awake to the ironies of Plato's formative Greek—or not immune to the Academy-generated tradition mak-ing him a dogmatic idealist—that the dialogue is a satire in the ex-hibitive mode of Pythagorean political intellectuality. Irony, as we know, was the weapon with which Plato's Socrates combatted the Sophists; but Plato's irony is not only Socratic and textural, it is architectonic, as we shall shortly see.

Note in the meantime that the Sophistic rhetorician also shares with Xenophon the downgrading of the manual and mechanical arts that became an un-Hellenic characteristic of the Hellenistic ep-och—un-Hellenic, that is, if the values of the Archaic age are counted as also definitive of the pristine Classical age. Whether Xenophon's works are indifferent to or indirect responses to Plato's, it is pos-sible to see them as a 'depythagorization' or de-intellectualization of pythagorist or Sophistic defenses of monarchy. It is quite prob-able that Xenophon saw the *Republic* as inimical to oligarchy be-cause satirical of it, since Aulus Gellius suggests that Xenophon's *Cyropaedia* was his reponse to Plato's *Republic* or part of it.[32] For, if Xenophon was indeed countering the *Republic,* he must have taken it in a sense inimical to his own preference for the rule of the few. As a *practicing* oligarch, spartanizer and gentleman (*kalos k'agathos*), and like Anytus in the *Meno,* he would have been predisposed against Sophists and against anybody who (like Plato's Socrates) used the term *kalos-k'agathos* ironically. As for Plato's gentler and subtler (but more complete) satire of Pythagoreanism, he likely would have seen it as barely intelligible feuding among intellectuals and mathemati-cians.[33]

The gentleman-militarist and the rhetorician from Elea do share some other significant conceptions. Xenophon's Socrates, like Simonides in his *Hiero,* makes the *aretê* of the kingly general depend entirely on his ability to make his followers happy (*Memorabilia* II.3). In the *Hiero*, the difference between a tyrant and a monarch depends on the willingness of his subjects to be ruled by him; while the condemnation at the end of the *Oeconomicus* of the tyrant who rules over *unwilling* subjects, shows that the consentingness of subjects to despotic rule is a matter of importance to Xenophon. This of course blocks, as it did in the discourse of the Eleatic visitor, any development of the place of law in reflective politics, whether in Xenophon's *praktikê* or the Eleate's *epistêmê*. But as to the happiness of the monarch the Eleate's Divine Shepherd, possessed as he is of kingly (basilikê) knowledge and a happy kingdom, he can be presumed not to lack it. Nor is Xenophon's Hiero kept from happiness as long as he knows how to keep the consent of his subjects.

Still, we find Hiero's interlocutor Simonides agreeing strongly to the need of the monarch for a mercenary guard which, however, will be put to uses that are good for his subjects as well; while Hiero well knows that the despot is "forced to maintain an army, or perish" (IV.xi). The implication, in Xenophon at least, is that the consent of the subjects (given human nature) is not enough to *sustain* a monarch who has it, even if it seems to legitimate him. For the Sophist, on the other hand, it is his "science" or knowledge that legitimates the one-man ruler; and the presumed success of the latter's inclusive "science" (which has included the supervision of generals, judges, administrators and other city-state functionaries) keeps the subject of the monopoly of force from arising in his discourse. But, of course, only a non-constitutional monarchist will believe that the *kingly* man's intelligence and great store of "scientific" ability is enough to legitimate his rule. And only a paternalist like Xenophon, with a militarist model of state-administration, would rationalize a tacitly dominationist system as something *willingly* consented to by those dominated.

Getting back to our Eleatic rhetorician, it is also not implausible to take him as trying to counter the condemnation of tyranny by Antisthenes the semi-Socratic, if Xenophon's use of the latter to condemn predatory despots has a historical basis (Xenoph. *Symp.*IV.36-37). In any case, a common belief that the Eleate (like Xenophon) is combatting is that of the inevitable *unhappiness* of the tyrant. And of course all good monarchists made the biggest possible difference between the legitimate monarch who made his people happy and the tyrant whose pursuit was his own interest and safety. More generally, however, we can see from the design of the *Politicus* that it owes its existence to Plato's desire to give *a fair hearing* to Sophistic at its unimpeded and discursive best, where in the *Protagoras* that great Sophist had had to dispute with Socrates, and where in his *Euthydemus* Plato had merely exposed the intellectual cheapness of two incompetent Sophists at their word-mongering worst.

In any case, the reader who listens to the Elean Sophist with the ears and eyes of the silent Socrates in the dialogue, namely, who listens from an Athenian, contemporary point of view with its traditional Athenian prejudices, such a reader will surely respond to the Sophist's defense of one–man rule with a skepticism and criticality rooted in the century-and-a-half of moderate democracy enjoyed by Athens since the constitution of Kleisthenes. This, at any rate, is how Plato would have expected his non-oligarchal Athenian readers (represented by Socrates in the dialogue) to respond. He will, at the same time, have shown the oligarchists what the best is that can be done for their theory, a best unacceptable to most Athenians. The limitations of one-man rule and weakness of the clever rationale for it, emerge under the modern reader's own eyes as he completes his session with the accomplished Sophist.

We need, lastly, to say a word about the pythagorization of the fourth-century climate of opinion. Beginning with the fragments of Philolaus from the end of the fifth century, we find a progressively stronger renewal of (what we know as) Pythagoreanism. I say "what we know as" Pythagoreanism because it is certain that many of the doctrines attributed to him, or even to the earliest Pythagoreans— who also left nothing in writing—are not original to him or them. And about the century-and-a-half of "*his* school" between him and

Philolaus we know nothing that is documentable. Outside of Archytas and Philolaus the first echoes of or reports about it occur in Plato and Aristotle; just as the first occurrences of the term *philosophos* and *philosophía* in our sense have been shown to occur within Plato's dialogues,[34] not in their school as claimed by later Pythagoreans. And this is relevant because it is clear that Plato and Aristotle did not think of him as a philosopher.[35]

It is certain, however, from the extant remains and the social history of Western Greece that they were supporters of dynasties and oligarchies, when not themselves rulers like Archytas the *stratêgos* of Tarentum. The brotherhood had been anti-democratic from its beginnings in Kroton. There, a combination of democratic elements and notables resentful of its excessive privileges finally expelled them, after protracted strife—a story to be repeated in other cities of Western Greece, timocratic or aristocratic as these appear to have been.[36] Thereafter, the only extant mentions of Pythagoras are by Xenophanes who ridicules his doctrine of the transmigration of souls, and by Herakleitos who ridicules his eclectic learning and craftiness, *kakotechnía* (DK22 B40, B81, B29). In the fifth century Herodotus knows Greeks who hold *Egyptian* doctrines but declines to name them (Bk.II.23), and Empedocles' fragment DK31 B129 would seem to refer to Orpheus, but some readers following Porphyry take it to refer to Pythagoras, while Iôn of Chios mentions him, in a much discussed fragment, in the same breath with Pherekydes the writer. And these, as scholars have duly noted, are the sum-total of the references to Pythagoras during that century.

Pythagoreans do next figure in the public consciousness as impoverished refugees, in the mixed company of the nature-philosophers, successful or unsuccessful Sophists, and school-teachers who had flocked to Athens in search of work; so that it seemed fitting to Aristophanes to give the name of Socrates to his comic composite of the three stereotypes because he was so well-known, and already becoming a legend in his own life-time in the last two decades of the fifth century.[37] But how the other legend grew that turned Pythagoras into a dominating influence over the intellectual climate of opinion, we can only dimly discern, given first that it was at first an oral-aural unrecorded process and secondly that, in step with the increased resort to the new medium writing and the pythagorization of the climate of opinion, *all documentary sources* mentioning or reflecting the process were themselves pythagorized as they came under the control of the sect. If the increased use of writing was in some way an explosive phenomenon, then that would have favored (and would also explain) the Pythagoreans' saturation of the culture with their writings. As a cult there was, of course, a conspiratorial side to it, and this would have translated into an effective attention to the public image and public relations of the movement.[38]

The attraction of Pythagoreanism as a new kind of knowledge lay in its institutionally enforced claim to be both mathematical or numerological, and a secret or revealed truth. 'Join my discipline and you'll know what to do with your life' was the message to the general public; to the nature-inquirers, Sophists, and intellectuals of the time the message was 'take what I have to say seriously, and your own teaching will be more easily accepted.' The culture had reached a time when the public wanted only answers, not more Socratic questioning: a time, therefore, in which Plato's dialogues— perpetuating and memorializing, as they did, both *the Socratic practice of irony* and of uncovering ignorance or confusion *by means of question-and-answer*—could not possibly succeed with the general public. Beautifully constructed as these dialogues were, however, they could not be allowed to be wasted or go unused.

So the use which the circle of Speusippos and his friends found for them was to turn the dialogues into a vehicle for the imposition of a system of doctrines both compatible with and *interactive with* the advances in knowledge being made by the Pythagoreans. This process was facilitated by the fact that what the dialogues dramatize is the intellectual, argumentative life of cosmopolitan Athens; as a consequence of this their abstractible content was very conceptual as well as full of arguments about knowledge itself. Speusippos, his friends and successors would in this way, namely, by pythagorizing the dialogues, benefit from both the public relations and the research of the Pythagoreans.[39] If, however, Speusippos was to keep himself and his academy from being completely absorbed into the pythagorean movement, he would have to wield and uphold some separate authority of his own other than Pythagoras. And this authority was there to hand, in the dialogues of Plato as interpreted by himself, his colleagues, and the succeeding scholarchs who would be in control of all access to Plato's works.

An analogy with the school of Isokrates may be found illuminating: if Plato had been the founder of the Academy it wouldn't have survived his death, as Isokrates's school did not survive him. Rather, as just suggested, the Academy was founded by Speusippos and his circle with the twofold purpose of appropriating Plato's fame and work to their own uses, and of distinguishing themselves from the Pythagoreans who (earlier in the century) had yet to gain public acceptance. The two centers are said to have come into existence within a few years of each other, and were equally attended by distinguished students from all over. Where Isokrates' school inculcated the art of oratory, the Academy inculcated what was basically only another species of idealism not really damaging to, or distinguishable from, the Pythagoreans' way of thinking. The price of this was the obliteration of the brilliant dialogism and exhibitive criticality of Plato's dramatizations of Athenian intellectual life.[40] But the gain to the Pythagoreans from this arrangement and the acceptance it won for them was enormous, and determinative for the whole history of Western thought.

Let us, in concluding this part of our study, meditate for a moment on the enormous intellectual difference, in the composition of Athenian opinion, as between *the turn into* the fourth century and *the end of* that century. The difference is doubly diremptive. Intellectually, the two moments represent twice over two different worlds; the culture has spread into different parts of the earth geographically. Not only is Athens and Greece becoming a visual-graphic culture from having been an oral-aural one (till about the death of Socrates), but it ceases (ten years after Plato's death) to be a conglomeration of free, politically sovereign communities and non-alienated individuals. On top of the fact that Aristotle had to live through the completion of the sea-change in the nature of communication and the loss of Hellenic autonomy and community, he also—at some point in the history of the group with which he had come to study—saw that very group turn the dialogues of the Plato they were surrounding into para-pythagorean tractates. And this no doubt was a contributing cause of his deserting the Academy in the late 340's. By this time the Academy was a school teaching and defending an orthodoxy, and no longer a discussion-group or a disinterested institution devoted to pure research. So that, when Aristotle returned from *his* researches and travels abroad, he naturally started his own separate school of inquiry and discussion, namely, the Lyceum. This is the school that was also called the Peripatos, and which, as we are seeing, was no more faithful to the humanist teachings and investigative spirit of the original Aristotle than the Academy had been to the satirical or critical spirit of the original, dialogical Plato.

The Platonist-Monarchist Doctrines of the Academy, and the Peripatetic *Politics*

In short, where, among Athenian intellectuals at the lively turn-of-the-century, there had been a fashion for (i) antilogizing, as in the discourses of Protagoras and Antiphon, for (ii) Socratic or semi–Socratic questioning, as in the semi–Socratics and Plato, and plenty of (iii) Sophistic rhetoric, (iv) Aristophanic humor and myth–making along with Euripidean rationalism, the picture in the last thirteen years of Aristotle's life is very different. The most significant thing that has changed (for our purposes) is that one could not, in the earlier milieu, be *both* intelligent *and* dogmatic decisive as one might be in other contexts. Verbally *unqualified assertiveness* would have been quickly mocked and refuted. As the far-ranging inquirer and systematic talent that his fragmentary remains show him to have been, Aristotle is still the complete intellectual of classical Athenian times. But the city-state rationality of which he is an exponent is disappearing all around him, as the city-states lose more and more of their autonomy. He has been collecting and studying the constitutions of these cities, one result of which is our text of *The Athenian Constitution,* and he is writing or making notes for a book on politics; and the result of this effort is our text of the *Politics,* much handled by the Peripatetics, then handed down to us. But his colleagues and successors in the Lyceum had not absorbed the values of *a polity* such as Athens had been; nor did they share either Aristotle's city-state rationality or his loyalty to moderate constitutionalism.

Having reviewed this much of the fourth-century intellectual background, we can now proceed to examine both the influence of this climate on the *Politics,* and the nature of the verbal echoes of Plato's *Republic* and the Academic *Laws* in the work. It will perhaps be best to begin by confronting what the *Politics* says about monarchy.

Analysts have rightly pointed out that the Aristotelian classifications of constitutions are not like the biological ones that describe actually existing species.[41] This is because observed constitutions so often exhibit characteristics belonging to more than one classification, although of course each type is defined by a principle or number of essential traits. So his division and categorizations of constitutions are abstract and formal, much like the "ideal types" of social theory such as "a command economy" or "a developing nation." And this is how he classifies the subdivisions of one-man rule, or monarchy (III.1285a2ff., 127933–4, 1279b5–6, V.1311a3–4).

After mentioning the hereditary monarchy of the servile Asiatics and the lifelong generalship of the Spartan kings, the text recalls the obsolete elective tyrannies or "asymneties" of archaic times, which were resorted to in emergencies, which were not hereditary but which often turned into lifetime dictatorships. It then lists the fourth class "royal hereditary monarchy according to law, over willing subjects in the heroic epoch" (1285b4–6). But, when not soldiering for their own upkeep or survival, when were 'subjects' ("heroic" times or not) ever such 'willing' subjects? While the conquest was still recent? If they no longer felt oppressed, what would be evidence of their uncoerced consent; and what uncoerced occasions, unprompted by largesse or relief from external peril, would there be to express it? Isn't this wording simply trying to make non-constitutional prehistoric monarchy look constitutional?

Discussion of what the text calls "absolute monarchy," *pambasileía*, comes last. But before ever beginning its list the text has made the case—starting from a critique of ostracism which condemns the banishment of men of exceptional *aretê* or excellence—for the person whom no one would think to to dominate (*archein*) any more than they would try to rule Zeus. Such a man, says the text, it would seem natural for all others to obey gladly (*peithesthai asmenôs*); "so that such a man will be an enduring (*aidíous*) king of cities." There are two jarring, artificious points here, and one with a distinct dynastic flavor. Is it credible that a self-respecting functionalist like Aristotle would allow that *any* citizen be exempt from being ruled, when he has earlier characterized the good citizen as someone who knows both how to rule and to be ruled?

Secondly, the phrasing of "it would seem natural" is a Sophistic appeal to the anti-nomothetic or anti-legislative side of the nature-versus-*nómos* distinction: when Aristotle says "by nature" it is just part of his genetic view of things-in-process. The assimilation of the exceptional—non–dominatable or dominant—person to god-likeness is dynasticist and an opening toward the Hellenistic cult of the ruler.

The subspecies of monarch called tyrants rule in their own interest and with a view to their own safety; but, says the text, kings govern in the common interest (*pros to koinon . . . sympheron*, 1279a34) and, the text continues at V.1311a1–8, their wish is to be protectors of property owners from injustice and of the people from being down-trodden; where the tyrant seeks pleasure, the king seeks what appears good (*to kalon*). The kingship is like aristocracy in being based on merit or good works (*euergesias*, 1310b34) or the ability to benefit the city or nation. And we the readers notice that this is no longer a description of, but an apology for, kingship. And it is an oligarchist apology or rationale. The examples given of Codrus of Athens and the Persian Cyrus (in so far as he liberated his people from the Medes) are within the bounds of law;[42] but the instances of the Spartan, the Macedonian, and the Molossian kings are examples of successful territorial conquest whose justice it doesn't occur to the text to question.[43]

The citation at 1285a4 of the Spartan monarchy as *believed to be* the most (*basileia malista*) "typical" (Rackham) or the "strongest" (Barker) form of "law-based" kingship makes a pretense to exactness insofar as the passage points up one or two limitations on this kingship. But it doesn't question the oligarchist or military-élitist "law" on which it is based. And am I not covertly spartanizing if I invoke the popular (but inaccurate) belief in it as the most typical or strongest kind of monarchy? As a kind of generalship the writer thinks it is legitimate—even when, as on military campaigns, its power is not only absolute but becomes (unqualifiedly) judicial. This is *fuzzy* because the text is not talking war, but focusing on the command *as kingly*; its subtext, here again, seems to be pushing statedly law-based monarchy in the absolutist direction of the Macedonian kingships.

This is not note-book obscurity or first-draft tentativeness, but Peripatetic obscurantism putting the best face possible on *all* the kinds of monarchy, and making sure they are—in whatever available respect—kept distinct from tyranny. Strategically, the subtext here is to keep the Macedonian monarchies from being called tyrannical. It's also unAristotelically fuzzy because, *as a classification*, this species of Agamemnon-like monarchy belongs quite as much under the text's fifth heading of absolute monarchy—so few are the limitations on it, except for the five Spartan ephors the king will report to when the campaign is over. And is it consistent to admit that the obsolete third species of kingship (the asymneties, 1285a32) are tyrannical although also *elective*, and not to allow that the Spartan kingship is also tyrannical although *hereditary*?

It is certainly dynastic to proceed as if kingships were more secure (*asphalês*, 1285a25) because of heredity (*dia to patriai*), and it is slyly oligarchist to invoke the native citizenship of hereditary royal bodyguards as a legitimating factor. For these would, in practice, be a bristling or honor-seeking élite and, in theory, an incarnation of the guardian-class of Plato's *Republic* literalistically understood.

But Aristotle's *Rhetoric* is quite clear, at 1366a5, that governments whose aim is self-defense (*phulakê*) are "tyrannical." This work, which circulated in Aristotle's lifetime and was thus less subject to tampering, also knows that kingship is tyrannical in just the measure that it is *not limited* (*aoristos*, 1366a3). And let us repeat, for the reader blocked from reading Plato dialogically: Aristotle, as a composer of dialogues himself, would have read the dialogues dialogically and perceived the irony and satire in them. He would not have taken them literalistically, as does the interpolator or editor who applies, or reuses literally, ideas formulated by speakers other than Plato in the dialogues. Nor would Aristotle have reformulated as categorical assertions in a *positive* spirit points (in the discourses of Plato's characters) brought into exhibition for inspection and response by Athenian auditors. Wouldn't Aristotle have rehearsed the given idea as loaded with the affect (negative or positive) given it by its interactional context, and then commented on it? Just such are the points made by the Sophistic rhetorician from Elea in the *Politicus*, in his pythagorizing defense of one-man rule. For he, in his turn, is being made by Plato to echo and take advantage of ideas about monarchy that came into play in Athens around the middle of the fourth century.

Moreover, as a matter of observation for the *Politics*, the kinds of states (*poleis*) and constitutions (*politeia*) boil down in practice to two, either democratic (*dêmokratikai*) or oligarchic (*oligarchikai*, IV.1296a22f). And this, while the text pretends—to mask its polarizing bent—that it's not easy to avoid the extremes of democracy or unmixed (*akratos*) oligarchy (1269a2). "That the middle form (*hê mesê*) of constitution is the best (*beltistê*) is clear," Aristotle had said at 1296a8, "for only it is free from faction" (*astasíastos*). "Democracies, also, are more secure than oligarchies and more long-lived (*polychroniôterai*), because of [the bulk of] the center" (1296a14f.). "And it must be thought signally compelling (*sêmeion*)," he adds, that "the best law-givers are from the middle sort of citizens" (1296a19).

We note that while, on one hand, this coincides with the functionalist recommendation at *Republic* 422a that both Wealth, *Ploutos*, and Poverty, *Penía*, be kept out of the city, on the other hand, it contradicts the *Laws'* fatalist, Hellenistic acceptance of the extremes of both which cause either oligarchy or democracy, respectively, to be the commonest of existing constitutions. But, weren't these extremes more common in the last decades of the century than in the first half of it, when the *Republic* was written?

In any case, whether his kind of constitution is democratic or oligarchic, says (the 'democratic') Aristotle, "the lawgiver must always include and feature (*proslambanein*) the middle class" (1296b36). Still talking to the avoidance of the extreme forms of constitution, Aristotle notes trenchantly and Solonically, "everywhere it is the mediator who is most trusted, and it is the one in the middle who is mediatory" (*diatêtês*) 1297a7). And he adds a warning which may well address the inclinations of his élitist friends, "those make a great mistake who, wanting to create aristocratic constitutions, not only give too large a share to the fortunate but also short-change or fob off the dêmos" (1297a9ff.). So that it is practically a political theorem for Aristotle that "the better the constitution is mixed, the more abiding will it be." And this is what can be extracted with credibility from the Peripatetic *Politics* as to what the original Aristotle thought the best realizable state should be.

By contrast, this brings into relief something about the way the passages on monarchy which we reviewed above (in their received form) were probably handled by lecturers using them in their unguarded state. It suggests that the passages dealing with monarchical constitutions were overwritten and enlarged *from the point of view of* Aristotle's foreign *oligarchist* colleagues, students and successors in order to adapt to the existing political situation in Hellenistic Greece, a situation in which the oligarchal class could hope for more benefits from their militarist, orientalized monarchs than from whatever their local constitutions might allow the cities in their merely nominal autonomy, a situation in which the old hoplite equals were no longer distinguishable from the non-citizens in point of political rights or participation.

Spiritually, it was also a situation in which *happiness* (*eudaimonia*) instead of *outstandingness*, in the sense of community-honored *bestness* (*aretê*), had become the goal of life, under an imperial system in which only Greeks willing to be servitors of the conquering power could be publicly honored for achievement. To such Greeks or orientals, democracy would mean nothing; career in the service everything. Ironically, one now went into a life of "public service" only out of self-interest, no longer in the interest of one's *polis* or as a matter of course. And this is how *aretê* came to mean *politico-military* ability rather than well-rounded or civic or *human excellence*. Aretê, so ambiguously mistranslated as "virtue," became something more like Machiavelli's *virtù* than like the responsive communitarian versatility or competence which it had been in the free city-states of the archaic and classical centuries.

To understand what is happening when the text of the *Politics* refers to "the ideal state," we must understand what is meant by that syntagm and how it arose in Athenian culture. There is not much difference in the Aristotelian text between the meaning of the locutions translated as "the best state" (*hê aristê politeia*) and what is called "the ideal," or "most wished for (*malista eiê kat'euchên*), state," since they are both grammatically superlatives and dianoetically ideal or perfective, namely, not *ultimately* achievable in practice, only approximateable. We need to understand, however, that earlier in the century, and as part of the motivating context of Plato's political dialogues, the concept of the *ideal* state, the state under discussion (*hê eirêmenê politeia*, Rep.499d5) originated as an oligarchist counter to the standing Athenian notion of the *ancestral* constitution (*hê patrios politeia*). The concept was the only respectable way in which *to appeal away from* the beloved, sloganized ancestral constitution (which went back to Kleisthenes, Solon and a hundred years of success) *to something else.* That unspecified something else was, of course, a constitution more oligarchic than the standing democratic one, but *more attractive in its ideality* or perfection than any existing (and therefore imperfect) constitution.

Let us look at the terms for it, in the dialogue which holds it up for inspection and satirizes it. At Rep.520c Plato's Socrates smilingly calls it "kallipolis," the "City Beautiful" or the "good looking city." At Rep.540d2 he ironically says about it that "our notion of the state and its constitution is not entirely a day-dream" (*mê . . . euchas*). And at 499b–c Socrates with mock solemnity says that "neither city nor constitution nor mankind will ever be perfected" until the uncorrupted and *knowing* philosophers (i.e., the Academic pythagorizers) take charge of the state, and adds that only if he said that this was impossible would he be ridiculed for entertaining day-dreams (*euchais*). Ridiculed by whom? By the Academic pythagorizers of course. At the end of Book IX Socrates concedes that "the city whose founding they have described in words (*tê en logois keimenêi*) . . . can be found nowhere on earth" (*epei gês oudamon . . .*). "But perhaps," adds Socrates, "there is a pattern (*paradeigma*) laid up in heaven (*ouranoi*) for him who looking, sees it, and can settle for it, or in it."

We notice that the standard translation "the ideal state" drains the affect from it: it is no longer a wish-dream of the pythagorizers in the Academy, but something for discussion. Here are two translations:

Barker: "the study of politics [which belongs to the practical arts and sciences] must be equally comprehensive. First, it has to consider which is the best constitution, and *what qualities a constitution must have to come closest to the ideal* when there are no external factors . . . to hinder its doing so. Secondly . . . (1288b23ff.)

Rackham: "it is the business of the same science to study which is the *best constitution* and what character it must have to be the *most ideal* if no external circumstances stand in the way, and what constitution is adapted to what people . . .

Notice that 1288b25:*poia tis an ousa malist'eiê kat'euchên*, translates more exactly into "the most to be wished" or "most desirable," not into "most ideal." The best constitution and the ideal constitution, then, are one and the same in the Aristotelian text.

But since politics is a practical science (as the chapter began by saying) the equivocation between *best* and *ideal* tends to make the best practicable constitution ideally normative, and the purely discursive, ideal constitution practical! This brings us to what the realities are that the text is recommending:

VII.1325b36: *poias tinas dei tas hypothesis einai peri tês mellousês kat'euchên synestanai poleôs*: "what the [necessary] conditions are for the state that is to be constituted in the ideally best manner" (Rackham).[44]

"We must therefore assume," adds the text in Barker's translation, "a number of ideal conditions, which must be capable of fulfilment as well as being ideal" (p.290).[45]

These conditions, on examination, all turn out to be oligarchist.

This state, for instance, "cannot have its citizens living the life of mechanics or shopkeepers, which is ignoble and inimical to goodness. Nor can it have them engaged in farming: leisure is a necessity, both for growth in goodness and for the pursuit of political activities" (1328b40–1329a, Barker). More generally at *Pol.*VII.1329a22, and in a phrase that stands out because it is lifted from *Republic* 500d: all others would have no share in the state who "are not producers of goodness" (*mê tês aretês dêmiourgon*). That "this also follows `by hypothesis' (*ek tês hypotheseôs*, b24–5), for being happy is necessarily included in (*hyparchein*) goodness," confirms our proposal that the assumption at work here is that the best state is an oligarchic state in which functional divisions are being turned into class divisions. So it is not an Utopia that we can take or leave that is being advanced here, but a state the conditions of whose realization are being spelled out by the writer. Note, in addition, that the words about this class of people as *not* being craftsmen who produce *aretê*, is simply a literalist echo of the phrasing in the *Republic* .

At 1327b30–35 the text talks as if the Greeks were all still free, with good political institutions and capable of ruling all mankind— *as if*, that is, the Greeks had not yet lost their dominance or autonomy; but that on the other hand, at 1327b39, the Platonist "guardians" of *Republic* are brought into the discussion of what the character of the citizens should be in the most desirable state as if the literalist reinterpretation of the dialogue was an established fact. But the counter-dialogical non-ironic reading of the work could not have become such a fact till after Plato's death, (unless perhaps that event was preceded by some drastic disability).

This would seem to suggest that the time subsequent to 347 B.C., which was made epochal by the Macedonian victory at Chaeronea in 338 B.C., was the time during which the Academy decided on and implemented the change in the way Plato's satirical dialogues were to be read. Not only was the early second half of the century the time when Plato's successors such as Speusippos, Aristotle, and Xenocrates were working out their own views. It was also the time when it became imperative for the Academy to avoid offending the conquerors, at the risk of being closed down. And it is quite likely that the Macedonians would have taken offense at the simultaneous satire of militarism and oligarchism in the *Republic* if they had had enough literary Greek to understand it rightly. Meantime the spread of Pythagoreanism in the mid-century must have been such that it became convenient for timorous or élitist intellectuals to ally themselves with the newly-popular supporters of oligarchs and dynasts from Western Greece. The successful enforcement by the Academy of the militarist-oligarchal interpretation of *Republic*—by means of a systematic de-dramatization of its interactions and a systematic purging of its verbal pregnancies and satirical allusions—could well have been the result of this combination of circumstances. And the change would be all the easier to bring off because the language of the *oikoumenê* was now Koinê Greek, and because "philosophy" no longer meant "the pursuit or love of knowledge" but rather adherence to a life-guiding orthodoxy.

Echoes in the *Politics* from the De–Dramatized *Republic* and the Academic *Laws*

Just as the would-be description of monarchy in the *Politics* turns out to be a defense of it, so will we see that some of the descriptions of "democracy" in the book-as-we-have-it turn out to be caricatures. At the same time, we have to bear in mind that the *Republic* has been brought into line with the new oligarchist and pythagorizing fashions of thought by the extirpation of its satirical irony and a propositionalizing of its content that (i) sunders things said from the way and tone in which they are said, and (ii) detaches them from the named character who says them and his interests. If you

purge from an extended satire of oligarchism, pythagorizing intellectuality, and militarism, its sardonic tone and pervasive, or architectonic, irony, the result will be to turn it into *an assertion, instead of
a criticism, of* these institutions. And this is what the Academy did
to, and with, Plato's masterpiece. It is because their origin is now a
de-dramatized *Republic* that the citations from it in the Peripatetic
Politics work to reinforce the oligarchist subtext of its exposition.

Thus, the text at 1261a6 has not an inkling of the irony with which
Socrates is speaking of the community of wives, children and possessions and, in deprecating it, speaks of it as a regulation
(*gegramménon nómon*)! The writer has misunderstood something
which Socrates knows will never be accepted by his Athenian auditors, to be a legal command—and humorlessly goes on to criticize it
as creating too much unity in the state. Can this be Aristotle who so
simplistically takes a suggestion designed to shock Sokrates' hearers, as a law to be observed by the guardians, and who has—we
also note—identified the whole state with the guardians?

Again, the text from 1290a10 to 1291b14 shows how uncritically
and non-holistically the overwriter is reading the *Republic*. He no-
tices that "the first (*prôtê*) city" projected in the work is different
from the second feverish city, without noticing that the difference
corresponds to the *need for remediation* of the second city (according
to the now sardonic Socrates), and without noticing the radical
change in tone of Sokrates' discourse as he gives up on the first
healthy (*hygiês*) minimally necessary (*anankaiotatê*) city in order to
consider Glaucon's luxurious (*truphôsa*) and feverish (*phlegmainousa*)
city. The difference between the two cities which he does take up is
that which will allow us to find justice in it (*to dikaion*, 1291a24). This
is the addition (he says) to the first city of a warrior class which is
more a part (*sic*) of the state, as the soul is "more a part" (*morion
mallon*) of the body, along with a judiciary class, and a politically
skilled (*syneseôs politikês*) one.

The writer here has quietly identified the military with the soul
of the state, where the standing Athenian wisdom from Isokrates to

Aristotle was that the *constitution* is the soul of the state. He also speaks here of the judiciary and magistracies as if they were part of the executive, like the public servants (*to peri tas archas leitourgoun, eiper . . . aneu archontôn*, 1291a35-6). And speaking of the city's need for a political élite (*tinas aretês tôn politikôn*),[46] he grants that the functions of soldier and farmer or craftsman may overlap, only however, in order to go on to *polarize* the state (unAristotelically) between rich and poor as classes that cannot possibly overlap and as the classes whose claims are overriding (*hyperochos*). Would Aristotle have left the middle class entirely out of a discussion of the components of the polis, and talked like the writer here as if *the state-apparatus only* was his focus rather than the city-state as a whole— (when it *was* a non-polarized whole, that is).

Next, 1316a criticizes Plato's Socrates for not discussing revolutions fairly (*kalôs*), because he picks on "the first and best constitution" as if it was the only constitution especially to suffer them. This shows that the text has not understood, first, the learnedly satirical shape of the passage beginning at 545d4, going on through the esoteric mathematical humor of 546b to 546d3 (about the *perfect number* which presides over God–blessed births), and ending with the degeneration (*metabasis*, 547c4) of "the best state" into a Spartan–like timocratic oligarchy.[47] Secondly, the Peripatetic text clearly believes that the projected, luxurious but spartanly *militarized*, feverish but *pythagoreanly remediated*, second city of Sokrates' sardonic fabulation[48] is literally both *Plato's* best city and that—rather than the target of Plato's satire—it is that on which the *Politics* may model *its* city-state.

This writer, finally, also completely misses the jest according to which the city-state is to be "purified" of its tendencies to excess and the guardians restrained from taking over the whole city, by a restriction of the musical modes allowed in it, and a prohibition against the use of all musical instruments except the lyre and the cither (*Rep*.399c–e). Would Aristotle have missed the outrageous humor of this, especially when the reader has been primed to it by that startling list of things—from *Republic* 395d4 to 396b8—which the guardians may not play-act or imitate: namely, if they do any acting (*eán de mimôntai*, 395c3), they may perform only what is appropriate to brave, *sôphron*, pious, free men; for it is to this kind of acts that they must be habituated. They will not be permitted to act the part of women, young or old, either quarrelling or calling on the gods, either inflating themselves on their good fortune or lamenting their grievous misfortunes. Still less may they imitate women in love, in heat, in labor or in sickness. Nor may they play the part of slaves of any gender, or of cowards, or imitate the misdeeds of mockers and cursers whether wrong-headed or drunk, nor those of bad or mad men or women. They will not even be allowed to imitate blacksmiths, oarsmen or their time-keepers; and neither may they neigh like horses, or low like bulls, or plash like rivers or sound like either the sea, the thunder-clap or any such thing. That the lively list of ignobilities is so long and some of it so improbable, stresses for the reader that the tone in which it is spoken is one of banter (*paidiá*) not of instruction (*paideîa*).

The author of *Laws* began by choosing a Cretan advisor and a Spartan legislator as the second and third speakers in it on a mistaken, i.e. literalist, understanding of what Plato's Socrates *sarcastically* says in the *Crito* and *Hippias Major* about the laws and intellectuality of these two states. His prejudice in favor of these oligarchic cities has blinded him to the irony in Socrates' words, and allowed him to take them as a truthful assertion of the superiority of their laws over those of (once) democratic Athens. To speak of ". . . Lacedaemon [or] Crete which you are always saying are well-governed" as Socrates does in the context that he's in, is like speaking of Peoria as "the city in which the best operas play, as you are always saying," or of Ryadh and Qumram as "the cities which, as we know, have the best wine-shops."[49]

That the main speaker in the *Laws* is an Athenian Visitor (*xenos*) is probably a response to the fact that the author could not have called him Socrates without contradiction, given that Socrates was known never to have left Athens except on military service. But the Academic "tradition"—as this bit of systematic misinformation is called——that the Athenian Stranger speaks for Plato, has served to sanction the interpretive notion that he is really a pseudonym for "Socrates." Behind these last two points, we see at once, are (i) a tacit admission that the purpose of *Laws* is expository, not dialogical (i.e. not dialectically interactional, not such that the author *cannot* be heard to be speaking in his own voice) and (ii) an attempt to reinforce the suggestion that "Socrates," in the dialogues that *are* by Plato, is Plato's spokesman *there too*.

Dialogical readers who recognize the *Republic* as the extended satirical fabulation that it is, will have no difficulty in perceiving how antithetical and alien to it the *Laws* are. The spirit of Socrates' discourse in the former is keenly riant throughout, indulging at every turn in some word-play, topicality or witty allusion. The superannuated speakers in the *Laws*, on the other hand, are irredeemably ponderous in their winding lucubrations, feeble in their occasional attempts at humor, and pathetic in their overdone deference to each other. Where Socrates' story proceeds with sequential liveliness from point to startling point: from the militarization of the minimally necessary city, the need for censorship, and the idea of God as an educational construct, to the community of wives, the purely musical purification of the city's fever and the inhibition by music alone of the standing temptation for the guardians to take over the whole state, the Athenian Stranger's discourse—in contrast—advances with the massive placidity of a shallow Meander. Where *Republic* is elegantly satirical of Pythagorean themes and interests, *Laws* is both Pythagorean in its presuppositions and proposing to implement Pythagorean programs.

Now the specific references to *Laws* in the Aristotelian *Politics* have all been found to come from between Books III to VII; and they are one thing. They are best understood in relation to the more general matter of the influence of *Laws* as representative of a mode of thought and a climate of opinion to be found respectively in the Speusippean

Academy and the culture of post-Chaeroneian Greece. That the idea
of a ruler ruling without laws was deeply shocking to Athenians in
Plato's lifetime is confirmed for us by the way it is dramatized and
contextualized in the *Politicus* dialogue. This is in striking contrast
to the unqualified ease with which Bk.IV of *Laws* speaks of the tyrant
as being above the laws. Such ease *betokens and is facilitated by* a time
when the imperial dynast was not bound by the home-constitutions
allowed to his subject cities under the nominal autonomy granted
them by the Macedonians. We are led to doubt that the author of
Laws can be the same as the author of the *Politicus* for the additional
reason that the institutions, which give the author of the latter his
generative context, are not at all the same as those the author of
Laws can have in mind.[50] So, when *Politics* 1264b27 says that "*Laws*
. . . was written (*grapsentas*) *later* [than the *Republic*]," we must allow
that *graphentas* may not mean 'written' in the sense of 'composed
by its author,' but could well mean 'written out' by—perhaps—some-
body else. And 'later' will be seen to—perhaps—mean 'after, or during, a time of radical change in the political institutions of Greece.'

Still within the contextualizing method we have been following,
let's look now at a sample or two of (i) the way in which some
themes and locutions from the Academic *Laws* and de-dramatized
Republic are echoed in the *Politics*, and (ii) the way in which *Laws*
itself literalistically rewords ideas borrowed from Plato's *Republic*.
Under (i) we have already noticed how the flagrantly counter-Athenian jest about the community of wives and children in the *Republic*
is taken by the reference at *Politics* 1261a8–10 to be an enforceable
prescriptive regulation.

Under (ii) we take note of *Laws* 681d7–10: "Let us now speak of
the occurrence of a third form of polity in which all the forms and
afflictions of polities, and of cities too, happen to come together."
*Triton toinun eipômen eti politeias schêma gignomenon, en hôi dê panta
eidê kai pathêmata kai hama polêon ksympiptei gignesthai.* (Note—about
the Greek—how awkwardly brief it is with its clumsy use of the

participle *gignomenon* and the conjunctive *kai hama*.) These words would seem to correlate with *Rep*.557c–558c6 in which Socrates characterizes with *ironic* enthusiasm the mixed, permissive and pluralist nature of the democratic constitution with an eye to its abuses—as required by his survey of deteriorated constitutional forms. Having just spoken of aristocracy and monarchy, the Athenian doesn't have to use the word 'democracy' but can call it the 'third' form of polity. And even though the wit in the *Republic* passage could easily have been made to fit extremist criticisms of democracy, the Athenian oligarchist's rehearsal of the the idea (*eidos*) of this kind of constitution completely abstracts from the ironizing humor of the passage.[51] Plainly, he has misread the prose in the passage that he has drawn on.

Here is another example of (ii). Where Plato's Socrates openly calls his discourse in the *Republic* a fabulation *hê politeia, ên mythologoumen logôi* (501£4),[52] the *Laws'* Athenian approximates such detachment only once in Bk.III. He says at 682a7f. "Now let us advance still further in *the tale* (*tou . . . hêmin mythou*) that now engages us; for possibly it may furnish some hint regarding the matter we have in view" (Bury); "Let us then now proceed onwards, *a fable* having just now come upon us; for, perhaps, it will make some sign respecting our wishes" (Burges, more accurately). His real attitude is represented by what he says at 683b, "all these matters must be discussed by us, as if from the beginning, unless we have any fault to find with what has been said." He is wanting, as we've said, to recommend and actually implement pythagorizing, oligarchist notions of government and kingship. He is not merely articulating a city-state in discourse, he is recommending for actualization a political program with special reference to a state-apparatus that will smoothen the functioning and legitimacy of the multi-ethnic Macedonian imperial system. His *polis*, in the reference of his discourse, is so much less in evidence than the élitist, professional and militarist *state–apparatus* that it becomes a symbol only of that apparatus and what-it-is-really-to-rule-over. And that which is to be ruled over, are the Hellenistic kingships that arose with and from Philip's victories and Alexander's conquests.

The most notable example of (i) is that in which the *Republic* is understood and quoted in an unintelligent, non-dialogical way by Book II of the *Politics*. Taking a startling *counter-cultural (pará to ethos, Rep. 452a6) irony* literally, the author of the passage not only says, "Socrates [in Plato's *Republic*] says that there must be (*dein . . . einai*) community of children, wives, and possessions," but takes the jest to be a *gegramménon nomon* a statutory law or written regulation (as noted above). He does not see that its discursive introduction is *not an argument* for it, nor that there is no reason to state "how [the measure] is to be carried through," since it is only a notion. Nor does he see that, notion that it is, it's not addressed "to serving the city" but only to stimulate thinking about the consequences of radically miltarizing the citizens into specialized fighting machines able to defeat Spartans and/or Thebans.

Another misdirected criticism of this author is that the measure would produce an excess of unity in the state: namely, he cannot have had in mind the functioning nonalienated sovereign community that democratic Athens was, and *that Aristotle knew* until his middle-forties. For, the unity in such a city—with all of its metics and slaves—is, and was *organic* or *endogenic*, and functionally reinforced by its self-administration rather than exogenically imposed and administratively maintained. Coherent unity in administered masses would, however, have been a threat to a heteronomous state-apparatus such as that of the Macedonian conquerors. Aristotle, furthermore, would not have complained about any part of Socrates' fabulation that it "has made clear (*diôriken*, 1264b30) entirely too little" in connection with the practical details of an *ideal* constitution which he knew Plato's Socrates had developed for the intellectual entertainment of his auditors.

The *Politics* says next that, in contrast to *Republic*, *Laws* "is mostly a collection of statutes and has said (*eirêken*, perf.ind.act.) little about [the form of] the constitution and, though wishing to make it more available (*koinoteran*) to cities, soon comes 'round to [the form of] the other constitution" (1265a1–4). Since *Laws*, as we have it, is not mostly a collection of statutes, the author of this passage knows a different *Laws* from ours—a shorter one, without (it would seem) the prolegomenous lucubrations of the work we know. Now the story given out by the Academy about the *Laws* has always been that it is an imperfect work of Plato's whose posthumous issuance was overseen by Philip of Opus, and whose imperfections are due to Plato's old age. But this means that Aristotle was no longer in Athens or the Academy when it came out, and that he would have had only remote, not immediate access to it. And the claim that Bk.II of the *Politics* *witnesses* that *Laws* is by Plato loses its force. So even if it is Aristotle, and not Theophrastos or a Peripatetic editor speaking, all we have is that some part of *Laws* are attributable to Plato. What parts? Contrary to expectation, the legislative *not the* cogitative or *philosophic* parts.

Book II of the *Politics* doesn't know *Laws* well enough to be sure who the speakers in it are; it literally takes Socrates to be the main speaker in it. And it calls *Laws* a Socratic discourse; but *Laws* in no way satisfies Aristotle's defintion of a Socratic discourse at *Poetics* vi.1450a19. Now, I have already rehearsed or cited, in Chapter 10 of *Plato's Dialogues One By One*, the internal and external evidence for doubting that *Laws* is by Plato. The point here is to show that it cannot be Aristotle who is speaking so inaccurately about a work he is supposed to have certified. Recollect, further, that the text of the *Politics* itself goes back only to the compilational efforts of Andronicus in the first century B.C. R. Shute believes that Cicero did not know our *Politics*; while Susemihl and Hicks think he knew it in an earlier form.

Cicero's *De Legibus* says about the *Laws* (at ii.6) that it practices in its preambles something recommended by Charondas; but the ex-

tant examples of Charondas's legislation in Diodorus Siculus XII.11–
20 are all of Neopythagorean origin. And as we in fact know, it was
characteristic of early Hellenistic political writings that they included
separable 'prooimia'—much like our *Laws*. In the next century L.A.
Seneca quotes Poseidonius (fl.100 B.C.) as saying "I do not approve
(*improbo*) that Plato's *Laws* should have the preambles added (*adiecta*)
to them" (*Epistle* XCIV, 38). And here it's not just a question of
whether the (philosophic) preambles belong in or with *Laws*, but it
is evidence that the work was still in editorial construction between
the fourth and the end of the second centuries.

As dialogical readers of Plato we have to ask, would Aristotle, a
composer of dialogues himself, have compared the fully dialogical
Republic to the monologous, dialogically (and logically) defective
Laws without noting the huge difference in their literary and intellectual quality or effectiveness?[53] If *Politics* 1265a4–5 intends that of
the *Republic* by "the other constitution" which (it says) *Laws* ends
up resembling then, again, it cannot be Aristotle who is assimilating a dialogical, non-programmatic work (with a tacitly
unimplementable constitution) to an expository, programmatic
work with a literally intended constitution.[54]

Where *Politics* 1265a13f. includes both the *Republic* and the non-
Socratic *Laws* under Socratic discourses, there lies buried also (i)
what looks like a textual remnant of Aristotle's original view, as
well as (ii) another bit of literary sloppiness. The latter consists in
the lumping of "all Socratic discourses" as 'searching,' 'fresh' and
'brilliant' into one category without distinguishing whether they
are Xenophon's, Plato's, Antisthenes's, or some other semi-Socratic's. But it is in fact the case, and something that Aristotle would
have perceived, that the dialogues that are by Plato are *zêtêtikón*,
kainotómon and *kompson* (searching, innovative, and wittily elegant).
Whoever is responsible for the text here neither knows Athenian
literary history nor has enough discernment to see a problem in the
synthetic allusion; and that could hardly be Aristotle.

Psychê in the 'Politics' and 'De Anima;' the Moderate Polity as a Mixed Constitution

Next let us briefly compare Aristotle's account of the soul in *De Anima* with the accounts of it in *Politics* I.1259b20–1260a19, and VII.xiv. 1333a18ff. The latter locus first divides the soul into two parts, one possessed in itself of reason and the other "not rational in itself but capable of obeying reason." It then "divides the rational part into two," because "reason is on one hand practical, on the other theoretical" (1333a25).[55] But the distinction *in Aristotle's other works* is *not dyadic* but tripartite: between practical reason (*praktikê*), productive or creative reason (*poiêtikê*), and theoretical reason (*theoretikê*). *Politics* Bk.I asserts that "to the soul belong by nature a ruler element (*archon*) and a ruled (*archòmenon*), each with a different function or excellence, the irrational and that which we call rational" (1260a6–9). The distinction, clearly, has been made in a parallelism with the polarized political realm according to which the difference between the established ruling class and those ruled is both reinforced and based in the nature of things. But in the non-polarized classical Athenian polity the distinction between the rulers and the ruled was an *alternating* one, and functional only, not related to social or economic status except accidently. We have to ask whether an original distinction of Aristotle's has not been reworded to suit the non-democratic situation of Athens under Macedonian rule and the ideology of the rulers.

The distinction is not so emphatically simple in the *De Anima*, and it is differently made. Not only is "the psychê . . . the first actuality (*entelecheia prôtê*) of a natural body with the power (*dunamei*) to live" (II.412a28), "in general . . . psychê [is] activity (*ousía*) according to reason or form (*katá ton lógon*, 412b10–12). *De Anima* adds "but it is sensation primarily which constitutes the animal," and, at 413b11f. says, "suffice to say that the psychê is the origin of the functions enumerated [e.g. of nutrition, touch etc.] and is determined by them, namely by the capacities of nutrition, sensation (*aisthêsis*), thought (*dianoia*), and motility." 413b21b2ff. speaks of "other varities of soul" thus, "if it [the organism or a part of it] has sensation, it has also imagination and appetency. For where there is sensation there is also pleasure and pain; and where these are desire (*epithumía*) also is necessarily present."

Aristotle continues,

"Now the psychê is that whereby primarily we live, perceive and have understanding: therefore it will be a species of reason or form-giving (*logos tis . . . kai eidos*), and not matter (*hylê*) or substratum (*hypokeimenon*). Of the three meanings of being, *ousía*, mentioned . . . form (*eidos*), matter (*hylê*), and what comes of the two together, matter is potentiality (*dynamis*), form is the entelechy. And since the whole made up of the two is endowed with psychê, the body is not the entelechy of the psychê, but the psychê is the entelechy or actualization of the body. Hence those are right who regard the psychê as not independent of body yet at the same time as not itself a species of body (414a13–20)."

Turning next to the seat of reasoning in the psychê, *noûs*, the text says—omitting (to our surprise) practical and productive knowledge,

"as regards intellect (*nous*) and the theoretical power nothing is yet clear; but it would seem to be a distinct kind of psychê; it alone is separatable (*chôrizesthai*) in the way that what is enduring (*aïdion*) is from what is perishable (*phthartou*) 413b24ff.

This omission is standard to Stoics and Neoplatonists, but not possible to a consistent Aristotle. And the hesitating clause ("nothing is yet clear") sounds both like a reference to an ongoing discussion and like the marginal comment of a non-Aristotelic reader which has crept into the text. Aristotle himself would have referred differently and detachedly to platonizing hypotheses about the separability of "intellect" (more even than of "soul"), in line with his objections to the separate existence of platonic ideas. If soul or psychê cannot exist apart from body (as stated earlier in *De Anima*), then neither can the part of it called intellect.

Going back to Bk.II of the *Politics*, as we go over the references to and comments about "the Spartan empire" at 1333bff. we find that they make much more sense if read from the point of view of a semi-Spartanizer who wants the Macedonian empire to do better. Now while we've already reviewed the question of Aristotle's intellectual distance from the Macedonians, and he is not on other points in sympathy with the Spartan system, the writer at 1270b17 is both paralogical and snidely anti-democratic when he states that the abuse of power by the Spartan Ephors turned that state into a democracy (!). I say snide because the sharing of power among five ephors—who may or may not have consulted or shared their bribes with the 28 nobles of the Spartan senate—turns the state into an oligarchy not a democracy. The paralogical and spiteful misnomer must come from elsewhere than Aristotle's original lectures or notes. What Aristotle might have lamented about Sparta was the corruption of what could have been a military aristocracy into an oligarchy of ownership,[56] just as what he would have feared for Athens was its deterioration from a free participatory government into a confused ochlocracy.

We have seen that the city-state in the *Politics* is a natural existence,[57] and that (like the family which is prior to it[58]) it is prior in the order of development to the human individual. But in so far as it is a function of human will, the institutional way of meeting mankind's needs, it is also a matter of convention. And if it is neither purely natural nor purely conventional, it is also therefore not the pure product of fear or force, namely, it is both natural and strives to be rational. As the human individual in his perfection is the best of animals, so,

when he is is separated from law and justice he is the worst of all . . .
the unholiest, the most savage, and the most abandoned to gluttony
and lust. For justice comes with political society (*Pol.*I.1253a36).

The society to which the individual belongs, says Aristotle, is for
the sake of living; but the state is for the sake of the quality of life
(1252b30). Accordingly it aims at creating the conditions under which
the individual can achieve his or her own good or, as he says at
1323b40–1324a2, his or her best life (*bios . . . aristos*), namely, happiness. His reasoning in this context leads to the conclusion that

> the best life, whether for individuals severally or in common for states,
> is a life wedded to excellence (*meta aretês*), equipped with the means
> (*kechorêgêmenês*) for it, and for taking part in good practices.

But the two ensuing questions in the text call for remark because
of the way they are formulated. "First, whether the life of participative politicality (*sympoliteuesthai kai koinônein*) is more choiceworthy
than that of the guest or stranger detached from political community" (1324a15–17)? This form of words is proper, in antiquity, *only
to an age of empire*—not to the era of the classical city-state in which
all citizens were (by definition) active participants to some degree
in the politics of their city. We also note that the idea behind the
question has become one of the *happiness* of the individual subject
rather than that of the aims of the state. And this idea is important
to Hellenistic monarchism because it becomes, in the absence of
laws consistently adhered to, one of the legitimating excuses for
kingship. But living well, for Aristotle the classical moderate, is doing
well; so that happiness *eudaimonía* is not only an activity but a condition of being-thought-well-of by the community of which the good
man, the excellent citizen, is a non-alienated member. And this is
very different from the happiness or solace which non-ruling members of a subjugated society can find for themselves in the absence

of a communitarian sharing-and-controlling of their destinies in a free, sovereign *polis*.

Furthermore, even though the text recognizes that the happiness of the individual is not strictly a political question, it *all the same* goes on to discuss it, as if it was a burning question. And this it indeed was to the Athenians in the Academy, although it could not have been one to the foreigners in the Lyceum, since "the life of politics" for the latter was not an alternative to "the life of philosophy." The question in fact overrides and absorbs the second strictly political question of "what the best constitution is under which anybody whatever can live happily and be his best in practice" (1324a25f.). In any case, the meaning which Aristotle gives to good living or happiness (*kalôs zên*, 1278b24) as the aim of the state, is also described as the common interest or common good (*to koinêi sympheron*, 1278b23). But as between 'the common good' of the classical city-state polis and the Hellenistic 'happiness' of which the text-as-we-have-it speaks, there is a vast difference which the equivocal text nonetheless manages to hold in suspension. But it is an unsalvable if also almost unnoticed suspension (a colloid, so to say, not a solution).

The Aristotelian *Politics* covers four or five different types of democracy (1291b16–1292a38). The first kind is so named because of its emphasis on equality. Under its law no economic class is sovereign (*kyrios*) and all share (*koinônountôn*) in the government (*politeia*). Here the dêmos is in the majority, so that its judgments are paramount. In the second variety of democracy the (otherwise exclusionary) property qualification for office is low. Another kind of democracy is that in which all full citizens can share in office, but all are ruled by the law (*archein . . . ton nomon*). But in still another variety not the law but the majority (*plêthos*) is sovereign (*kyrion*). This happens when the decrees (*psêphismata*) of the Assembly override the laws (*nomoi*).

"In states where democratic governance (*katá nomon*

dêmokratouménais) is guided by law," the text continues, "demagogues do not arise, and the best of the citizens do the presiding" (1292a9). But when the laws do not prevail then demagogy arises, and the dêmos becomes king (*monarchos*). Notice that the ensuing text about Homer's objections to this, identifies monarchy as "not being ruled by law and being despotic, so that flatterers are held in honor." And this is at variance with all those passages in the *Politics* that try to dissociate monarchy from despotism and courtiership (so to call it).

The text itself goes right on to associate demagogic democracy, as we will call it, with tyranny. The resolutions of tyrannical democracy are like those of the tyrannical king, they become supreme and not the laws. The demagogized dêmos is equally susceptible to flatterers, with the demagogue ruling over the opinions of the dêmos now become sovereign. And when the law–suits and courts are also taken over by the dêmos the magistracies are disauthorized (*kataluontai*). "There would seem to be good reason (*eulogôs*) then to estimate (*epitimân*) that this kind of [demagogic] democracy is not a constitution. For when the laws do not govern, there is no constitution. It ought to be," says the text extending itself on this subject, "the law that rules over all while the magistrates rule on particular cases. This," it insists, "is what's judged to be constitutional. So that if democracy is [to be] one of the [forms of] constitutions, it is obvious that such a counter-system (*katastasis*) in which everything is managed by decree is neither mainly a democracy nor can a voted resolution be accepted as a general rule" (1292a35–38).

Notice firstly the critical intentness of the wording here, where it is a matter of democracy. Secondly notice the slippage according to which demagogic democracy blends into, is not distinguished from, democratic democracy, so that the apparently moderate words "there would seem to be good reason for judging that this kind of democracy is not a constitution" have application to normal, as well as to demagogic, democracy. Whatever Aristotle's spoken, dictated or written words may originally have been, it is clear that they have been tampered with in conformity with the doubts of an editor or later lecturer about *any* kind of democracy.

But we do get out of this (by a sort of implicit antithesis) a positive criterion of good constitutions: constitutionality must be based on the supremacy of the laws. But this at once brings into view a contradiction that the *Politics* as we have it muffles, namely, that *any* kingship will also be tyrannical if it does not bow to the supremacy of the laws, *pace* all the other things the *Politics* says in defense of monarchy. It remains to discuss what can be abstracted from the *Politics* about the most preferable form of constitution on Aristotle's classical criteria, in addition to that of the rule of law. Two of the interrelated criteria are that it obey the principle of the mean (*to mêson*, 1294b3, 5, 18) and that it be mixed (*dia to memîchthai . . . to meson*); for, in matters of politics, moderation is achieved through balance.

Such a constitution then will be "a mixture (*miksis*) of oligarchy and democracy," says the text, and "it is customary to give the name of polity only to those constitutions that incline towards democracy" (1293b34f.). Given that there are several ways in which the mixture may be put together (1294a36),

> the mark of a good mixture of democracy and oligarchy is when it is permissible to speak of the same constitution as a democracy and as an oligarchy; for, when this can be said, it must be because of the thoroughness of the mixture (*to memîchthai kalôs*). And this can also be said of the middle [form]; for in it each of the extremes (*tôn akrôn*) is exhibited (*emphainetai*, 1294b18–20).

And this is a believable criterion, if we remember that by democracy Aristotle here is going to mean something open but not entirely open (such as membership in the Assembly on the basis of only a small property qualification), and by oligarchy something restricted but not severely restricted or, else, meritocratic (such as assigning some offices by competitive election rather than by democratic lot). The result "in a well-mixed constitution" (*en têi politeia memigmenêi*, 1294b35) will be both "aristocratic" (i.e., selective) and "politic" (*politikên*, i.e., acceptable to the citizens). The text in the environment of these points is turgid; but by 'aristocratic' Aristotle appears to mean 'government by the best available' and by 'politic' something both acceptable-to-all and constitutional.

Given that we are discussing *the best constitution*—which the text sometimes calls 'polity' and sometimes 'aristocracy' (cf.esp. 1294a28–29)—what is surpisingly counter-Athenian *and* sophistical here is the citation of *non-Greek* Carthage and *inimical* Sparta as examples of properly mixed "aristocracy." The latter example is sophistical because Spartan citizens—whom the text calls the dêmos[59]—were also all "peers" among themselves (*homoiôn*, 1306b31) and a military élite, lording it over the *períoikoi* and abusing the non-enfranchised helot masses. The former is inapposite because Carthage (*Karchêdôn*) was an *active enemy* of all the Greeks, and endemically at war against them over Sicily.

Now the text at II.1272b24f. had said that the Carthaginians seem to have a good or well-regulated (*syntetagménês*) constitution because "their dêmos willingly adheres to the political order so that it neither has serious civil strife nor has a tyrant arisen there." The mention of the willingness of the subjects is standard apologetics for kingship since Carthage, like Sparta, had kings too. At the same time the defects of the Carthaginian system are weakly excused as "those common to all constitutions" (1273a3f.). We observe that it had long been standard among Greek oligarchists and Spartanizers to appeal to political examples other than Athenian ones; but (i) it is not in character for Aristotle the moderate to have also done this, for (ii) it is unlikely that Carthage would have been one of the states whose constitution he or his students collected for study. It is also unlikely that Carthage came to be used—in addition to Sparta and

Crete—in oligarchist invocations of other constitutional systems before Alexander's conquests and Aristotle's death.[60] The fact that there was only one term for both the good and the bad forms of democracy (where oligarchy and tyranny were names for the degenerate forms of aristocracy and monarchy) is probably what leads the *Politics* to use the term *polity* for the good form of democracy. But this of course means that *by then* 'democracy' had become, in the new political climate, an especially derogatory term. Now, if we refer to the *Ethics* (VIII.1160a34f.) we find that the good form, namely "a democracy of assessible (*timêmatôn*) or productive citizens," as we could call it,

> is properly called a *timocracy* and the *majority customarily* calls it 'polity' or 'constitution' (*politeia*).

If we remember that this is being said out of a background of a hundred-year *majority* attachment to 'the ancestral constitution,' we will not hesitate to equate 'polity' with '*the* constitution' as the Greek does (and which is weakly Englished as 'constitutional form of government' or, sometimes, 'republic').[61]

Another catch, here, is that *timê* (='corresponding value') also meant 'esteem,' and naturally puns with *timaô* (='to honor'); so that, in both Greek and English, it is easy to conflate 'meritocracy' with 'tax-paying democracy' as the meaning of polity or moderate democracy, though it is anti-oligarchic. But the semiotic pregnancy would be neither anti-Aristotelic nor anti-Athenian. On the contrary, it would fit the criterion according to which the offices of state are filled by the people thought to be best by the dêmos which elects them (and by the demes which choose them to fill the rotating offices in which the demes must be represented).

Now it is just where in Book VIII the forms of constitution and their respective deviations (*phthorai*) are said to be three (1160a30–38), that the usually more subtle oligarchist-monarchist editor bares his pro-Macedonian bias saying, "the best of these constitutions is kingship, the worst timocracy." And this *even though* he is going to say a few lines down (1160b21) that timocracy is the form the deviation from which is the least harmful. This is only consistent if he has taken *this* to mean that timocracy is the closest to its deviant form of constitution and *therefore* the worst. On the non-idealist, practical criterion that the least pervertible form might be the best form, aristocracy and kingship come off as the worser and the worst respectively because the latter, *when it is above the laws*, is ipso facto a tyranny and the former has oligarchy built into it from its origin and is *never unfailingly meritocratic*, namely, it never remains a government of the functionally most qualified and cannot avoid nepotistic lapses. The writer, whose apologetics thinks it is avoiding these negative outcomes for his own preferences, has to be an idealist for whom the glamor of the *ideal constitution* overrides practical considerations. The *Ideal* State is indeed the best *form* of constitution; the only trouble is, it never comes into existence. We may doubt that Aristotle, the anti-idealist nature–inquirer who conceives of politics as a *praktikê*, could be the author of such a paralogical jumble. It is the old fallacy of getting the public to accept the worst because something better *is not the best*.

We may conclude by returning to the recoverable Athenian core of Aristotle's political thinking in the uninterpolated *Politics*. The historical fact is that the Athenian political tradition begins with the example, in the sixth century, of Solon's practice of a successful political *mediation* between the economic classes that had got themselves into an extreme situation. It continued and was more formally refounded by the constitution of Kleisthenes at the end of that century. This constitution, by leading to the enfranchisement of all economic classes and assessing them proportionately with regard either to liturgies, eisphorai, or military service, facilitated in practice just that balance among interest groups that Aristotle was to desiderate in theory as a condition of the stability of the city-state (IV.1295b37–39).

It is surely Aristotle's voice that we hear when the text says

> it is desirable for the city-state to consist as much as possible of equals and similars, and this affinity occurs mostly in the middle class; so that the middle class *polis* necessarily fares best politically in being constituted by that of which we have said it is naturally composed (1295b26–29).[62]

In despite of this the historical paragraph beginning at 1296a34, which mentions the hegemonic influence of both Sparta and Athens and accuses both of putting their own interest above that of the cities they dominated, goes on to claim that, for reasons such as this, "the middle form of constitution either never comes into existence or seldom and in few places" (1296a38f.). This mainly reflects the hostility of the interpolator to constitutional polities, and his interest in proving that "most states are either democratic or oligarchic" 1296a23–24; but it is also *a historical inaccuracy* that Aristotle would not have committed. Was not Athens itself in the classical century such a polity, regardless of how insistently oligarchists called it a *radical* democracy. And had there been no democracies among the members of the Athenian or Delian leagues?[63] If the imposed or protected democracies among the latter had (as they often did) the support of the people, they could not rightly have been called oligarchies. And if Athens was the 'exception' confirming the oligarchist 'rule' in this passage, would not Aristotle have commented on the exceptionalism of its polity?

That the overwriting of the *Politics* by Theophrastos and the Peripatetics also involved *structural* adjustments *in the* intellectual *design* of the overall text, emerges as a possibility once we have perceived that its undoubtedly authentic (or 'Aristotelic') parts are those that speak *without animus*—critically or not—about the constitutional form called the 'polity.' This is because we are then forced to ask why Aristotle has not made the polity (the timocratic democracy) rather than the ideal (*kat'euchên*) constitution (the wishfully constructed state), the standard of comparison by which to judge other constitutions? As we have seen, the Ideal State, in Greek political and intellectual history, was an anti-democratic invention of positive consideration only among thinkers accepting of Academic or Pythagorean idealism, who favored dynastic or oligarchic rule. It was a device, namely, that we would expect Aristotle to have critiqued *as a rhetorical device* (whether positively or negatively), not only in its reference as our *Politics* does, but also consciously—as the author that he was of a book on rhetoric. It seems unlikely that a nature-inquirer and critic of idealism who, like Aristotle, was also a social observer and empirical collector of constitutions would have made the *ideal* constitution the *key* idea *generative* of an eight-book discourse, as in the *Politics*. The state of the text-as-we-have-it, however, *in its very texture* makes it endemically difficult to decide whether a given institution or a given species of constitution is being argued for or described. There is, indeed, what we have to call *a descriptive sophistry* to the discourse of the *Politics* that simulates impersonality, but whose overall duality and bias—which we have been trying to point out—was after all well noted by Kelsen when he called the alternation between its two points of view a disjunction between a disarming apology for "moderate democracy [or polity]" and a rhetorically cautious defense of "hereditary [and competent] monarchy."[64]

Kelsen's insight, however, has to be qualified by the weight of the anomalies noted, and by the fact that any development in Aristotle's thinking could not have been *towards* idealism.[65] Naturally enough, the Aristotle that emerges from our review is not the same as the Aristotle which the platonizing tradition tries to project. But *it is the Aristotle reflected in his The Athenian Constitution a work composed in the last five years of his life.* And while our view of him does not retract whatever criticisms of 'democracy' were his, these, we can also see, don't much differ in nature from the kind of gripe expressed by Churchill when he said that democracy was a terrible form of government but that any other form was worst. And this is just the *non-*

utopian way of saying that democracy, with all of its noticeable defects, is the best form of government that we can get *in practice*. The trouble is that the reception-history of the *Politics*, on top of its interpolated state, has failed to see that its strategic appeal to the *ideal* constitution turns it into a *utopian*, theoreticist political tract rather than the "scientific" text which it is claimed to be. The *Politics* turns out to be not a *praktikê* as Aristotle's own system requires, not a knowledgeable observer's handbook of practical political conclusions and suggestions, but an ambivalent multi-authored presentation of some of the ways in which democracy, kingship and oligarchy approximate or fall short of the Ideal State. But the concept of 'the ideal state,' in its historical context, is no more or less than an oligarchic inheritance to which the pythagorizing Academy gave literary substance by deliberately misreading and de-dramatizing Plato's satirical *Republic* as the best example of an ideal state.

The question with which we may conclude then is, does not a reading of the *Politics*, that both avoids flouting Aristotle's talent for consistency and honors his political values more aptly, justify the permissible conjecture that the lectures on which the *Politics* is based had reference *originally* to just those phases of the Athenian constitution and its history which realized in exemplary or epagogic fashion the political modalities which were to give the work its functionalist and moderate democratic, or timocratic, force?

Notes

1. "Aristotle and Hellenic–Macedonian Policy," *Articles on Aristotle 2* Ed. by J.Barnes, M.Schofield, and R.Sorabji (N.Y.: St. Martin's Press 1977); pp.170–194.

2. "In response to the actual situation . . ." certainly; but Kelsen did not ask, as we must now ask, whether and to what degree the response was Aristotle's or his Peripatetic editor's?

3. The connection between monarchism and platonism, as they co-oc-

cur in what Sorabji has called the "transformation" of Aristotle, will be taken up in the sequel. Cf. *Aristotle Transformed* The Ancient Commentators & Their Influence (Cornell U.P. 1990), an illuminating set of essays on the history of the transmission of Aristotle; and "In Search of the Unplatonized, Prescholastic Aristotle," below.

4. As David (Elias, VI c. A.D.) the commentator says, "He [the exegete of Aristotle] must know all of Plato's work, in order to show, by making of Aristotle's works an introduction to Plato's works, that Plato is always consistent with himself" *In Categ.* 123. 7–9. Or as Themistius (IV c.A.D.), the devoted paraphraser of Aristotle, had said (*Orat*.20): the study of Aristotle serves as the *proteleia* [preliminary instruction] to the *epoptia* [initiation into the mystery] which is Platonism.

5. "In Search of the Unplatonized Prescholastic Aristotle," below, gives fuller bibliographies for the research tracking the intellectual changes that go with the history of his transmission. That chapter also broaches the problems that result from full acceptance of the fact that Aristotle, the author of a *Poetics*, was also a composer of dialogues and could, *therefore*, not have himself been the author of all of the numerous *anti-dialogical references* to "Plato" in the edited corpus of his works, or in the works edited into existence such as the *Metaphysics*.

6. In unhistorical handbooks of philosophy.

7. W.W.Tarn *Hellenistic Civilisation* (London: Edw.Arnold 1930); p.291.

8. *History of Greece* Vol.XIII, p.201. (The reference which Grote gives to the *Deipnosophists* should be to Bk.xiii, *610* not 601).

9. H. Rackham translates the passage in a way that limits the revising to the author's own work: "If an author reads his work, he must re–write it. Always to shirk revision and ignore criticism is a course which the present generation of pupils will no longer tolerate" (Loeb Library edition).

10. *Aristotle and the Earlier Peripatetics* Tr. Costello & Muirhead (London: Longmans 1897); Vol.II, p.411. We note, in this connection, that while H. Shute speaks, on one hand, of "the free way in which Aristotle's immediate successors (Theophrastus, etc.) seem to have treated the master's works" (Hist. of the Aristotelian Writings, p.28f.), and of Theophrastus's being "a good deal more than a mere repeater and cautious editor" (p.26f.), he also, on the other hand, thinks it indisputable that at the time of the death of Theophrastus a regular curriculum of lectures was organized, in

which . . . the subjects treated of by the master . . . were dealt with . . . to a great extent in Aristotle's own words, but with considerable latitude of addition and criticism allowed to [the] lecturer (op.cit. 33).

11. There is a rapid survey of some of these changes in my "The Intellectual Content of Hellenistic Alienation," *Proceedings of the Fourth Intl. Conference on Greek Philosophy*, Rhodes 1992.

12. The acceptance of this impoverishment in the scope of philosophy is reflected in Cicero's account of the Peripatetics at *De Finibus* Bk.V. section iv. Cicero's wording would also seem to imply that the emphasis, in the *Politics*, on how kinds of constitution should vary with the circumstances is Theophrastus's rather than Aristotle's.

13. (N.Y.: De Gruyter 1973); and Tarán, *Gnomon* Band 53, 1981, p.721–750, as well as his *Speusippus of Athens* (Leiden: Brill 1981).

14. *On the History of the Process by which the Aristotelian Writings Arrived at their Present Form* 1888 (N.Y. Arno Press, reprinted 1976); p.26.

15. Strabo Bk.xiii. sec. 45 (or pp.608–609); and Athenaeus, who speaks of "Aristotle or Theophrastos" in the same breath (e.g. Bk.II.44b, XIV.654d), Bk.I.2d–3b. Athenaeus' text consists, of course, of what his epitomator quotes him as saying.

16. XIII.i.54 (or,C 609): *zêtôn epanorthôsin tôn diabrômatôn . . . metênenke . . . anaplêrôn ouk eu . . . hamartadôn plêrê.*

17. Shute takes *theseis* to mean "general questions as to the nature of a subject," similar to *aporêmata* (matters in doubt or dispute), *op.cit.*147.

18. *Commentaria in Aristotelem Graeca* Vol.XVIII, ed. A.Busse (Berlin: Reimer 1900); p.115, line 3ff. (224v33–36).

19. *Die Schule des Aristoteles*, Texte und Kommentar 10 Parts (Basel–Stuttgart: 1944–1959); vol.3 Klearchos. Athenaeus IX.393a mentions an essay by Klearchos "On the Mathematical Passages in Plato's *Republic*." Plutarch's life of Demetrius Poliorcetes identifies Demetrius of Phaleron as "ruling [Athens] nominally as an oligarchy, but really as a single man" (*Demetrius* x).

20. Hermippos did not include it in his list of Theophrastos's works, and Andronikos (c. 85 B.C .) did not know of it. Nikolaus of Damascus (c. 25 B.C.) was the first to ascribe it to Theophrastus.

21. *Metaphysics* ed. & tr. W.D.Ross & F.H.Fobes, 1929 (Chicago: Ares 1978)

22. Seneca *Quaestiones Naturales* VI.xiii.1.

23. *The Cambridge History of Later Greek and Early Medieval Philosophy* (Cambridge U.P. 1967); Cf. Ch.6, "The Peripatos."

24. About which context, more below.

25. In 336 B.C., for example, the dêmos expressly decreed immunity for the slayer of anyone aiming to install a tyranny. *Hesperia* 21 (1952), p.355f. note 5; and M. Ostwald "Athenian Legislation against Tyranny and Subversion," *TAPA* 86 (1955). It's worth noting, on the other side, that even the anti–democratic pamphlet *The Constitution of the Athenians* sees no possibility of changing a polity so carefully balanced and preserved as the Athenian (CA I.5, III.5–7).

26. The Homeric term for this concept was Anaks; but Isocrates does not use it in this sense, perhaps also because of the superior numbers and power associated with the war–leader Agamemnon. He does use the term (in the plural) as applying to princelings in his eulogy of Evagoras, king of Cyprus. But he also does not use the polysemic *basileus*, since what he is discussing is a generalship or super–generalship. These avoidances are true to the classical Athenian distaste for monarchy. The fourth–century term was *polemarchos*.

27. Cf. e.g. H.B. Dunkel, "Was Demosthenes a Panhellenist?" in *Philip and Athens* (Cambridge: Heffer 1973), as well as W. Jaeger's, Pickard–Cambridge's, and P. Cloché's biographies of Demosthenes (U. Cal Press, 1938; N.Y. Putnam,1914; and Paris Payot, 1937, respectively), as well as the latter's *Isocrate et son Temps* (Paris: Les Belles Lettres 1963).

28. (London: MacMillan 1913, 2 ed.); p. 834f.

29. *Florilegium*, (2 vol. in one) Tauschnitz ed. of 1838; *Peri Basileas* II.61–65.

30. For a fuller treatment of this question see my "The Politics of a Sophistic Rhetorician," *Quaderni Urbinati di Cultura Classica* 41.2 (1992), p.99–123. For the *Republic* and *Laws*, see *Plato's Dialogues One By One*, Chapters 8 ("The Remedial Constitution") and 11 ("The Question of Form, and the *Laws*); N.Y. Irvington 1984.

31. For an up-to-date account of the Macedonian monarchy, see E.N. Borza *In the Shadow of Olympus* The Emergence of Macedon (Princeton U.P. 1990).

32. *Attic Nights* 3 vols. text & tr. J.C.Rolfe (Harvard U.P. 1948–54).

33. For an introduction to the mathematical humor and other ironies of the *Republic*, see my "Plato's Ironies: Structural, Textural, and Allusional: On the Mathematical Humor in *Republic* Books VIII and IX," *International Studies in Philosophy* XXVI,4 (1995).

34. W.Burkert "Platon oder Pythagoras? Zum Ursprung des Wortes 'Philosophie'," *Hermes* 88 (1960); p.159–177.

35. See Burkert's full-length study of the phenomenon of Pythagoreanism *Law and Science in Ancient Pythagoreanism* tr. E.L.Minar (Harvard U.P. 1972). I concur with Burkert on this point (*op.cit.* p.298). Additional references will be found in the bibliography; but except for H. Thesleff's work, none of them, in connecting Platonism to Pythagoreanism, rise above the doctrinal or *literalist*, and therefore counter–dialogical, interpretation of the dialogues.

36. J.B.Bury *A History of Greece*; p.317f., and T.J.Dunbabin *The Western Greeks* (Oxford U.P. 1948), Ch. XII.

37. A. Melero Bellido *Atenas y el Pitagorismo* (Universidad de Salamanca 1972).

38. "Attachment to Pythagoreanism," says G.C. Field, "does not seem to have inculcated a very high standard of historical truth. And there is probably no philosophical school which has produced so many forged documents and misstatements of fact. . . . some of the . . . absurd falsehoods about Plato that were circulated . . . seem to have been conceived . . . in the interests of Pythagoreanism. . . . There is . . . evidence of . . . a not very scrupulous propaganda going on for . . . generations . . . with the object of claiming all the credit possible for philosophical and scientific developments for Pythagoras and the Pythagoreans" (*Plato and his Contemporaries*, p.176f.).

39. Aristotle's *Ethics*, as we know, identifies Speusippos as "seeming to follow the Pythagoreans" (1096b8). The anecdote claiming that there was an inscription over the gate of the Academy that read "Let none enter here without Mathematics," would, if true or reflecting some truth, reinforce the indistinguishability of the Academy from the Pythagoreans. Perhaps academicians were simply non-initiated intellectual pythagorizers who did not follow the ascetic and purificatory prescriptions of the sect.

40. For more historical detail, see my "The Hellenistic Obliteration of Plato's Dialogism," in G. Press, ed. *Plato's Dialogues New Studies and Inter-*

pretations (Lanham: Rowman & Littlefield 1993); p.129–146. Aristotle's Lyceum is the 'exception' that confirms the rule. The Peripatetics were no truer to Aristotle's naturalism, humanism, and democratic functionalism than the Academy was to the *dialogical* Plato. As Teichmüller says (in making different assumptions about this), "Die Schüler machen die Schule und nicht umgekehrt" [It's the members who make it a school, and not the other way 'round], LFVJ II.37.

41. E.g. Mulgan in his introductory *Aristotle's Political Theory* (Oxford U.P. 1978); p.64ff.

42. That this is not an implicit recognition of the right to rebellion, is shown by the failure in the next sentences to question the legitmacy of military conquest.

43. This contradicts the moderate sentences at VII.1324b27–30, where it is recognized that tyrannizing and ruling over unwilling neighbors might be unjust, and that planning to do so is unworthy of a statesman.

44. If we translate the last prepositional phrase as "with a care to its desirability" the game is even more transparent.

45. But if it can be fulfilled, it is plan of action not an *ideal*.

46. Cf. *Laws* 689c6–d3 which would entrust government *exclusively* to political experts.

47. See J. Adam's *Republic* Vol.II, ad.loc. and Appendices to Bk.VIII for the solution to the numerical operations proposed (Cambridge U.P. 1903). W.H.D. Rouse's clear translation of the passage rehearses Adam's explanations succintly (*Great Dialogues of Plato*, Mentor Books). My "Plato's Ironies: . . . On the Mathematical Humor in *Republic* VIII and IX," highlights and contextualizes the irony and humor of it (*Intl. Studies in Philosophy*, 1994).

48. As Socrates says at 376d9: "as if we were telling *myths* = *hôsper en mythôi mythologountes;*" and at 378e3: "the *stories fabled* = *memythologêmena;*" and at 379a2: "we must know the patterns . . . on which . . . to *mythologize*" = *typous prosêkei eidenai . . . en hois deí mythologein.*

49. Cf. *Hippias Major* 2283e8f. and 285b5–7: *Soc.* "But surely Lacedaemon is well-governed." *Hip.* "How could it not be"; and *Soc.* "Then, my friends, we find the Lacedaemonians to be law-breakers in even the most important matters, although they are thought to be so law-abiding."

50. The same inference is justified by the passage at *Laws* 683a7–8: *polis,*

ei de . . . ethnos. To add to the connotations of *polis* (city–state) that of *ethnos* (nation, people, hordes) would not have been possible before the Macedonization of the Greek city-states. This suggests that *Laws* is later than Chaeroneia.

51. Tory translators of this passage, as well as P. Shorey, all translate *eksousía* here as "license" when it actually means *'potestas,'* 'capacity,' 'wealth of means.'

52. And 376d9: "Come then and let us educate these men [the guardians] in our discourse as if we were fabulating (*mythologountes*) fables (*mythos*)" . . .; or, 592a9f.: "the city whose founding we have described, reposing in words (*en lôgois keimenêi*), for I think it can be found nowhere on earth," and of which "perhaps there is a pattern laid up in heaven" (*en ouranôi . . . paradeigma*).

53. While the inferior *intellectual* quality of *Laws* is quite masked, for Greekless readers, by the careful English finish of translations such as Jowett's or Bury's, denials of *its inferior prose* by readers of the Greek do not obviate an inferiority due to much more than copyists' errors. August Boeckh long ago documented the deficiencies in the prose of the first three books of *Laws* in his *In Platonis qui vulgo fertur Minoem eiusdemque Libros Priores de Legibus* (1806). F.Ast, as well as Zeller (in his *Platonische Studien*, 1839) also seriously doubted that *Laws* could be by Plato. R. Burges' scrupulous translation (1884), annotating as it does many of the difficulties in the original, gives the English reader a truer impression of it. Gerhard Müller's *Studien zu den Platonischen Nomoi* (Munich: Beck 1951) is a more recent discussion of the question.

54. Within the editorial dimension of the transmission of Aristotelian or Peripatetic material, the confusion that calls *Laws* a "Socratic" discourse could well be related to the fuzziness—uncharacteristic of Aristotle—about what a Socratic discourse is, at *Poetics* 1447b11.

55. We note that the distinction in Aristotle's other works is tripartite, and between practical reason (*praktikê*), productive or creative reason (*poiêtikê*), and theoretical reason.

56. For all the loci that draw attention to Sparta's so-called 'monarchical' or 'aristocratic' features, there is a plain admission at 1296a36 that, of the two hegemonic states that were models for the rest of Greece, Sparta was an oligarchy.

57. (Whether or not the comparison of it, in *The Movement of Animals* 703a29, to an animal organism is genuine.)

58. Just as man is "a pairing (*synduastikon*) animal even more than he is a social (*politikên*) one" *N.Eth*.VIII.1162a17f.). The city-state, however, seems to be prior to the *oikía* the household (*Pol*.I.1253a19) though not to the (biological) family. Does the fact that coupling is rated as *prior to community* imply that molecular aloneness (*Zweisamkeit* as Nietzsche called it in contrast to *Einsamkeit*) has become a possibility in the culture? And if so, at what stage in the transition of Greek society from tribalism to non-heroic individualism did it become possible; i.e., at what stage did individual alienation become possible in the history of that sovereign political community, the Greek polis?

59. Barker translates *dêmos* here as "numbers" (p.174), Rackham as "the common people" (p.315) and Franz Schwarz as "Volk" (p.218: *Aristoteles Politik* Reclam 1989), all of them falling into the equivocation and reinforcing the sophism.

60. The 158 constitutions which are said to have been collected for study by Aristotle and his students, were all of *Greek* states. According to Barker, "the names of some seventy or more of the states described" are referred to in the ancient sources, and "they range from Sinope on the Black Sea to Cyrene in N.Africa . . . [to] . . . Marseilles . . . to Crete, Rhodes, and Cyprus. . . . thus includ[ing] colonial constitutions as well as ... metropolitan" (p.386f.). Barker's note is based on V. Rose's *Aristotelis qui ferebantur librorum fragmenta* (Leipzig 1886) which I have not been able to consult; Rose's *Aristoteles Pseudoepigraphus* (1863) includes an earlier collection of historical and political notes on Greek states attributed to Aristotle.

61. Taxes in our sense were never felt as usual in ancient Greece, although Peisistratos seems to have had regular recourse to them in the sixth century; otherwise we might call timocracy a 'tax-payer's democracy.' Military and eligibility classifications in Athens were based on a measurement of agricultural produce. I use 'productive citizen' for 'tax–payer' here in order to avoid both anachronism and the oligarchist flavor of 'property–qualification.'

62. *bouletai . . . polis eks isôn einai kai homoiôn . . . touto de hyparchei . . . tois mesois: hôste anankaion arista politeuesthai . . .* (1295b26–29).

63. Such as Selymbria in the former, or Phlius in the latter; cf. M.N. Tod

Greek Historical Inscriptions I.88, and Xenophon *Hellenica* IV.iv.15, V.3.16, respectively.

64. "Aristotle and Hellenic-Macedonian Policy," *Articles on Aristotle* 2 Ed. J. Barnes, M. Schofield, and R. Sorabji (N.Y.: St. Martin's Press 1977); pp.170–194.

65. In spite of the centuries-old insistence of his Byzantine commentators that Aristotle was a platonist. See "In Search of the Unplatonized, Prescholastic Aristotle," below.

5

In Search of the Unplatonized, Prescholastic Aristotle

How Aristotle Was Turned into a Platonizing Logician: Randall's Aristotle as the Heuristic Hypothesis Generative of this Essay

If what we have just uncovered is the history of how Aristotle was made to look more critical of democracy than he actually was, this chapter will be about some of the attempts to make Aristotle look like a 'platonist,' and to make him interpretable as one. It will not be about the Aristotle that we know from the Latin and vernacular translations in which his works are mostly read. Nor is it about the Aristotle of substance philosophies, of neoclassicism or aristotelianism, whether generalized or applied. For, the story that must be brought into view is that of his 'platonization.' This means that we must show, at least in outline, the feasibility of research leading to the recovery of what I call the Hellenic Aristotle, as opposed to the Hellenistic Aristotle, to the Greek as opposed to the Latin Aristotle. This is the methodic humanist, nature–inquirer and lover of old plays who emerges from J.H. Randall's reading of his works. He is to be distinguished from, or at least added to, the syllogistic and encyclopedic Aristotle of 'the tradition' whether Latin or Byzantine. Shorthand for this Aristotle will be 'Randall's Aristotle;' with the qualification that Randall himself—in proposing that there was such an Aristotle—went only a short way towards recovering the naturalist and humanist dimensions of Aristotle, sometimes even subtracting from his own conception of Aristotle as a humanist and naturalist. The idea of 'Randall's Aristotle' is the heuristic hypothesis which, if followed up, is expected to lead to the clarifying of aspects of Aristotle's thought that have been obscured or veiled in the process of his transmission.

The Platonization of Aristotle in the Neo–Greek Intellectual Climate

We see evidence of the inclination toward deductivism that is to accompany philosophy for the rest of its history, in the fact that the editor of Aristotle's treatises, Andronikos, places the treatises on demonstration first and *starts out* with logic as the doctrine of demonstration (*apodeiksis*), believing it to be the form of philosophizing used in *all* systems of philosophy, and therefore the first that ought to be known (Philoponus *in Cat.* 5,18ff.; Ammonius on *Anal.Prior.*, and Arist. *Metaph.* IV.3. 1005b11). We also see how far Andronikos is from thinking of Aristotle's *dialogues* as what had come to be called philosophy. Boethus, the Peripatetic but stoicizing successor of Andronikos, believed for his part that philosophical instruction should begin with physics. "We find," as Überweg says, "in . . . the Peripatetics of this . . . period . . . an approximation toward Stoicism" (*HPU* I p.184).

The "period" in question is the mid-first-century B.C. While the main concern of Strato, head of the Lyceum after Theophrastos, was also physics he at least did not break with Aristotle's naturalism. For him, according to Plutarch (*De Sol.Animal.* ch.3), perception and thought are continuous with each other, and there is no intellect (*noûs*) separate from the body. The Peripatetics then, in the climate of opinion brought about by the Macedonian conquest of Hellas, have themselves tacitly acceded to the Stoic abandonment of poetics and rhetoric as the *philosophic* disciplines which they were in Aristotle as part of the organon, namely, as prerequisites to and preparation for the pursuit of knowledge.

It is also true, however, that a number of authors interested in history, literature, rhetoric, and the new statecraft were students of Theophrastus. One such is said to have been the comic dramatist Menander. Another, according to Cicero (*De Fin.*v. 19,54; *Laws* iii. 6,14; *De Off.*i.1.3), was the oligarchist and grammarian Demetrios of Phaleron (Plutarch *Phokion* 35), who was active in founding the Alexandrian library, and for whom D.Laertios lists some fifty works (cf. also Plut. *Demetrios*). Are we seeing here the end of genuine Aristotelian polymathy, and the beginning of the separation—*in the Lyceum itself*—of literary studies from natural history?

The historical fact is that the Aristotelianism of the Peripatetic successors was defective, and much invaded by the stoicism and platonism of the intellectual climate of the Hellenistic *oikoumenê*. It is also the case that what we call Aristotle's school–treatises (*pragmateia*) were relatively unavailable or neglected until Andronikos's publication of them in the mid-first century B.C.[1] Thus the Commentaries on Aristotle's works did not begin till about the middle of the first century B.C.—after 150 years of obscurity due to this dormancy of the *pragmateia*. The burst of activity which followed Andronikos's edition gave way to a lull which lasted until the middle of the 2d century A.D. (*AT* 79). We seem obliged to infer that the public availability of Aristotle's published dialogues was not enough to insure the survival of authentic Aristotelian views, even among the immediate successors who downgraded the dialogues,[2] but must have had some sort of access to the treatises.

We shall also see that availability of the systematic treatises did not suffice, either, to keep Aristotle from being platonized. The treatises themselves give evidence of what can be called *editorial* interpolation by their users, not only of scribal accretions.

The historian Philip Merlan, in his essay on the Peripatetics, allows his own bias towards theoreticist platonism to become visible when he says about them that:

First, philosophic–speculative interest is . . . replaced by interest in . . . special and empirical knowledge, this knowledge no longer to serve as foundation for something higher, but terminal. Secondly . . . philosophic interest . . . often finds its satisfaction in non–theological, naturalistic, or even materialistic doctrines.

This reflects the new climate of opinion, for the dominance of which Stoicism and the pythagorizing Academy wer^ competing in the time after Aristotle's death.[3] Like the platonists, Merlan thinks of Aristotle as primarily a speculative philosopher not interested in the special knowledges as such. He neglects the input which Aristotle's interest in special knowledges had into his classification of, and respect for, these knowledges as *co–ordinate* with the theoretical (theology, physics, mathematics, i.e. the divisions of 'first philosophy'). Merlan also makes the (platonist) claim that Aristotle agreed with platonism in believing that "thinking (intelligizing, whether intuitive or discursive) is entirely different from sensing" (*op.cit.* p.112). For, pseudo–Theophrastos reduces '*first* philosophy' to theology alone, in the so–called metaphysical fragment.[4] And he takes for granted (which Aristotle does not) the idealist division of all reality into the spheres of the intelligible and the sensible. This even though Theophratos himself knows, in the *De Sensibus*, that Parmenides for one did not make a big difference between thinking (*phronein*) and perceiving (*aisthanesthai*),[5] and Aristotle's *Poetics, Rhetoric* and *De Anima* do not make such a difference.

In beginning our pursuit of Randall's Aristotle, we need to note that the unity of the several themes treated in this inquiry can only be perceived by reference to the coherence among the original subdivisions of the interconnected system which is Aristotle's philosophy. This philosophy is diversified by subject–matter, because it is encyclopedic; the diverse disciplines encompassed by it, have to have (on his own account) different starting points or premisses; while, as he also reminds us, methods suitable to some inquiries are inappropriate to others. Aristotle's system, insofar as it achieves coherence, does so *without reductionism*. So, if he can be claimed as a humanist, it will be because of his interest in "the philosophy of human affairs" (*N.Ethics* X, 1181b22), as in the *Ethics, Politics, Rhetoric, Poetics* and *Analytics*.

His claim to naturalism rests not only on his biological inquiries, but on his view of society and the state as the natural products of human association. It also rests on a philosophy of the "sciences" (the practical, productive, and theoretical knowledges) which understands their products as coming-to-be either by art, by nature, or by chance (*Metaph.* XII,1170a7–8), namely, through processes which, for the most part, can be made intelligible either on the analogy of nature or the analogy of human production (*Phys.* II.8. 199a).[6]

Let us see first how Aristotle fared among the most notable and most 'Aristotelian' Peripatetics, Andronikos of Rhodes (fl. 70 B.C.), Alexander of Aphrodisias (c.200 A.D.), and the late Hellenistic Themistius (317–c.387 A.D.). Living in Rome as he did, and late as he was, "the contents of Themistius's works," says H. Blumenthal, show that he was predominantly a Peripatetic. . . . the last major figure in antiquity who was a genuine follower of Aristotle" (*AT* p.123). In Athens itself by Themistius's time, however, the study of Aristotle—mostly of his *Categories*, and his logic as presented by Porphyry—was considered to be *only* a preparation for the study of Plato. Themistius, the devoted paraphraser of Aristotle, did not disagree with this.[7] As H.D. Saffrey says (*AT* p.178f.): "in the Neoplatonic school at Athens, the . . . study of Aristotle had always been considered as preparatory to the study of Plato. . . . This is also Themistius' point of view (*Orat*.20). . .; Aristotelianism serves as the *proteleia* [preliminary instruction] to the *epoptia* [initiation into the mystery] which is Platonism." This practice, of course, is part of the history of Byzantine philosophy; but as an episode in Western thought it is another instance of one over–manned school of thought assimilating into itself an institutionally out–numbered school with different ideas. In the West, although Aristotle was platonized to the degree which we are seeing, he kept the separate identity and equal importance which allowed him to become the foundation upon which medieval Scholasticism and much modern philosophizing is built.

Andronikos (fl. 70 B.C.), in his own work *On Division*, a platonist subject, tries to synthesize the views of both Plato and Aristotle on the matter. Porphyry (233–301 A.D.) used this work in his introduction to Plato's *Sophist*, the Greek of which is lost, but which is believed preserved by Boethius's Latin adaptation of it, *De Divisione*.[8] Porphyry was not an Aristotelian, but he commented on Aristotle in order to make him usable by platonists, contributing in this way to the platonization of Aristotle. Of course, nothing can contribute *in the long run* to the (future) recovery of the authentic Aristotle as much as Andronikos's sorting out and publication of the lost treatises—even though some among these may not be by Aristotle and are interpolated to various degrees, and even though Andronikos's edition may have cemented into the text an unspecifiable number of inherited interpolations.

In his own *Peri Psychês* and *Peri Eimarmenês*, the Aristotelian commentator Alexander of Aphrodisias (philosopher of the Peripatos in Athens from 198–211 A.D.), defends Aristotle's views of chance, free–will and destiny against the Stoics. He is remembered for believing, in his own right, that general concepts exist only in the mind, for not abandoning naturalism entirely, and for his division of mind (*noûs*) into physical or material noûs (*hylikos*), habitual noûs (*epiktêtos*), and formative or active noûs (*poiêtikos*). His doctrine of the over–all unity of the Intellect, in which individual minds latently participate, was influential down to the time of the Renaissance. This doctrine has, of course, to be the result of platonist influence upon him.

For mnemonic convenience, even though he wasn't a Peripatetic himself, we can take Ammonius Saccas (first half of the 3rd century A.D.), namesake of the contemporary but lost Peripatetic Ammonius, as marking the close of this phase of the platonization of Aristotle by the Peripatos itself, since Ammonius was the dominant commentator on Aristotle between Alexander of Aphrodisias and the Athenian neoplatonist Simplikius (527–565 A.D.). This Alexandrian Ammonius had been an auditor of Proclus, and was a tutor of Plotinus. About him A.C. Lloyd says:

> He claimed that Aristotle meant the prime mover to be an efficient cause. His argument (if it is his) that *Physics* II.194b29–33 showed that the cause of change is efficent cause is plain silly, but his explanation of Aristotle's . . . God is interesting: efficient causes seem to work within time, while the first cause and its effect, the movement of the heavens, are both eternal.[9]

R. Sorabji says of him that "the 'Neoplatonization' of Aristotle was Ammonius' main achievement" (*AT* p.231) . . . This 'Ammonian' Neoplatonism is to be found in Asclepius . . . and . . . Philoponus." Ammonius is indeed characteristic of the road that led to what H.J. Blumenthal calls "that superimposition of Platonism on Aristotelian texts which is the hallmark of the Neoplatonists" (*AT* p.115).[10]

The extreme degree to which the thinkers of the Neoplatonist school platonized Aristotle may have been good for platon*ism*, in giving it logical and categorial ballast; but it turns Aristotle from a classical Greek philosopher into a Hellenistic dialectician who was not a humanist, and a nature–inquirer who was not a naturalist. And this is what motivates us to try to recover what we can of the unplatonized, prescholastic Aristotle. The neoplatonists, in fact, turned this critic of platonist idealism into enough of a neoplatonist as to seem to be the best introduction to their own views.

In his book on Hellenistic philosophy, J.H. Randall quotes B. Russell as saying that "the rational vision in which logic culminates" is that "of a completely intelligible universe."[11] And this is not different, I would say with Randall, from the mysticism of Plotinus's (204–270 A.D.) neoplatonist logic, that peculiar derivative from Aristotelian logic. But about Russell we have to add that the vision in which Russell's conception of logic culminates, in so far as it is 'rational', is *only mechanistic*. It does not make the universe fully intelligible; it only makes it technologically manageable. But, in making intelligibility purely *computational* and serving only material need, this 'vision' makes the universe uninhabitable psychologically because it ignores the imaginative and affective components of *human* rationality itself and human need.

Now this sort of intellectualism is not *per se* wrong, any more than practicality in itself is. The deficit in the intellectualism of Plotinus and Russell is that it makes knowing the basic and inclusive good; so that, for Russell as for Plotinus, the good is a kind of truth— rather than the truth's being one among many kinds of good. In any case, for Plotinus himself reality is only what is intelligible. And for him, the source—the *archê*—of everything, of being and existence, is perfection: *the One.*

The intellectualism of Aristotle, on the other hand, went together with a practicalism which recognized art and artisanship, conduct and human action to be *knowledgeable* activities. Aristotle recognized *as 'sciences,'* to.use our latinate word, *all* the practices, professions, crafts, and divisions of regularizable *human* action and production.[12] *Politikê* and *rhetorikê, poiêtikê* and *iatrikê technê* (medicine) are all *'knowledges'* for Aristotle—as they are in fact and as needs to be repeated—quite as much as physics or quantum chemistry. And they are not less knowledges because they are not theoretical, and their discourse is not deductive. Yes, Aristotle believed the intellectual excellences to be the greatest, and activity based on knowledge and excellence to be the happiest.[13] So, in this sense he is an intellectualist. But he is not theoreticist about it; the *archê* of conduct is the good at which the human individual aims. What is good is conditional and relative to the being seeking it; there is no one, 'transcendental' Good, unconditional and apart (*haplôs, chôristos*) from everything else or upon which everything else depends. The motivating principles of politics and ethics for Aristotle are the human well–being of the society and the good of the individual, not perfection or the contemplation of the idea of the good. We can, however—if we draw out an implication of Aristotle's poetics—find the experience of perfection or completeness in art and literature.

The story of how Aristotle was turned into a Byzantine scholastic is philosophically worthwhile in its own right; but it is not the story we are telling here. Here, we must go on to inspect what sort of a thinker Aristotle emerged as—had been transformed into—by the Middle Ages and Renaissance. So far, we see him going into the former as a platonist logician. We must now look at aspects of the process in which a classical Greek thinker, whom we think was a nature–inquirer and a humanist, became a Latin scholastic.

Getting Past the Latinization of Aristotle

Aristotle's logic was transmitted to Latin Christianity by Boethius (c.475–525 A.D.). He translated all of the *Organon*, as well as Porphyry's introduction to it, the *Isagoge*. He also wrote commentaries on the latter, on Cicero's *Topica*, and Aristotle's *Categories* and *De Interpetatione*. Boethius became a Roman senator; but he seems to have learned his methods and philosophy in—or better—*from* the Alexandrian school of neoplatonist philosophers. "The last major commentator before [Themistius] who may claim to be a genuine Peripatetic," says H.J. Blumenthal, "was Alexander

. . . (a century before him). . . . his explanation of Aristotle is overridingly Peripatetic" (AT 113). *Yes but*: as we have seen, the Peripatetics were *themselves already platonizing him*. As A.C. Lloyd remarks in his essay on later neoplatonism (*CHLG*, p.281), the later neoplatonists "took for granted . . . a Neoplatonizing interpretation of Aristotelian doctrine about intellect. . . . [it] had certainly been made before Plotinus, and possibly by the respected Peripatetic Alexander of Aphrodisias."

The last Roman and the first scholastic, as Boethius (475–524 A.D.) has been called, was no less a platonizer than Alexander (fl. 200 A.D.); but where Themistius's (fl. 352 A.D.) non-philosophic writings were concerned with magic, Boethius's are about other arts-and-sciences or about reflective spirituality.[14] In other words, Boethius avoided the tendency in neoplatonic speculation of combining philosophy with a defense of theurgy and polytheism. A Roman senator in Gothic Italy, with a neoplatonist *and* Ciceronian education, Boethius is a personification of the lay intellectuality of his time. The task he set himself of translating Plato and Aristotle into Latin is exactly what was required for spreading and preserving Greek learning in the West. But we have to remember that operationally, in the educated circles which he addressed, this meant making Aristotle intelligible in neoplatonist terms. The Aristotle being latinized, we see, was *an already platonized Aristotle*.

This granted, some details of the process by which Aristotle's conceptualizations were latinized are worth stopping at. For instance, when Boethius comes up with the term 'intellectibilia' as his translation for *noêta* (what is known), the connotation which the latter has of being the result of intellectual processing *dianoia*, is lost.[15] So that experiences which come from responding reflectively to such complex signs as works-of-art—and are therefore objects of thought (*noêta*)—are either excluded or assimilated to the entitative abstractions of neoplatonism. He reinvents or resurrects Cicero's term 'visum' (image) as the equivalent of *phantasia* (imagination;

Boeth.*in Isag*.2 25): this also is rather too static. For *Organon* itself he had had to use 'ferramentum et quomodo supellex', terms too strong to become lexically routine as dead metaphors.[16] For *axiôma* he gives 'probamentum,' and that seems dynamic; it is we who have lost the sense of *axiôma* in the Greek as something worthy of approval or proof.

Of greater consequence was Boethius's use of 'essentia' for *ousía*. Whether he invented 'essentia' or not, he certainly secured its acceptance. In the case of this term, we can see quite clearly that the way in which Aristotle was latinized was also the way by which he was turned—from being more process–philosopher than philosopher of substance—into only a substance philosopher. As it happened, *substantia* was already in use (in Marius Victorinus and Augustine) as the equivalent of *ousía* and *hypóstasis*. Seneca and Quintilian had used *substantia* as contrasting with *imago* or *mendacium* (the imaginary, the unreal).[17] So when Boethius translates *ousía* as *essentia*, the latter had to coexist with *substantia*. At the same time, *substantia* was also the equivalent of *hypokeimenon*, the substratum or *subiectum* (subject).

Now, as between Roman culture and the culture of archaic and early classical Greece, there was a big difference in world–pictures. Among the Romans, nature (*natura*) was more spatial, the great receptacle containing innumerable separate things–with–attributes. In contrast, the archaic and classical view was of nature (*physis*) as a teeming, a plenum, of patterned processes. *Physis* was growth or process, chancey and constraining, a prevalence or enduring and an alescence or arising. Where there was only the space between things in the Roman view, in the Greek view there were the *relations* among them, and time was felt to be more deeply associated with, or a cause of, change than among the Romans. It was taken for granted that the world had always existed, that it had had no beginning—even if what existed now had followed upon chaos or some degree of it. Another inherited belief of Greek culture relevant to our story was that passivity is a bad thing, and that the good natural thing to be, was to be active.

By the end of the classical age and later antiquity, however, the new interest in cosmology and the creationism of the prevailing religions had had their effect on the climate of opinion. So we find the late classical and post–classical commentators (Aristotle, for instance, and Theophrastos) *on previous* Greek thinkers—such as the Presocratics so–named—looking for light on the subject of cosmic origins in them, even when (like Solon, Xenophanes or Zeno) these were not cosmogonists. Because later creationists were especially interested in *just this subject,* many of these reports have come down to us where reports of Presocratic views on other subjects have not.

Then, because nineteenth century philologists and editors repeatedly collected these fragmentary quotations from, or reports on, individual thinkers under the heading of *peri physeôs* (on nature), *all* the Presocratics came to be thought of as "nature–philosophers." And "philosophy" itself was said—in line with positivist preconceptions—to have begun with nature–inquiry, when reflection that includes self–reflection, as it must to be philosophic, actually begins with Solon's reflective political poetry. The term 'philosophy', in our modern sense, is first found in Plato's dialogues (POP, *Hermes* 88, No. 2, 1960) according to Burkert's research on the subject. Its newer meaning of "knowledge–seeker" or "lover of knowledge" would seem to have arisen in the fifth century. Before that, men of knowledge were called *sophoi* or *sophistai.* Down to the earlier fifth century, it is worth remembering, *sophía* was the word for 'knowledge' and had meant 'informed competence;' so *sophos* meant 'competently versatile or knowlegeable,' not "wise" in some detached anti–worldly sense, as I have already pointed out in my study of Solon.[18]

But by late antiquity, 'being,' Aristotle's *ousía,* is understood against a background in which knowledge is now spectatorial, and nature has become static constituted out of elements in which relations are not processual but hierarchical.[19] And philosophic activity is based on platonizations or porphyrizations of Aristotelian logical works.[20] So, Boethius's *essentia*, scholastic *substantia*, and Thomas's *esse* come through the Renaissance into the modern age loaded with non–classical, non–Aristotelian, and non–functionalist implications. Because Thomas Aquinas's *esse* means 'the *act* of being', it is closest to Aristotle's *ousía*, but it departs from Aristotle in turning 'act' into 'actuality,' and pure being into pure actuality.[21] There is no process–word in Latin, such as *energeia* in Greek, for 'activity' or being–in–the–act. Latin 'motus' and 'agitatio' reduce activity to a state.

Aristotle implies that the application of *'energeia'* to motion is the primary usage, and that other uses derive from it, at *Metaphysics* 1047 a30–b2:

the word *energeia* applied to the word *entelecheia* has also been passed on, from motions especially, to other things . . . what is not yet in existence is never said to be moved, although other predications are made of them, such as, 'thinkable' or 'desirable' but never 'moving.' This is because, while not being in act (*ouk onta energeia*i) they *will* be in act; for, something that is not yet, is potentially; but it does not exist because it is not in actuality (*entelecheia*i).

At 1048a 30ff. he tells us what he means by being in act and being in potency:

Activity, *energeia*, is the thing's being there (*huparchein*) otherwise than potentially (*dunámei*). We say e.g. that the Hermes is potentially in the wood, and the half is in the whole, because they might be separated out. . . . Opposed to this is that which is in act. From particular instances by induction what we wish to say becomes clear, and we need not seek a definition of everything but may appeal to analogy. The actual is to the potential as a man building is to a man who *can* build. . . . We will differentiate one of the terms in each case as act (*energeia*), the other as potentiality (*dunaton*). Not all things are said to be in act in the same way but only by analogy. As this is in or to that, so that is in or to this; for, some are as motion is to the power to move, others as being is to some matter.

Note that in the last sentence *ousía* is spoken of as what activates or gives an existing form to some matter. And this reinforces our sense that *ousía* means the being or *mode of* existence of a thing, not a separate 'essence' or idea of it. Relying on the distinction between activities which are their own end and those which are not, Aristotle says that, when the work is the end, the activity is itself the product or work. Here it is also the *entelecheia*, namely, it has the end in itself. When the product is something that results from the exercise of the power, another distinction can be made; the act or activity can be said to be *in* that which is being made, as the poetry is in the poem being made or the art of weaving in the woven. Thirdly, when the activity results in no product, both the activity and the end can be said to be *in* the actor—as seeing is in the seer, thinking in the thinker, and life or living, and being happy are in the psychê (1050 a35–b1).

Having emphasized the distinction between the activity and its outcome, Aristotle then says that "it is evident that the being or form is the activity" (*hôste phaneron hoti hê ousía kai to eîdos enérgeiá estin*, 1050 b2). And this is the wording which contrasts with the *substantialist* scholastic formula which translates the same passage as "the substance or form is actuality." And I call it substantialist because the scholastic 'actuality' refers to the *result* of the activity instead of the activity, and because the first subject of the sentence, 'being,' a process-word, has also been turned into a noun-substantive, the scholastic's 'substance.' The discussion of 'end' in relation to 'process', at *Metaph.h* IX.1048b18f. and 1050a21ff., shows that Aristotle thought of *entelecheia* too as active completion of a process or the realization of the latent end in it (*telos enechein*).

Confirmation that *ousía*, being, is *energeia*, activity, can be found in *De Anima* where psychê is said to be the *archê* or principle of living things (I.i.402a7). Psychê thinking or psychê choosing is what moves the human organism (I.iii.406b24f.). *Metaph*.II.i.412a19f. says that "psychê must be the form of a natural body capable of life; in this sense, its mode of being (*ousía*) is its realization (*entelecheia*)". Aristotle is telling us "in general what the psychê is: what its mode of being is, according to reason" (*ousía gar hê kata logon*, 412b10f.). "Psychê is the primary activity or realization of a natural body having life," 412a28–29, repeats the view that being alive, namely, to be alive at all—to be organically—is the active realization of a potency.

Aristotle's Humanism and Naturalism

To keep a long history within the compass of one essay, as well as to keep our question operational we need to ask: if 'platonism' is a significant ingredient of Aristotle's philosophy, was this platonism read into it entirely by the commentators, or was Aristotle a sometime platonist who developed into the non–platonist Aristotle that (following J.H. Randall) I have posited as worth looking for and reconstituting?[22] If he was the former, is platonism something to be found only in his early work, and out of which he grew; or, did he retain elements of platonism throughout his works? Alternatively, again, is the platonism that might be found in mature works, the result of interpolation, of interpretation, or genuinely Aristotle's? Most important of all, what is meant by platonism? One thing that is certainly *not* meant when it is said that Aristotle may have started out as a "platonist," is that he was *like Plato in having composed dialogues.*

Do we not mean by "platonism" the doctrine that can be extracted from Plato's dialogues when they are (i) de–dramatized and read non–dialogically (ii) in the dogmatic interests of pythagorizing idealism, and (iii) without any specification or legitimation of the decision-procedures by which something said by a speaker in the dialogues is attributed to Plato himself as his belief. We can no longer postpone forever the finding of satisfactory answers to such questions as, why Plato *never speaks in his own voice* in the dialogues; why the first of the dialogues in the dramatic order, the *Parmenides*, includes a knock–down *refutation of the theory of ideas*, upon which what is called platonism so basically depends—and with which Plato's Socrates, if we attend to his behavior in the dramatized interactions staged by his creator, seems to be playing as he improves it and satirizes it, by allowing its weakness's to become visible. Nor should we omit such other questions as, why Plato's Socrates appears to contradict himself by banishing the poets in one dialogue and praising them in another (the *Meno*), by putting them—in point of knowledge—on an equal footing with the statesmen who have been saviors of their country?

After Plato's death and as far as the record goes, the only thinker (besides the *dialogical* Aristotle) who might have thought that the doctrines voiced by the speakers who confront each other in the dialogues were not assertions by Plato himself, was Arkesílaos. This is plausible because, in trying to restore the method of question and answer in the Academy, he would have used the dialogues as exercises in argumentation and refutation, namely, he would have viewed them *antilogistically*. And this view, even when failing to see a dialogue of Plato's as the work-of-art which it is, at least sees that speakers' assertions are held in the suspension of a dialectical *medium*, and that the interactions between them are encounters staged by their author.

Otherwise, after Plato's death, thinkers or commentators who refer to "Plato," *all* intend a non-dialogical Plato. There is no doubt that by "Plato" they mean "platonism;" for, they all use the same illicit locution, "Plato says," no matter which speaker's words they are quoting—very often without citing the dialogue in which the interaction from which the words are abstracted, took place. When the locution occurs in an Aristotelian treatise, we have to wonder whether they are Aristotle's words, since he wrote dialogues himself, and did not leave the Academy till soon after Plato's death.[23]

By this I mean that, if there was a difference between his own style and use of the dialogue-form and Plato's he would have been aware of it, and used formulas that *responded to this knowledge*. Cicero tells us that, eloquent as Aristotle's dialogues were, they usually featured a main speaker whose views represented Aristotle's position. If this is accurate and not itself a de-dramatization of Aristotle's lost dialogues, then even while wanting readers of his own works to take the leading speaker literally, Aristotle would have known that this should not be done in the case of Plato's dialogues. Now we *do* have Plato's dialogues, and the collection has come down to us with works mixed into it that are not by him. The spurious works can usually be separated from the authentic with some certainty; but when there isn't enough certainty about Plato's authorship of a dialogue, or convincing clues that it's not by Plato, we classify it as doubtful. In other words, when there is a quantum of dramaticity in a non-authentic dialogue that is a good imitation of Plato, other evidence than lack of dramatic quality would have to be found to make it questionable. By other evidence, I mean for example the use by Socrates of locutions uncharacteristic of his speech in the undoubted dialogues, or historical or linguistic anachronisms, bad writing of which Plato could not be capable, mistakes that an Athenian contemporary of Plato's could not have made, etc. and, finally, external testimonia.

So, because Plato's dialogues presuppose a detailed acquaintance with the affairs of his time and the intellectual climate of his city–state, and because they are dramatized, intellectually interesting conversational interactions, visibly the products of great literary skill, *we* may not pass over in silence the lack of response to (or silence about) Plato's literary skill which we find in works attributed to the author of the *Poetics* when these refer to Plato's works. How to account for the silence of Aristotle the literary theorist and expert on rhetoric, is one question; the other question is to account for the insensitive locutions typical of the Aristotelian corpus, when reference is made to the doctrinal system of platonism.

Often when such reference is made, "Plato" can surely be taken as lazy shorthand for "the system of platonism." Many parenthetical occurrences of "Plato" in this sense must be post-Aristotelian, Peripatetic or editorial, such as the parenthesis at *Metaph.B* III.i.13 "(as the Pythagoreans and Plato stated)," or *Metaph.C* IV.v.25, "(as indeed Plato says)." The pythagorean habit, we note, was to say "Pythagoras" when what was meant was "the pythagoreans." So when, for instance, the text has "Plato speaks of 'the great and small', the Italians of the *apeiron* . . ." (*Metaph.A* I.vii.2), "Plato" (singular) clearly means "the platonists" (plural), in view of the contrapuntal reference to "the Italians."

An allusion to "Plato" may not only be a textual accretion itself, the translator into a modern language may pile his own platonism on top of it, as does Tredennick at *Metaph.A* I.ix.3, "again, of Plato's more exact arguments some establish ideas of relations . . ." Plato's name is not in the Greek: . . . *hoi akribésteroi tôn logôn* . . . Or, at *Met.B* III.ii.21, where the "we" in "we say" (*legomen*) is impersonal (as in "are said") Tredennick translates "in what sense *we Platonists hold the Forms to be both causes and independent substances* has been stated in our original discussion. . ." making it appear that Aristotle has called himself a platonist—else, it's the interpolator-editor rightly calling himself a platonist. The "original discussion" referred to is at I.vi.1–3; it is a brief rehearsal of the rise of the theory of ideas. Does the appearance that this passage has of wanting to take Socrates' inductive searches for definitions or generalizations (*to katholou zêtountos*) as an early assertion of the theory of ideas, show that it is not a disinterested rehearsal, or is it Aristotle being faithful to the point of view he is reporting? The first sentence of the passage starts with this phrasing, "after the philosophies above–mentioned came the treatises, *pragmateia*, of Plato . . ." Can someone who thinks that Plato wrote *treatises* be Aristotle? If the reference of *pragmateia* is generalized to "works," then the author of it must think Plato composed both dialogues and treatises, or didn't know the dialogues, or else, hadn't seen them, and is comfortable omitting mention of them. But if *pragmateia* means "concerns," then we see that Plato is being assimilated into the school of Pythagoras and the systematic concerns of the pythagorizing Speusippos.[24]

Most often the allusions not only don't give the name of the speaker quoted, they also don't name the dialogue he's in. And these cases break down into those in which *we are* able to come up with the particular reference, and those in which we're not. The latter throw light on the nature of the former. For example: "Plato at least says that it is another kind [of number]" (*Met.A* I.viii.24). But where in a dialogue does a speaker say that the pythagorean numbers under discussion at *Met.* 990a 18ff. must be different in kind? Or take *Met.D* V.xi.7: "This distinction was used by Plato. . ." Do we know just where a speaker in the dialogue uses the distinction.?[25]

Among the many locatable allusions we list *Met.C* IV.v.25, "(as indeed Plato says)" which refers to *Theaetetus* 171e, 178cf. But *Met.E* VI.ii.3 "Hence Plato in a way is not wrong in making sophistics deal with what is not in existence (*to mê on*). . ." refers, seemingly, to *Sophist* 254a. And *Met.K* XI.viii.3 repeats this same allusion to "Plato," seeming to refer to the same locus in the *Sophist*. The speaker in the *Sophist* is, of course, the copious rhetorical sophist from Elea who is busy defining and subtly putting down the eristic sophists with whom he wants to lump Socrates. But we notice that the allusion is again not exact, "Plato wasn't far wrong in saying that the sophist spends his time with the non–existent (*to mê on*)." What the visitor from Elea says is,

"The sophist rushes off into darkest non–existence, clutching (*prosaptomenos*) it with knack (*tribêi*), and hard to discern because of the darkness of his position."

The author (or editor) of these two passages in the *Metaphysics* has not looked it up; he must be citing from memory. But notice that his phrasing takes the deprecatory humor out of the visitor's words; the allusion reflects only an interest in the sophist's ability to probe and vanish into a dark subject.

The author of the allusions would seem to be someone who has been through a complete course of training in the system of platonism, rather than someone who read the dialogues for their witty polemics or entertaining arguments and discourses. Since such a training or system did not exist in Aristotle's time at the Academy (or was at best in–the–making), when Plato's dialogues were coming out *one by one* and Aristotle was growing into the philosopher he became, and beginning to produce his own works (whether they consisted of dialogues, treatises or piles of notes), the beneficiary of such training—reflected in the citational style just noted—has to be either an editor or an interpolator of the text. The fact that some of the citations are not locatable in the dialogues would mean that they are quoted, or imported from lectures or notes *about* platonism as a doctrinal system, whether that system was put together by Speusippos, orally expounded by Plato himself (the *ungeschriebene Lehre* thesis), or derived from a posthumous de-dramatization of Plato's dialogues. For, in these cases there would be no need to cite any dialogue at all.

But why, then, is a dialogue cited in many cases, though not in all cases? On the assumption that Aristotle was sensitive to the dialogue–form, the formulas used by the citations prohibit them from being his. For, on the other hand, if Aristotle—contrary to hypothesis and in response to the dogmatic systematics pervading the post-Platonic environment—had decided to treat "Plato" in a *purely* doctrinal way, he would not have had to cite any dialogue at all either. As we are saying, a *literarily* sensitive Aristotle who had actually read and handled Plato's dialogues, would not then have proceeded to mishandle them with the insensitivy reflected in the kind of citational locution we have looked at. To be able to be exclusively doctrinal about "Plato", in the way expressed by those locutions, Aristotle would have had to avoid them altogether. But the dialogue presupposed is often named and namable, and it is impossible that Aristotle did not read Plato's dialogues.

I list a few more allusions to "Plato" or platonists in the Aristotelian corpus in the hope that their style and systematic nature will persuade other researchers to pursue the question, in itself and in relation to the dominance of platonism and the transmission of Aristotle in Hellenistic times, and in spite of the quality of Aristotle's thought—or, perhaps, because of its functionalism, naturalism, and humanism. *Met.I* X.x.5, "thus it is obvious that there cannot be forms such as *some thinkers* maintain," is an allusion to platonists not to Plato alone. It is probably not to Plato among others, because if Plato had been the outright inventor of theory of ideas, then why not allude simply to "Plato?" But if the allusion *is* to Plato among others, then we see him being associated with the pythagorizing Speusippos and his followers in the Academy. Since Plato didn't write treatises, the "treatises" referred to at at *Met.A* I.vi.1–3 could then well be those now represented by the fragmentary remains of Speusippos and his associates or successors in the first Academy.

In contrast, *Met.Z* VII.ii.3 says "thus Plato (singular) believed[26] the forms and the mathematicals [to be] two kinds of beings, and in the third place the being of perceptible bodies; and Speusippos still more kinds of beings (*ousías*). . ." We note that, if this refers to the pages in the *Republic* in which Socrates diagrammatizes the theory of ideas, it's not quite accurate; wouldn't Aristotle have tried to be completely accurate in connection with a *locus classicus* like this? The reference of *enioi* (some), a few lines down, is to those who "say that ideas and numbers are of the same nature," namely, to pythagorizing idealists such as Xenocrates, Speusippos's successor. In connection with "the cause of the forms," *Met.Z* VII.viii.7 has "as some are wont to say;" the reference would seem to be to both platonists and pythagoreans calling themselves platonists, whatever the distinction between them was.

Interestingly, when, as it ends, book Lambda objects to a plurality of governing principles (*archas pollas*), saying that this would be bad management of what there is (*ta de onta . . . politeuesthai kakôs*), the author quotes an old oligarchal-monarchical tag from Homer "rule of the many is not good; let there be but one ruler" (*Iliad* II. 204). Would this tag not have sprung more easily to the lips of a pythagorean sympathizer than to those of the moderate democrat who authored the uninterpolated *Politics*? And this cannot be Aristotle lingering in the point of view of those he is here reviewing, because he has just rejected the view reviewed. More words would have been needed to indicate to the reader that he is invoking one of their own principles in one field, in order to highlight the unsatisfactoriness of the same group's principles in another field. Conversely, Aristotle could be said to be invoking a pythagorean political principle, to rhetorically reinforce his own critique of pythagorean mathematical pluralism. But would he have done so without even hinting at his own disconnection from the notorious association between pythagorism and monarchism?

Platonism, and Randall's Aristotle

The thesis that Aristotle's thinking progressed from platonism in his youth to an almost exclusive interest in historical and empirical research in politics and nature–inquiry has great plausibility, and was the assumption generative of Werner Jaeger's *Aristotle*, devoted to the "history of his development."[27] Now J.H. Randall, to the extent that he grants Aristotle's dialogues to be early and to the degree that he allows them to be platonist, does not really differ from the thesis in its broad outline, simplistic as he also finds it. And this, even though Randall notes that the dialogue *On Philosophy* contains "a critique of the 'Ideas' of the Platonists taken as scientific concepts," and "particular criticism of the Pythagorean number theory [as in *Met.N* XIV]." Randall adds (RA) that "Aristotle speaks of himself as the true follower of Plato," in contrast to Speusippos, who "is departing from the master." The phrasing `Aristotle speaks of himself' is peculiar. In a *dialogue*? Only of course if he is a character called Aristotle in the dialogue.[28] Otherwise, what the dialogue contains is somebody saying that *he* rather than Speusippos has understood Plato better. And this brings us face-to-face again with the multiplex problem of what was meant by "Plato" here, and how Aristotle could have intended "platonism" by it, or been in competition *as a platonist* with Speusippos rather than as a *dialogue-writer*?

Having broached this complex question already—the answer to which calls for a program of research into the dialogical Aristotle, and the systematic references and cross-references to Plato and platonism in the corpus—I would suggest that it is also necessary and would be productive to question standing assumptions about Aristotle's early platonism. Consider: if what is preserved of Aristotle's thought in the *Organon* is early, could not the platonism that has been found in it rather be the result of Peripatetic and platonist additions of and editions to that work? Can we get an idea of how much it is the latter?[29]

Well, one of the fragments of *On Philosophy*, from Alexander of Aphrodisias (*in Metaph*. 117.23–118), reads "Aristotle brings out (*ektithetai*) their view (*to areskon autois*), of which he also has spoken in the *On Philosophy*." See how Ross translates this: "Aristotle sets out the Platonic dogma, which he has also stated in the work *On Philosophy*." This wording makes it sound as if Aristotle approved "their dogma," forgetting (i) that the speaker in the dialogue might not be Aristotle and (ii) that when he "sets [it] forth" in the *Metaphysics*, his purpose is to criticize it. So, in the case of the *Organon*, when the logic (deductive or inductive) is untangled from the superadded doctrinal comments, what we have is Aristotle's invention, his ontology-neutral syllogistic and his methodology. And logic is only an instrument not a point of view, while about method we have learned that it too is either doctrine-neutral or associatable with *any* doctrine. The suggestion then is that whatever is not logic or strictly methodology, could well be the contribution of the platonist or Peripatetic transmitters of the logic and the methodology. The latter, of course, opens more quickly into philosophizing.

We also know that, from before Boethius, Porphyry's *Isagoge*, written as an introduction to the *Categories*, was always the first in order of the works included in the *Organon*. Boethius himself turned this platonist tractate into an Introduction to *all* of Aristotle's logical works.[30] And it is probable that the *Organon* owes its existence *as a set* of treatises (which always included Porphyry's introduction) to the fourth century because, as Solmsen says,

> This is the time when the Neoplatonists became the guardians not only of pagan intellectual civilization in general and of the Aristotelian legacy in particular.

If the purpose, then, of both the platonized and the Latin *Organon* was for long into the Middle Ages and Renaissance, a neoplatonist one, it is no wonder that more than a platonist aura should cling to it. But if, as Ebbensen suggests (AT Ch.7), Porphyry was really trying to transmit an ontology–neutral *Organon*, then its platonism would be due either to earlier interpolators not perceived as such or to later editors—if, that is, it is not due to Aristotle himself, in which case the non-platonist Aristotle of my heuristic hypothesis must be a very mature Aristotle.

So, what, if anything, is non-Aristotelian about the transmitted *Organon*, and the *Isagoge*? Classical Greek, for instance, didn't have a word for our 'object.' The object of *poiêsis* or *poiein* was a *poiêma*, the cognate object of *noein* was *noêma*; but we find Porphyry using *pragma* for English 'object' or 'thing,' when defining his terms in the

Isagoge. In the commentary on Aristotle's *Categories*, the categories themselves are said to be *phônai sêmantikai tôn pragmatôn (in Cat.* 56).[31] This usage detaches the product of a *process* or *activity* from the producing, and changes the thing felt-as-an-'event'-or-'affair' into something non-processual. Do we not see an effect, here, of the Roman world-picture pushing Greek into semantic affinity with Latin and the Romance languages? Would Aristotle have said, dualistically and like Porphyry, that "a concept (*noêma*) is a concept of a thing (*pragma*)"? In very general terms, we can say that Porphyry wanted his readers to accept Aristotle's *Categories*, on the condition that their aplicability be restricted to the sensible world; with this restriction they can be taken as a guide in our explorations of the sensible world, of the realm of becoming. Note that this in its way, is already dualistic in a non-naturalist way and not Aristotelian—if (by heuristic hypothesis) Aristotle was the naturalist suggested by Randall; for, it asserts an impassable discontinuity between the naturalist's all-inclusive nature and what, for the naturalist, remains to be included in nature by further inquiry.

Also, if we accept M. Frede's evidence and reasoning that the book we call *Categories* is after all a whole, and look at its reception-history as well,[32] then we must consider that if it is by Aristotle (though it is incomplete) it ought to be trying to be coherent with itself, even in the case that its parts were not originally attached to each other by Aristotle. Porphyry, we know, commented on all fifteen chapters, not only on the first nine of the book, evidence that he believed it to be a unity;[33] and his title *Isagoge*, doesn't name what it is an Introduction to. So, it is only correct *not* to call the book the *Predications*—given that chapters 10–15 are called the post-Predications (*Postpraedicamenta*)—if the assumption that chapters 10–15 are not authentic, is true. For, if 10–15 are really about *more* predications or kinds thereof, then chapters 1–9 must have been thought of by their author as also about predications. In other words, its subject–matter would have been appropriately titled if it had been given the name it has in the recent French translation, "*Les*

Attributions," by I. Pelletier.[34] As a book *only* about nonsupersensible predications, however, it would not have been usable as the introduction to substantialist metaphysics that other platonists and neoplatonists wished it to be.

Randall also says (RA 16) that "the platonic period shines through the fourth and fifth chapters of Book III of the *De Anima*, about the *noûs* that `makes all things,' and is `separable,' and deathless and eternal—and completely impersonal." The two other places in which he finds patent Platonism are, first,

> the *Posterior Analytics*, in which the doctrine of the *Theaetetus*, that *logos* must be added to "true opinion" or knowledge of facts to make epistêmê or "science" is . . . made precise: the theory of science as demonstration . . . presents a very Platonic . . . ideal of science as completely formalized on the model of geometry.

and, second,

> Book Lambda of the *Metaphysics*, with its Platonic feeling for the Idea of the pure Good, 'apart from' the world, which Aristotle calls 'The Unmoved Mover,' and describes in the 'likely language' of the Platonic myth.

This "early religious and theological interest," says Randall, "is also reflected

> in the very notion of the science of . . . 'metaphysics' as 'the science of the things of *nous*,' as opposed to the things of the senses, the view that controls the thought in Books Alpha, Epsilon, and Kappa of the *Metaphysics*.

Let us examine these subtractions by Randall from his own postulation of a naturalist Aristotle.

It's an overstatement to call "platonic" what are only intellectualist claims about the activity of *noûs* in *De Anima* III.iv–vi. These chapters make it clear that as an activity (*energeia*, 429a24), a mode of existence, *noûs* is not corporeal: it is not a body but a functioning of the body's psychê. As a power or potentiality, a capacity, it is o.k. to say, Aristotle continues, that *noûs* is 'the place of the forms', namely, that the forms can be found there potentially (429a28ff.); but as an activity it is not a place. Speaking generally, *noûs* is separable from what it thinks in the same sense that things are separable (*chôrista*) from their matter (429b22f.). Of course, in the case of things without matter (430a4ff.), the thinking and that which is thought are the same; "for theoretical knowledge and what it knows are the same thing." And it is clear from this that the activity of *the power of mind* is formative: "it makes all things . . . as light makes potential into actual colors" (430a16f.). "Mind in this sense," Aristotle is saying here, "is separable (*chôristos*), not acted upon (*apathês*),[35] and unmixed (*amigês*) since it is *an activity*." Aristotle concludes, "when isolated (*chôristheis*) it is just what it is, and it is only this that is deathless (*athanaton*) and eternal (*aïdion*) . . . and without this nothing thinks" (430a22–25).

As for the doctrine quoted by Socrates in the *Theaetetus* that *logos*, a rational account, must support a judgment which is true in order for the judgment to become knowledge, that is certainly a doctrine valued by platonism. That Aristotle makes precise what is meant by a rational account in terms of his syllogisms as *the form of deductive demonstration* which, when added to premises inductively reached, produce knowledge, does not make him a platonist. But it does bring out clearly what is deductive about knowledge. And what is deductive is, of course, formalizable; and the formalization, for Aristotle, as for all later logicians, is just a validity-test of the argumentation not a platonization or idealization of it.

The second of Randall's remarks about *Metaphysics* Lambda, above, commits the fallacy of composition. The Aristotelian core of the *Metaphysics*, like that of the *De Anima*, does not oppose *noûs* to *aisthêsis* as dichotomously as Randall carelessly grants here and as Books A, E, and K are said to do; so it is a mistake to characterize the *Metaphysics* as a whole in terms of Alpha, Eta, and Kappa. We also remember that as writings the *meta ta physika* are an editorial composite, more than just an Aristotelian treatise with a mixed Peripatetic and platonist overlay—though it has that aspect too. Even Edith Johnson's remarkable attempt to abstract only what is Aristotle's from the *Metaphysics* as we have it, does not entirely succeed.[36] And it doesn't succeed, in addition to the above reasons, because it too easily grants too much of the reasoning in Book Lambda to be Aristotle's very own.[37] It does not consider the possibility that the lapses in the book are due to the platonist interpolator or editor who is using Aristotelian *hypomnêmata* about *noûs*, and causes and the first cause for the purpose of synthesizing conclusions about the universe-as-a-whole that would be acceptable to neoplatonists.

What, then, of Randall's first remark above on *Metaphysics* Lambda, and "its feeling for the Idea of the pure Good, 'apart from' the world, which [it] calls the 'Unmoved Mover,' and describes in the 'likely language' of . . . Platonic myth"? The memorable opening pages of the *Nicomachean Ethics* come instantly to mind, in which *goods*—not *the* Good—are plural and relative to the organisms whose goods they are. Isn't it, rather, these conditional goods that the 'Idea of the pure Good' is very much 'apart from'? The idea of an absolute good is a platonist or neoplatonist notion, alien to Aristotle's system of thought; even in Plato's dialogues it is to be found only peirastically, not clearly asserted. Socrates in the *Republic*, having refused to answer Glaucon's question about what the good is, and as part of the virtuoso turn in which he diagrams the theory of ideas, desiderates it as a non-hypothetical or unconditional starting-point for knowledge, as an extrapolation from the top end of the Divided Line *in terms that are themselves conditional*, as follows—and to repeat a key point made in an earlier chapter:

Socrates had categorized the special knowledges or sciences as being all of them conditional, at 5110b5–511e. But in his exhibitive rehearsal of the theory of ideas he suggests that there is "a portion of the intelligible . . . which reasoning itself grasps by the power of dialectics, treating its hypotheses . . . as springboards to enable it to rise to that which requires no assumption and is the starting–point of all" (511 bff.). This is Socrates's ironic answer to those who complain that the special sciences have starting–points that aren't really, or don't feel like, terminuses. He is suggesting here (and at 532a) that *if* there is a knowledge that transcends the hypothetical nature of the special sciences, and it is achievable by the pure reasoning (*dia tou logou . . . aneu pasôn tôn aisthêseôn*) of a well–trained man with synoptic power, and it relates all the ideas of the arts-and-sciences to the idea of the good as their first principle, *then* it will provide a secure anchoring for the special knowledges and a terminal for the knowledge-seeker. In avoiding *arbitrary* starting-points, and as the completion of the dialectic, it *would be* the goal of intelligence. We note that the demand for the unconditional arises within an unavoidably conditional situation. I am not just paraphrasing or interpreting as wistful the spirit in which Socrates speaks here; *hotan tis toi dialegesthai epicheirêi. . . dia toû lógou . . .ep'autôi gignetai tôi toû noêtou telei* is conditional and entirely subjunctive: "In this way *whenever*[38] someone by dialectic were to try, through pure reasoning apart from all sense-perception, to get to what each thing is in itself, and *were not to give up* until he *were to grasp* what the good in itself is, he [would] come to the end [and/or goal] of the intelligible."

If this is the passage in Plato's dialogues from which the idea of an absolute good *derives*, the derivation is indirect and obscure. Would a dialogical Aristotle have remained silent about how he derived it, had he ventured to de-dramatize and propositionalize something said *ironically* and *peirastically* by Socrates; would he not have noted the conditionality of the desiderating of an absolute good? Whoever is postulating an absolute good as platonist doctrine is not only antidialogical, but is taking cues from a prestablished set of doctrines and not saying so—if he claims to find the doctrine in a dialogue.

The neoplatonist equation in Book Lambda of the absolute Good with the First Cause would seem not to be Aristotle's for several reasons. The equation is patently the best way in which to Aristotelianize the absolute good or, conversely, to platonize the purely physical but immaterial first cause of the *Physics* and *Metaphysics*. The immateriality of the first cause, however, does not make it platonist. It is a scientific or "physical object" in the same sense that H_2O, $NaCl_3$, or $E = mc^2$ are, or rather, in the sense in which these laws can be the case; it is, so to say, the necessity according to which there is order, and according to which there is something rather than nothing, i.e. according to which chaos never was total, namely, according to which there never was nothing. The first cause is the *aïdion* (everlasting) *ousían* (1071b5) process or isness, the necessary processuality, of what there is; and, given that there is and always will be something, it is unchanging (*akinêton*) and everlasting. But it is not an entitative "substance" or thing.

Much less is it a person. It is not likely that Aristotle, the nature-inquirer, would have personified the first cause. We know that his sense of the All was, already, of it as an organism: so, what need did he have to personify it? Had he done so, being Aristotle, he would have had to explain the eternity of this personal being in parallel with (and in duplication of) his explanation of the necessity and everlastingness of the physical first cause. The attribution of personhood to the first cause would, also, have introduced contradictory attributes into its connotations, not the least of which turns an "it" into a "him" or "her," into an *efficient* cause instead of the *final* cause which-is-also-a–first-cause that it is in Aristotle's thinking. And isn't *too specific* a concern for *the* origin of the world incompatible with Aristotle's belief in the eternity of the world? What he discusses, in his criticism of the Presocratics, is *their* views of the originating principle(s) of *physis*, of the processes of nature. And that does not commit him either to the view that nature had an origin at all, or to the mixed platonist-creationist view that what there is derives from a supreme being who is a person. What is most un-Aristotelian and unphilosophical, finally, about the equation between the first cause and the absolute good, is its equivocation between *a mode of* existence, isness in the sense of ordinality or processuality, and *an* existence. The former is immaterial, the latter has to be composite of matter and form. And only a *mode of* existence can be purely "form" in the sense of active, ever-active or actual. Given what there is and that it is, the first cause must have been ever-active; for, if it had ever been inactive nothing would exist.

Notes

1. But see L. Tarán for the details: Review of P. Moraux's *Der Aristotelismus bei den Griechen v. Andronikos bis Alexander v. Aphrodisias Gnomon* Band 53, 198); 721–50.

2. H. Shute *History of the Process by which the Aristotelian Writings Arrived at their Present Form* (Oxford U.P. 1888)

3. *The Cambridge History of Later Greek & Early Medieval Philosophy* (Cambridge U.P. 1967); Chapter 6.

4. *Metaphysics* ed. W.D.Ross & F.H.Fobes, 1929 (Chicago: Argo 1978)

5. *De Sensibus* ed. & tr. G.Stratton 1917 (Chicago: Argonaut 1967)

6. Cf. *Aristotle* J.H. Randall Jr. (N.Y. Columbia U.P. 1960); also Chapter VI of my *Modes of Greek Thought*, and Chapter V of *The City-State Foundations of Western Political Thought*.

7. *Themistii Orationes* ed. W.Dindorf 1832 (Olms 1961); Oratio.XX.235c–236c.

8. *D'Aristote à Bessarion* P. Moraux; p. 23ff.

9. Simplicius *In Phys.* 1360 Diels; in *Cambr.Hist. of Later Gr.& Early Med. Phil.*, p.317.

10. It may help the reader to know that another Ammonius was the earliest Ammonius; he is mentioned by Eunapius, and is best remembered

as the teacher to whom Plutarch turned in Athens, in the first century A.D. Lastly there was also an Ammonius, surnamed Hermeiou, who lived and taught around the end of the fifth century in Alexandria. In addition to commentaries on Porphyry, *he* also wrote commentaries on Aristotle. Cf. *The Cambridge History of Later Greek Philosophy, Aristotle Transformed,* and Dillon's and Whittaker's books on Platonism and Neoplatonism, in which note is taken of the confusions that have existed among these homonyms.

11. *Hellenistic Ways of Deliverance and the . . . Christian Synthesis* (Columbia U.P. 1970). Russell made this claim during the platonist phase to which he admits in the autobiographical introduction to A. Schilpp's *The Philosophy of Bertrand Russell* (Northwestern U.P. 1946). Below, we shall also be referring to Randall's *Aristotle* (Columbia U.P. 1960).

12. *kai oudemía oute technên estin hêtis ou meta logou poiêtikê heksis estin, oute toiautê hê ou technê. . . (Nic.Eth.*VI.iv.1140a8–10). "Nor is there any art which is not a rational disposition concerned with making, nor any such disposition which is not an art."

13. *Nic.Eth.* Bk.VI.vi, and Bk.X.vii.1177a23–24.

14. In Boethius's time, pagan magical rites were prohibited and capitally punished by Theodoric's legal code. E.R. Rand quotes the relevant clauses from the *Edictum Theodorici Regis* (ed. F. Bluhme, 1870) in *Founders of the Middle Ages,* p. 311.

15. *In Isagogen Commenta,* ed. S.Brandt, CSEL Vienna 1906, xxivff.; AT 362.

16. Boethius *In Isag.*1 10; *In Isag.*2 93; AT 374.

17. C. Arpe *Philologus, 94* (1941), p. 65ff.; R. Eucken *Geschichte der Philosophische Terminologie.* Im Umriss Dargestellt, 1879 (repr. 1960).

18. In "Solon the Presocratic," Chapter II of *The City-State Foundations of Western Political Thought* 2 rev.ed (Lanham: U.P.A 1993).

19. The word "hierarchy" does not occur in classical Greek, and first appears in Pseudo–Dionysius and late Hellenistic inscriptions (E.A.Sophocles *Greek Lexicon of the Roman and Byzantine Periods*).

20. We should note that while neoplatonists do invoke and honor process, they do so within the constraints imposed by the strongly hierachical organization of their systems; and it is not *natural* process. The Latins, on the other hand, worked under the constraints of their noun–based

language. As J.H. Randall liked to point out, nouns are substantive or abstractions, verbs stand for acts or activities.

21. *On Being and Essence* (*De Ente et Essentia*), Tr. Intro. Notes by A.A. Maurer (Toronto: Pontifical Institute 1949)

22. It can be shown, in connection with the changes which transformed the classical city-state climate of opinion into that of the subjugated Hellenistic age, that the connotations of the technical terms *mythos* (as 'plotting') *mimêsis* (as 'mimetic–making') and *katharsis* (as 'aesthetic' or ritual 'purification') in the *Poetics* were expressionist, but that they were not given their technical Aristotelian meanings when translated from the texts of Hellenistic grammarians. Likewise *thumos* was dyadic or communitarian and socio-existential in classical times. *Aisthêsis* and *phronêsis*, in Aristotle, are not sharply dichotomized as in Hellenistic times or the platonists; *hamartía* means "mistake" not "flaw," and is understood by Aristotle as it is in a shame-culture rather than in a guilt-culture. *Aretê* still meant human or civic excellence in Aristotle, not just inner goodness; and his *physis*, is given its classical meaning of growth or process in this essay. It is on these key concepts that Aristotle's humanistic naturalism hinges. But it was on just such slippery semantic slopes that platonism and Hellenistic alienation got their intellectual legs. Cf. my *Art and Human Intelligence* (Appleton 1965), and "The Intellectual Content of Hellenistic Alienation," *Intl.Conf. on Greek Philosophy*, Rhodes 1992.

23. A.-H. Chroust, drawing on Düring, makes a strong case for Aristotle's having left the Academy before Plato's death. I. Düring *Aristotle in the Ancient Biographical Tradition* (Göteborg 1957; Stockholm: Almquist & Wiksell); and A.H. Chroust *Aristotle New Light on his Life and Work* 2 v. (U. of Notre Dame Press 1973). There is actually no evidence, other than "tradition," that the Academy was founded before Plato's death, or that he founded it rather than Speusippos.

24. If we take *pragmateia* as psychoanalytically pregnant, namely, as a symptomatic manifestation of what the scribe or *diorthôtês* is here suppressing, then its latent content would be "affair." What is referred to but suppressed is "the Plato business," the Academic "affair," which must have caused great conflict, in which Plato's dialogues were turned into the matrix of Speusippos's dogmatic system and, when referred to, *treated* (equivocatingly) as *treatises*.

25. What if we find the locus, but it isn't voiced by one of the traditionally approved characters who are (wrongly) claimed to speak *for* Plato?

26. The verbs in the surrounding text of which "Plato" is tacitly the subject, *dokei* and *oiontai*, actually call for datives; so some translators supply "Plato" with some such verb as "believed;" but Tredennick (typically) has "posited."

27. *Aristoteles. Grundlegung einer Geschichte seiner Entwicklung*, Berlin 1923. Translated by R. Robinson (Oxford U.P. 1934 and 1948)

28. My intent here is only to strengthen Randall's thesis about Aristotle's functionalism and naturalism, not to criticize Randall himself who had good perceptions of both Plato's dialogism and Aristotle's humanism.

29. We bring to mind F. Grayeff's strong conclusion, quoted by Randall as an over–statement (RA 25, n.9): "What has come down to us as the Corpus Aristotelicum is, in fact, *hē bibliothēkē Aristotelous kai Theophrastou kai tōn met'autous*, i.e., the Corpus Peripateticum, or the School Library of the Peripatos. For contradictions, critical objections, discussions, differing viewpoints and varying standards are found in the Corpus to a degree that it seems impossible to attribute any part of . . . some length, to one individual author," "The Problem of the Genesis of Aristotle's Text," *Phronêsis I* (1956), 105-22. Insofar as this reminds us of the possible indefeasibility of the problem, it is not an overstatement. But we should not let a sense of the difficulties and amounts of suppressed evidence deter our inquiries.

30. Cf. F. Solmsen "Boethius and the History of the 'Organon,' *Amer.J. of Philology 65* (1944); pp.69–74.

31. As part of a logic of terms, Aristotle's categories classify terms simply, that is, independently of the truth of the propositions they might be in. The predicables in the *Topics*, on the contrary, are ways in which terms are predicated and dependent on the truth of propositions.

32. In "The Title, Unity, and Authenticity of the Aristotelian Categories," Ch.2 of *Essays in Ancient Philosophy* (U. of Minnesota 1987). That *Categories*, as he says, "shows signs of the activity of a later editor" (EAP 13) is just what has created the doubts about its authenticity.

33. H. Chadwick (*Boethius* 125) is certain that Porphyry covered the Postpraedicamenta, chapters 10–15 of *Categories* so–called, because

Boethius's exposition of these chapters twice acknowledges that it is following Porphyry, naming him at 263B, and 284A.

34. (Montréal: Bellarmin 1983; Paris: Les Belles Lettres). "Categories" in one sense is not really a misnomer for a book about predication. But in the sense that "categories" applies to metaphysical predications, i.e. predications of the widest possible application, *Categories* becomes a book about both ordinary predication and transcendental ones, *if your philosophy posits a super-sensible existence.*

35. *Apathês* means "impassive" not "impersonal;" but we note that if applied to the universalized, personified *noûs* of the neoplatonists, "impersonal" is an attribute or connotation of "impassive" that contradicts the personification. This is worth noting because whoever is responsible for *Metaphysics* Lambda as we have it, is manifestly trying to synthesize his own neoplatonist conception of *noûs* with Aristotle's.

36. *The Argument of Aristotle's Metaphysics* (N.Y. Lemcke & Buechner 1906)

37. This, in turn, happens because she identifies abstracting *the argument* in the *Metaphysics as a continuous sequential whole* with rehearsing Aristotle's own words and reasoning. But making the argument coherent is just what an over-writer or editor would most attend to in putting together related *hypomnêmata* of Aristotle's. Ingemar Düring's methodological remark comes to mind: "An editor of the text of a compilation . . . can never be sure whether he is restoring the author–compilator's original text, or making it better than or different from the original" (AIBT 26). Commentators and interpreters are subject to the same difficulty.

38. *Hotan* is followed by the subjunctive in Greek: it means "*if* ever."

6

Philosophic Historiography and the Reception—History of Plato and Aristotle

How to Avoid Misreading Ancient Greek Texts

Plato's Dialogical Mode of Thought

If the purpose is to read Plato's dialogues as their perceptible but neglected design tells us they want to be read, the practice of Berkeley and Hume in the eighteenth century and of Xenophon and the semi-Socratics in antiquity, has proved misleading. The characteristic of these dialogues that has misled later readers—when, by exception, they think of Plato's dialogues as dialogues at all—is the one that Cicero ascribes to Aristotle's dialogues in his description of them, namely, that there is a leading speaker in them who represents their author's point of view (*To Atticus* xiii.19).[1] Given also that the Stoics eliminated rhetoric and poetics from the organon with which philosophers, like others, need to be equipped in order to be good inquirers or good analysts of texts, modern applied logicians with insufficient feeling for literature have had no way to read Plato's conceptually sharp, thoroughly literary masterpieces other than propositionally, namely, as other than tractates expounding a system of doctrines which are encrusted here, there, and everywhere with brilliant metaphors, allegories, and word–plays—only some of which, however, are admitted into discussion as literary tropes, and none of which are admitted to be as determinative of the meaning of the "tractate" as 'the content' that can be propositionalized.

In the case of Plato's dialogues, there is no leading speaker as there is in those of Berkeley or Hume, although there are speakers who, for the nonce, hold the floor or are allowed dominion over the attention of the auditors. We have to accept that there is no one speaker or set of speakers who represent or defend beliefs that we can be sure are Plato's own: Not the pedagogic but polite Parmenides in the *Parmenides*,[2] nor the foreign visitor from Elea in the *Sophistes-Politicus* dyad. Nor is Socrates Plato's spokesman when he is taken literally or purged of his ironies. Likewise, if we have perceived that the *Laws* are an Academic production and not by Plato, the Athenian Stranger will of course not be claimed to be speaking for Plato either.[3]

The decision-procedures by which these characters have been singled out to be speaking for Plato himself have never been validated or made explicit enough. They have never been shown to be non-arbitrary or based on compelling clues provided by the dialogues themselves. That if the decision-procedure were made fully explicit, its steps could still not be validated is shown by the fact that, to the degree that in the past it has been made partially explicit, to that same degree has it been disputed by rival platonists among themselves.[4]

The consequences for the history of philosophy that we have to face when, in taking a source-critical approach to its literature, we re-read Plato's dialogues *dialogically* and Aristotle's *Nachlass* with *source-critical skepticism*, are serious. But had the field of philosophy in the English language not become so unhistorical the case, as a case of misreading, would be less extreme. After all there have been Americans who, from the late nineteenth century to the times of

Woodbridge and Randall, knew that the dialogues were brilliant ironical constructions abounding in wit and concerned with the way such matters as human excellence, knowledge, and the state ought to be conceptualized. It is true that in the German language, philosophy has not been as unhistorical as the fashion for "Analysis," as it calls itself, has made it. Nor can German classicists be ignorant of the work of Jauss and Iser on the need for reception-history in connection with literary works.[5] The trouble with German Plato–scholarship has been that the idealist biases within which it had to work have blocked it from perceiving how extrusive to the design of the dialogues, and disturbing to the effectiveness at which this design aimed, is the claim that the theory of ideas is centrally generative of Plato's work.

But, we need to reiterate, the theory of ideas is no more the inclusive intellectual framework out of which the dialogues grew than are the theory of one-man rule (as in the *Politicus*) or the constitutional cycles through which the state is said to pass in the *Republic*. These are simply important parts of the materials to which Plato applies his formative talents, both literary and conceptual. The minimum of necessary collateral information required to understand an Athenian author may not be limited, as the dogmatists limit it in the case of Plato, to only what the pythagorizing Academy wanted said about him when it appropriated him to their own uses—especially where the information seems questionable historically or is self-serving. The inclusive context should rather be, as with any author, all the socio-intellectual conditions and antecedents under which Plato's dialogues were produced and to which they were a response.

Viewed semiotically, the theory of ideas is no more an endogenic part of the interpretant of the dialogues than the practice of the Sophists is in dialogues other than the *Sophist*, *Politicus*, and *Euthydemus*. It is instead an allothentic interpretant, namely, a distraction from the relevant contextual conditions that in some way are determinative of the intellectual product. On the other hand, where the theory of ideas is the subject-matter of the dramatized conversation there it naturally is an endogenic part of the interpretant, just as the notion of 'the One' is in the last sections of the *Parmenides*.

Determinative of the Academic re-interpretation of the dialogues, on that side of our history, is the fact that Speusippos was himself an idealist, that Aristotle identifies him as a pythagorizer (N.Eth.I.1096b8–9), and that he seems to have collaborated with the Macedonian conquerors of the Athenian democracy. It is also relevant to Speusippos's interpretation of "Plato" that what the intellectual fashions wanted by the time of Plato's death was prescriptive maxims and dogmatic answers not Socratic questions, Socratic indirection, or Socratic irony. This change favored the platonist's elimination of the extended, often subtle ironies of the dialogues. It also favored their masking of the intellectual open-endedness or inconclusiveness of both the aporetic and monumental dialogues. Positive answers to questions left standing could always be gotten by a post-dialogical (and externalist) appeal to the theory of ideas. And this, even when the design of the dialogue itself may have been to sharpen the question as a question by dramatizing a better formulation of it than a Meno or a Hippias could have been capable of.

While Plato's artistry is such that only on a closer re-reading is its operation visible, his dialogues do abound in 'self-focusing devices,' as Umberto Eco calls them.[6] This is the name for the *self-reflective* literary *trope* whereby an author draws attention to the form of what he is doing. One such trope which is missed by non-quizzical readings of the *Republic*, but without which what happens next cannot be understood, occurs in Book VIII, 545d–e.

Waxing poetical Socrates asks rhetorically, don't change-overs in the constitution happen only when "those who have the rule" are divided among themselves? So shall we pray to the Muses, like Homer, to tell us how faction first fell upon the princes;[7] and say that they are speaking in a tragical high–flown way, pretending seriousness but having fun with us as if we were children (545e–546a)? Since destruction overtakes everything that exists anyway, Socrates continues, our *polis* too will be undone because *the best calculations* on behalf of those bred to be the rulers—and here comes the jesting about the nuptial number—will not prevent unblessed breedings out of season. This is because, for the begettings to be godly (*theoi*, 546b4), they have to happen at a time governed by a complete (*teleios*) number. For human births, Socrates now says, come under

> the first number in which increases by root and square are given three dimensions, with four marking–points of things that make like and unlike, that wax and wane, and make all commensurable together and rational, from which numbers, three and four wedded with five and cubed produce two harmonies, one square, so many times a hundred, one oblong: one side being one hundred squares of the rational diameter of five less one each, or of the irrational diameter less two; the other side one hundred cubes of three. This whole number, geometrical, master of gestation on earth, is controller of better and worse births (W.H.D. Rouse)[8].

Plato is doing something very humorous but arithmetical here, with his Socrates. Auditors who laugh at Socrates' words because they think they're only majestic-sounding mumbo-jumbo, will not have the last laugh. For, there *is* a solution to the problem of carrying out this calculation; but it calls for such outstanding arithmetic skill as to be a challenge to the mathematical pretenders who abounded in the pythagorizing environment. Socrates however is not only laughing at the mathematical pretenders, he is, as elsewhere in the *Republic*, continuing to play with and gently satirize some of the latest intellectual developments in Pythagorean or pythagorizing circles. The complexity of the calculations called for is also a way of laughing *with* both those who can solve the problem and those who don't have mathematical or pythagorizing pretensions. Here is the solution, in the words of Rouse's summary:

> "The exact meaning of this [passage] depends upon an arithmetical sum, which however, is clear. Those who wish to understand the details may find them in Adam's admirable excursus to Book VIII, to which I am much indebted. The general idea is that every birth is symbolised by a circle with a moving circumference. At the beginning is the begetting: and if the circumstances are all favourable, the birth takes place when the circumference completes the circuit; if not, all goes wrong. The numbers are numbers of days in the seven-months birth 33 + 43 + 53 = 216, and the number of days in a divine birth (3 x 4 x 5)4 = 3,600 x 3,600 (a square) = 4,800 x 2,700 (an oblong) = 12,960,000. The perception of the number is connected with Pythagorean beliefs; Cf. p.399, n.4. These things belong to a commentary, not to a translation; and I am content to give renderings of the mathematical terms, which no doubt delighted the Athenian audience, who loved such speculations."

As I say in the essay cited above, Plato, with his Socrates, is making a gift to his pythagorizing acquaintances of some very interesting *mathematizable* but *mythical* correlations which he knew they would enjoy. Trapped into the mythification by the mathematics, they would be smiled at as mythifiers[9] by rationalists but pleased with themselves over the *pythmagoric*—if I may invent a term—accession to their stock of numerological treasures. But like the Muses earlier invoked, and as announced, Socrates is having fun with the pythagorizers as if they were children—even while the overall effect of the jesting is a serious criticism of a key modality in the preservation of the ideal, most-to-be-wished-for state. About this example we should note, lastly, that it also involves a not explicitly verbalized signalling of the humor to be enjoyed; namely, the very elevation of language in the passage defining the 'complete' number is so visibly an affectation that it turns, in its technical pomposity, into a satire of its own elevation.

Some self–focusing passages are architectonic in their reference to the structure of a dialogue *as a* constructed *whole*. Such, for instance, are the lines at *Republic* 376d9, at which Socrates warns that he is "educating these men [the guardians] in [his] discourse as if we had the leisure and *as if we were telling stories or fables*" (*hôsper en mythôi mythologountes* . . . 376d9). Such too is the passage in which Glaucon says (592a8–b1): "I understand: you are speaking of the city laid out in discourse whose establishment we have just completed, for I do not think it exists anywhere on earth." Isn't this telling us that what Socrates has been dealing with is a utopian construction, a counter-utopia actually, not a political program?

Sometimes it is a drawn–out play on words that has the effect of focusing the reader's attention on the way in which Plato is doing what he is doing, as well as on the fun he or his characters are having while doing it. For instance, we can begin to take the Elean visitor's discourse in the *Politicus* as more than a defense of one-man rule by a Sophistic rhetorician with oligarchist-pythagorist affiliations, when we pay closer attention to the way in which he sometimes parades his skill at punning, *as if* he was *in competition* with the punning practices of Plato's Socrates in the dialogues.

Speaking of arts that are "kindred" (*ksyngenôn*, 280b4), for instance, he goes somewhat out of his way to distinguish them— while being echolalic about it—from arts that are "closely cooperative" (*engus synergôn*). Also somewhat out of the way of the dichotomies he's engaged in, is the remark about "kinship" (*oikriôtêta*)—picking up from "kindred" (*ksyngenôn*) two lines earlier—which repeats the distinction between clothes and rugs according to which it is like that between kin who wrap [themselves] around [us] or spread [themselves] under [us]. *peribolê* = a wrap-around, *hypobolê* = a spread-under. And this has been preceded as well as followed by frequent echolalic occurrences of words compounded with the root syllable *blêm–*, *ball–* (blê[m]– or ball-): wool as a defense against weather (280e3), the manufacture of defenses (*problêmatourgikês* 280d6), defenses (*problêmata, problêmátôn* 279d1), hand-made defenses (*problêmatos* 280e4), standing out for study (*problêthéntos* 285d1), whatever is there (*proballómena* 285d3), what is to be taken up (*probéblêtai* 285d5), defense perimeter (*períblêmata* 288b3), the class of defensive things (*próblêma* 288b4, 288b6).

It becomes clear that he's not only a Sophist, namely, professionally skilled in the art of words; he is also in an intense agonistic relationship to his skeptical listener in the dialogue, the elder Socrates. Not that, as a virtuoso, he is not having fun: he has just gotten away a few moments earlier with using *thakos* (288a6)—with its double meaning of "throne" or "privy"—in a diäiretic definition of it as "found on land or water, it wanders and is stationary, it is honorable and dishonorable . . . and has one name because its kind is to be sat upon by someone, and it exists to be a throne for someone" (288a3–7). Granted that the humor of the clever (*deinós*) Sophist is not as agile as that of the ironic Socrates, the fact remains that Plato's formative prose has clued us into how to understand him. It is, accordingly, a complete misunderstanding to read him as literally advancing a rationale for one–man rule on behalf of Plato, the stage–manager who has characterized him as what he is and made his discourse what it is.[10]

Similarly, speaking historiographically now: it is not legitimate intellectual history to take things said in a debate between hostile or friendly interlocutors as *evidence* about anything, and as in no need of qualification. But this is what Mogens Hansen, among other classicists, does in his otherwise valuable book on Athenian democracy.[11] If it is historiographically necessary to keep in mind when dealing with the speeches of Aeschines or Demosthenes, that the one was anti–Macedonian and the other pro–Macedonian, then it is just as necessary—if we want to infer something from the *Gorgias* about how assembly democracy worked in the fourth century—to be clear that Plato's Socrates (SocP) in the earlier phase of the discussion with Gorgias, Polos and Kallikles is leading them on by drawing out implications and consequences of the practice of Sophistc rhetoric—both in his refutation of Polos, and his several refutations of the Kallikles whom he reduces to perfunctory agreement. We also have to note that it is Gorgias who, as a rhetorician and *as is to be expected of a rhetorician,* makes the claim (at 452e) cited by Hansen (*ADAD* 16) about the value of his own rhetorical, Sophistic art. It is not Plato who has made the claim, nor can we infer from it alone the factual truth that rhetoric reigned as "supremely" and as "dangerously" in fourth century Athens as the bare citation suggests.

Come to think of it, the *Gorgias* could better have been cited—when taken as an integral whole—as showing the *limitations* of Sophistic rhetoric when it is a matter of practicing honest politics for the good of the *polis* as a whole. Actually, in his refutation of Polos, Socrates had sarcastically made the irony explicit, that *Sophistic rhetoric is of no use whatever* to the man who has no intention of doing wrong (481a–b). And this is what had brought Kallikles impatiently into the argument. Responding to the challenges hurled at him by Kallikles, Socrates gets him to concede that the ordinances of the assembled many are superior because they are those of the many who by nature are superior (*kreittous,* 488d5f.) to one, so that they also are by nature "fair" (*katá physin kalá,* 488e4). And this allows Socrates to conclude, from Kallikles' own words, that it is more degrading to *do* wrong than to suffer it *by nature as well as by convention,* because it is the opinion of the many that it is more degrading or fouler to do wrong than to suffer it. And this is the first of three more refutations which Kallikles has to suffer in the rest of the dialogue. In a final development Plato's Socrates turns the tables on the professional politicians by categorizing their rhetoric as mere flattery of the public instead of the attempt it should be to make the public better. The irony is that the Athenians whom

Socrates, with true but painful technê (521d,522a), has tried to make better, are no more grateful to him for it than they are to the political flatterers and Sophists who do them no good (519b–d). For, Socrates says, if some wrong-doer (*ponêros*) decided to prosecute me it would be no marvel (*oudên ge atopon*) if he succeded in getting me condemned to death (521d). The self-irony of these cool words of the dramatic Socrates suits both the modesty and strength of his character and are a pregnant allusion to the fate of the historical Socrates.[12]

Let us, then, bring together and summarize what our results entail for the purposes both of appreciating Plato's dialogues as dialogues, and of using them as historical evidence. It is a violation of the principles of evidence to use decontextualized utterances of speakers in the dialogues as certifying anything about the socio-historical facts of fourth-century Athens. Who the speaker is, and what his assumptions and interests are, have to be taken into account as determining the way a given speaker sees things. The interlocutory situation the speakers are in, namely, the tensions between them and the pressures they are under, are to be respected as controlling their responses. For, as in any dramatization, the action which unfolds is generated by the 'central' situation in which they find themselves. And, as Aristotle says in the *Poetics* (1450a21–22), the characterization of the speakers will be dependent upon the nature of the action (the 'plot') as it develops (*ta êthê synparalambá nousin dia tas prakseis*).

Readers must learn to catch on to the tone of voice in which speakers' words are couched; for, the tone in which something is said severely qualifies the meaning and effect of what is said. Something said with a grammatical surface-form that is assertive will, in fact, be a denial if it is said ironically. Readers must also adjust their attention-span to that assumed by communicative interactions in a culture which was just becoming literate, rather than oral-aural. For, in oral-aural and semi-literate culture the attention–span of communicants was both sharper and much greater than ours. And, in a culture where conversation could be an entertainment, not just informational, there were unstated formalities or quasi–rules that speakers observed among themselves. Attention to context and character will also help the reader make sense of what a speaker says in one dialogue if it appears to conflict with what he says in a different dialogical situation.

As good readers, in other words, we will be responding to dialogues in their wholeness, both as instructive and as entertaining, rather than hunting for confirmations, developments, or echoes of doctrines we were told about in prior accounts that purport to be interpretations of the dialogues. For, these accounts are external to the dialogues, not based on any clues or cues internal to them but based, rather, on interests demonstrably other than those of the dialogue itself in its complex integrity. Individually, the dialogues turn out to be units, in a series augmenting and exonerating the image of Socrates, which dramatize the communicative encounters that were the essence of his intellectual life. The collection of dialogues that are by Plato turns out to be, when we have read through them, a putting under observation—a putting on exhibit— of the disputatious intellectual life of fourth-century Athens.

If there is any positive lesson in the literary theory of Deconstruction it is precisely this: that interpretations of literary works are easily and ever deconstructible because they are either (i) *only* interpretations or (ii) *allothentic* interpretations. The experience of the literary work itself, in its integrity, is always a *reconstruction* of the work responding to and guided by its design as it carries the reader through to its completion. It cannot be a deconstruction of the work itself, because deconstructions do not give or enhance the aesthetic experience of the work. Deconstructions deconstruct only interpetations of works, and are themselves therefore deconstructible. Readings of a literary work that facilitate or enhance its enjoyment or intelligibility will not be deconstructible if they are based on endogenic interpretants of the work, and on the collateral information relevant to its integrity and scope. Reconstructions by different readers will naturally be *individually* differential as verbalized, but they will be congruent and not deconstructible to just the degree in which they are based on endogenic interpretants of the work.[13]

Better and Worse Readings versus Misreadings

Now, there is a view among literary theorists and interpreters of texts that all meanings (interpretations) of complex signs can only be arbitrary because there is no way of distinguishing meanings merely imputed to the sign from meanings generated by the sign itself. This is plausible to such thinkers because they take the meaning-process to be merely *dyadic*, namely, to consist of a *signifier* that relates to a *signified*. But this leaves out of consideration a third necessary component of the meaning-process: the relationship itself which mediates between the sign and its object. This relationship is the intellectual component which brings the process of reference to completion in a grasp or understanding of the object. This pivot or phase of the process is called the *interpretant*. The interpretant is to be distinguished from the interpreters of the sign; it is the thought or sign which people share when they have grasped the object determined by the sign. If getting to the object of a sign were an unmediated process, there would be no possibility of error in grasping said object: either because the imputed object will be determined by *any* interest, or because it is inseparable from—directly determined by—its sign.

The reader can already see that, on the triadic view, not any meaning attributed to a text is as valid as any other. And that's because, on this view, it is the mediating activity of intelligence that determines what the object of the sign can be; and, if the mediation is errant the nature of the object will have been misperceived. As, for example, when the luminosity of a sign is overwhelming and—

taking that luminosity to be the only interpretant—its object is said to be merely an optical phenomenon. If the object was in fact material we have missed the other clues in the sign that point to its materiality. But when, by means of tinted glasses, the interpretant is rectified or rounded out by these other clues, then the true nature of the object emerges. Note, however, that if our spectacles or filter import features that are not part of the object into what we're looking at, then we will again be misinterpreting the sign. Such non-endogenic features are said to be *allothentic*, namely, they lead away from the object determined by the sign: they posit something *other* than what the sign determines, as its object. The immediate interpretant will be the reader's emergent impressions and understandings of the work in hand. The final interpretant is what decides his more definitive grasp of the work.

So, with the help of semiotic theory, we may say that when the sign is a literary composition, that composition must include the determinants of its interpretant which will in turn determine the object of said composition taken as a sign. Speaking most generally, the object of a composition is the aesthetic experience which it provides for the reader; and this simultaneously includes the pleasure to which it is giving intellectual form, the cognitive gain embedded in the way it has assimilated-and-presented its subject-matter, and the increase in perceptivity or responsiveness which it promotes in the reader.

What the reader brings to his/her understanding of the sign can be called his *collateral* information. This will include acquaintance with works *in the same genre* as that which he has before him. The genre of a work (and of its components) is of itself already a sign, an initial determinant, of how the work wants to be taken. The genre both tells something about the form that the work is taking, and is not allothentic; it is in fact partly constitutive of the work, and will count as an endogenic interpretant of the work. More concretely, if a composition has the shape of a dialogue with named speakers challenging and responding to each other in it, then it must be read as a dialogue, and—if it is to be understood as a whole—not treated as an essay, tractate, sermon or poem. So, to treat a dialogue as other than a dialogue (tacitly or explicitly) is to impose a form upon it which is allothentic, is to be already misreading it as something which it is not.

If, as an example, a convent-bred young lady takes *Tom Jones* to be a novel about the spiritual development of a sensitive young man, then she has misread a *picaresque* novel as if it was a *Bildungsroman*. Here, the illegitimate interpretant upon which her interpretation of *Tom Jones* was based is a systematically misleading idea about about its nature. Similarly, if we call the *Timaeus* dialogue a cosmic hymn to nature we have taken a part for the whole, and characterized it on the basis of aspects of a part of it. We have abstracted from the communicative interaction within which the cosmogonic discourse arose, where there might be things in that interaction which tell the reader how to take the discourse. If we describe the *Politicus* as an outright defense of the theory of one-man rule, we may forget that the defense is *what is only to be expected* from a Sophist with Pythagorean affiliations, that what he says is falling upon the skeptical Athenian ears of Socrates, and that he is also trying to out-mythologize the latter in his inventive abilities because he is in a competitive verbal relationship to the Socrates at whom he does not fail to throw a barb or two.[14]

In the particular case of the *Republic*, and as we have seen, even when it is nominally taken as a dialogue, it is not taken as the monumentally satirical dialogue which it has the visible marks of being. And the discourse within it on the best possible, or most-to-be-desired, constitution is taken as a literal political program instead of as the extended critique-by-satire that Socrates' tone and language signal it to be. So much can works be denatured by misreadings based on interpretants alien to its design, that the *Republic*—in the literalist pythagorizing way of taking it—comes out as enforcing the opposite of what it was constructed to imply. So it isn't only the compulsive concentration on doctrinal content and the relentless propositionalization of expression that causes 'philosophers' to misread Plato's dialogues; it is, just as basically, a habitual blindness to their constitutive form that is to blame. "Habitual" because of the tendency in propositionalism ever to neglect the 'form' of what is being said in favor of the 'content,' on the mistaken assumption that the two can be separated without affecting the meaning of the expression.

Nowadays deconstructionism has in practice reasserted the old Hermeticist belief that there are no limits to what a text or work may be made to mean.[22] In this, when it is a matter of Plato's dialogues, platonists and logical analysts are at one with the hermeticists and deconstructionists. But not only are some readings of works better than others, not only is it a matter of better and worse readings; some readings must be dismissed as wrong because they are *not of the work* in hand. And they are not of the work because they are based on interpretants that have the reader referring to *something other* than it. Thus, when it is asserted that the *Ion* or the *Euthyphro* represent phases in the development of the theory of ideas, the *Ion* ceases to be the witty *exposé* that it is of some Rhapsodic techniques, and the *Euthyphro* is turned away from being an enactment of the difficulty in defining "piety," practioner of it that Socrates in the dialogues always is, and central as the notion is both to his life-cycle in Plato's dialogues and to the trial which he is soon to undergo.

Detaching What Is 'Aristotelian' from Less–than–Aristotelian Texts

The trouble with the corpus of 'Aristotelian' works that we have inherited from their platonizing editor the Peripatetic Andronikos, is that the transmitted texts are at least as Peripatetic as they are Aristotelian. For, the Peripatetics were no truer to Aristotle's naturalism, humanism, and political functionalism than the

Academy was to the *dialogical* Plato. The two previous chapters have pointed out some of the contradictions to and revisions of the views of the original Aristotle by Theophrastos and others who are inaccurately labelled his followers. The differing extant doctrines of succeeding Peripatetics can be found in Wehrli's collection of their remains.[17] Dikaiarchos, for instance (a favorite of Cicero's), was no less a spartanizer than the arch-oligarch Demetrios, even while appearing to favor mixed constitutions.[18] Seneca, we saw, reports some of them as believing in supernatural causes (*Q.N.* VI.xiii.1.). The question of 'supersensibles' is discussed by most of the Peripatetics in terms that are not Aristotle's and in a spirit quite contrary to the account of *noûs* summarized above. For Klearchos and others, the *psychê* is (in line with their other dualisms) separate from the body. Other Peripatetics besides the author of the pseudo-Theophrastean "metaphysical fragment," dualistically separated 'objects of sense' from 'objects of reason' (I.i) in a way that Aristotle did not.

More research than has ever been attempted is needed, if we are to separate Aristotle's own views from those of his successors satisfactorily. A rereading of the accounts in Zeller, Ueberweg, Heinrich Ritter, Bréhier or Copleston does not suffice, at this date, to remove the impression of how very contaminated by the views of his successors is our view of Aristotle's doctrines, and how very much that is attributed to him really belongs to Theophrastos or the Peripatos. Perhaps we have to start again from where H. Shute's*History of the Process by which the Aristotelian Writings Arrived at their Present Form* left off in 1888, but with the understanding that Aristotle was always his own original thinker and categorizer, that he did not start out as a 'platonist' (i.e. as a Speusippean or any other kind of idealist), and that he himself never set any foot upon that road toward unification with Neoplatonism that his Byzantine commentators wish he had. In the meantime, the contradictions and deviations of the Peripatos, their new distinctions based on principles alien to Aristotle, together with the details of the sociohistorical and intellectual context of the transmission of the texts, are enough to warrant skepticism about the reliability or faithfulness of the process by which the texts of the Aristotelian corpus have come down to us.

We have seen how the practice of the stoicized and platonized Peripatetics sanctioned the ignoring or contravening of Aristotle's fundamental distinctions between the practical, poetic, and theoretical knowledges in reading the 'Aristotelian' texts themselves. We have also seen how the Peripatetics were confused enough to believe not only that the *psyché* is separate from its body, but also that the theoretical power of *noûs* might be able to subsist separately in the same way that "what is enduring" (*aïdion*, 413b24ff) is able to exist independently of what is perishable (cf. MS p.135). As the platonist doctrine that this is, if it is imputed to Aristotle as his own, then of course Aristotle comes out as a platonist.

Aristotle, in the "syllogistic" part of his *Analytics*, was indeed the inventor of deductive logic; but it was not he who started or sanctioned the preference for deductivism that so much philosophizing has shown since Andronikos's edition of his lecture-notes. Nor was Aristotle responsible for the down-grading of the dialogue-form as a medium for reflective critique. In practice, his own resort to the dialogue-form was suppressed and, although taken notice of by Cicero, not well reported by others. To this day, words and phrases from the fragmentary remains of the dialogues are used as if they were not dialogues but expositions of doctrine.

Aristotle was a nature-inquirer, as well as a humanist and lover of the poetic arts of his culture; but he is not responsible for the identification of philosophy with natural philosophy that started with Boethus, the Peripatetic successor of Andronikos, and which seems to have trapped modern editors of the Presocratics into omitting the self-reflective Solon from their list, and believing that philosophy began—this time—not with deductive logic but with speculation about nature at large. And this, to the point where Parmenides, the critic of nature-philosophic speculation, is presented as a speculative nature-inquirer himself.[19]

We also saw how the stoicizing practice of the Peripatetics dropped the study of rhetoric and poetics from the organon with which Aristotle had sought to prepare researchers for their investigative tasks. For, the Stoics had not only reduced the organon to logic alone, they also restricted philosophic search—the pursuit of knowledge—to just the subjects of physics and ethics. Peripatetic practice, in any case, was not diversified and encyclopedic as Aristotle's had been; but led to the separation of nature-inquiry from inquiry into human matters. There were too many specialists among them: Theophrastos was a botanist, Aristoxenos was a pythagorizing music theorist, Demetrios Phalereus was a political apologist for oligarchy as well a bibliophile and grammarian, and the pseudo-Theophrastos who authored the metaphysical fragment was a platonizing and stoicizing theodicist. Philip Merlan's chapter on the Peripatos, in his version of the events, manages to lay stress on the empirical researches of the Peripatos at the same time that he thinks of Aristotle as primarily a speculative philosopher not interested in the special knowledges as such.[20] But Aristotle was actually both an empirical researcher himself, and a reflective and self-reflective (i.e, methodological) commentator on human affairs.

What Merlan's account of the "School of Aristotle" unintendingly shows is how far along the road to Neoplatonism the Peripatos already was at the turn of the century. In under-emphasizing Aristotle's interest in the special knowledges, Merlan neglects—just as the Peripatos itself neglected—the way in which this interest gave rise to Aristotle's classification of the special knowledges as co–ordinate with the theoretical (i.e., the divisions of 'first philosophy'). So Aristotle is, again, not to be charged with the persistent predisposition to see the different kinds of knowledge as only sub-species of theoretical knowledge. For Aristotle, the special arts-and-sciences (including *praktikê* and *poiêtikê*) were co-ordinate with the theoretical sciences, and are to be pursued with different methods for their different subject-matters. Nor did Aristotle believe that their different starting-points or premisses were necessarily compatible, as the Neoplatonists wanted them to be, and as unity-of-science postivists and reductionists still hope they can be shown to be.

Corresponding to the separation of *psychê* from *sôma* among the Peripatetics, and just as fateful, is the gap they introduced between sensation and intellect. They turned the latter into a substance instead of the function which it is in Aristotle, and reduced the former to pure (unprocessed) sensory input. This last move has the effect in turn of making intellection a purely formal or calculative activity *unmixed* with feeling.

In connection with the Neoplatonists' "One" as the cause of all there is, and because Aristotle was a pluralist about causes, we may not assume without question that he was as much interested in *first* causes (*archai*)—or in *The First* Cause of all things—as his platonist commentators make him out to be. If we take Aristotle's account of the four kinds of antecedent conditions to which *effects* respond as his best explanation of causation, then he has to be seen as a functionalist and process-philosopher but not an idealist. For, his material cause (*aitía*) is that-from-which an effect or thing arises, while its efficient cause is the agency by-means-of-which it came to be. The formal cause, thirdly, is the pattern according to which the effect came into existence or got made; but it does not subsist separately from the material in which it operates. Similarly, the final cause, the that-for-the-sake-of-which the thing came into existence, is not separate from its functioning since it is an actualization (an activation) of the thing's possibilities. So knowing, the activity of making things intelligible, is a realizing (an actualizaton in thought) of the determinate identity of a thing in terms of its functioning, its uses, its generative antecedents, its connectedness with, and implication in other determinate processes. It is not participation in a previously assumed cosmic intellect, or the action of said intellect in us.

What thinking (the activity of *noûs*) actualizes are forms present, the order potentially present, in the subject-matter. And thinking ("*noûsing*"), like sensing, is a selective *responding* of the human organism. It is a response to the action of the process or thing we want to understand or think. In Peircean terms, the signitive thing to which thought is responding is functioning as a sign; and that which it is a sign of becomes intelligible as its interpetants arise in our response to the sign. *Noûs* is an aspect of our human capabilities (*dynameis*); it is the power to actualize the regularities or order that constitute the integrity of what is being made intelligible. Because it is a capabality of actualizing whatsoever form it needs to actualize, *noûs* (intellect or intelligence) cannot itself have a pre-existent structure of its own. As the *dynamis* which it is, its only form or structure is its capacity to take on the form or structure which the sign is determining it to assume.

Interestingly, and as J.H. Randall points out, it is so much less structured as a capacity that, as a pure capacity, *noûs* is practically a pure potentiality: a formless ability to take on any form that it encounters. And this befits the transparent or impassive nature of the intellectual function. If it were not impassive, it would distort the intelligibility of what it apprehends. On the other side, the action of the sign upon the intellectual capacity (*noûs*) does not alter it; *noûs* brings the determining power of the sign into operation. And this capacity, Aristotle points out, is separable from the human organism only in discourse, in the same sense (he says) as "when we think of mathematical objects, though these are not in fact separable from their matter, we do conceive of them as separate" (*De Anima* III.vii.431b15–16). So Aristotle's *noûs* may not be taken as it was by his Hellenistic commentators to be capable of existing separately and independently.

As *noûs* is nothing without the organism of which it is a function, so it cannot function without images. That is to say, its functioning begins with sensing (*anankaion gar hypárchein to aisthêton*, 417b25) and requires images abstracted from observation. But the text of the *De Anima* does not follow this up; it says instead that, in addition to the power which responsive intellect—*noûs pathêtikos*—has of knowing (by abstracting or taking on the form of universals), there also has to be a power which responds to and makes things into "definite qualiti[es]" (430a14–16). "It is this intellect which is separable and impassive and unmixed, being in its essential nature an activity" (Hicks) . . . while the affected (*pathêtikós*) intellect is perishable and without this [activity] does not think at all" (430a 24–5). The memorable analogy in the text here is with light, without which nothing would be visible. So too, in Peripatetic–platonist thinking, qualities and possibilities could not be grasped without what they called "active intellect" or *noûs poiêtikos* (a syntagm not found in the text itself). Clever as the analogy is, however, it remains extrusive to the tenor of Aristotle's otherwise naturalist analysis of the psychê and its capacities. It is to be doubted that Aristotle himself would have granted *the acquiescence presupposed here* with the platonist notion of a "soul of the world" which is being implicitly appealed to, to make the analogy work. *Noûs* in Aristotle was not the cosmic power or cause that it became among the Neoplatonists.

About the First Cause, the previous chapter has given the reasons for rejecting as Aristotle's the Neoplatonist equation of it with the Absolute Good as inserted into Book Lambda of the *Metaphysics*. The immaterial first cause in Aristotle is what we now call a "scientific object;" Peirce would call it a regularity or "law," according to which there is order, and according to which there is something rather than nothing, i.e. according to which chaos never was total, namely, according to which there never was nothing.

To return to the problem of the 'Aristotelian' *Politics* and the Peripatetic efforts to make Aristotle interpretable as a monarchist as well as a platonist, let us remember that it isn't likely that Aristotle, as a city–state person himself, would have found doing his political duty any more onerous than the Athenians among whom he lived. Yet the *Politics* asks questions of a form proper only to metics who might be aspiring to become (by exception) citizens, or else proper only to citizens living in a non-participatory, subjugated *polis*. These questions, as we saw, call for remark because of their peculiar wording. "First, whether the life of participative politicality (*sympoliteúesthai kai koinônein*) is more choiceworthy than that of the stranger or guest detached from political community" (1324a15–17)? This form of words is not proper to the epoch of the classical city-state in which all citizens were (by definition) active participants to some degree in the politics of their city. But it does create the opening for monarchist theory to invoke the happiness of the subjects as a factor legitimating kingship. Such wording also helps us gauge the success with which the Peripatetics succeeded in making over half-or-more of the 'Aristotelian' *Politics* into a critique of Athenian democracy from the oligarchist, rather than from the democratic, point of view.

We recapitulate the points that most disqualify the *Politics* from being entirely by Aristotle, and that show it to be a heavily edited and amended product. First, the editorial lesson of the *Metaphysics* is that it was possible for a whole work accepted as Aristotle's to have been edited into existence. Like other Aristotelian works it is based on what are said to be lecture-notes. And under "lecture-notes" we must include, as well as *hypomnêmata* of Aristotle's, notes taken by students of oral presentations, or notes made or obtained by a Peripatetic "successor," who will have received them from a Scholarch or lecturer. This, secondly, draws attention to the fact that the references to Plato and platonism in the Aristotelian corpus are both over–systematic and *ex post facto*, namely, there are references in (what we think of) as the earlier work to (what we think of) as later work. There are also a few quotations with no dialogue specified, whose text cannot be found in the dialogues at all. This is why we spoke, above, of the "near-thoroughness" of the editorial effort; its incompleteness tells the tale.

This anti-dialogism, thirdly, is reinforced by *dialogically insensitive* nature of the *locutions* regularly used to refer to what are claimed to be doctrines of Plato. These references, besides not naming the dialogue he is is in, very seldom name the speaker being quoted. The fact that some of the citations are not locatable in the dialogues would seem to show that they are quoted or imported from lectures or notes *about* platonism as a doctrinal system. Now if this was the case, no need would have arisen to cite any dialogue at all—*except for the plan to attribute the doctrines to Plato himself.*

An Aristotle sensitive to the dialogue-form would not have used locutions destructive of the literary integrity of the dialogue-form. A minimally dialogical way of quoting from the dialogues would be: "as Socrates says in the Meno;" or, "as Socrates said in the *Republic;*" or, "as Socrates says in the *Phaedo;* or, "as he says in the *Charmides.*" Maximally dialogical ways of quoting from Plato's works would be: "as Socrates peremptorily said to Anytus in the *Meno* . . .; or, "as Socrates replies to Thrasymachus in the first book of the *Republic* . . ."; or, "as he jestingly says in the *Phaedo;*" or, "as he ironically says in the *Charmides* . . .." But note, on the other hand, that *if*—contrary to hypothesis and in response to the dogmatic systems now competing in the Speusippean-Xenocratic Academy— Aristotle had decided to treat "Plato" in the *purely* doctrinal way that the dogmatists do, he would not have had to cite any dialogue at all either.

Can we believe that Aristotle—"the master of those that know," as Dante called him—did not see the irony or verify for himself the mock–Pythagorean numerology of the passages in the *Republic* that refer (i) to the unblessed breedings out of season that will bring down the ideal state, and (ii) to the arithmetizable distance between the happiness of the kingly man and the tyrant? Aristotle would've had not to read the *Republic* at all to miss them; but this is excluded by the fact that his editors quote from the notes of his lectures in a counter–dialogical way. Moreover, as appreciators of the dialogue-form would insist, a reference to or quotation from the dialogues by a composer of dialogues would not use the counter-dialogical locutions that the text of the *Politics* uses. We have to conclude that the references are either the work of an editor or (if *not entirely* his) that they have been amended with *dogmatic* as well as "systematic," intent.

Moreover, *if* you are the Aristotle of the *Poetics* and his dialogues, *and* you are treating the tenets of or variants in the dogmatic system of idealism about which there is a course of lectures, and which was in every Academician's mind, there would have been no reason to refer to Plato's dialogues at all. The references would have been to what Plato had said, or was heard to have said in the supposed lecture(s), *not* to what doctrines from his lecture(s) happen to be echoed by speakers in the dialogues. And, as for the view that Aristoxenus's report of an *akróasis* (namely, a recital) on "the good" was once publicly delivered by Plato without being at all understood, the report rather suggests that the recital was *a reading* about "the good" *from* one of the dialogues.[21] It is not a verification of the claim that Plato gave lectures either on *his* or *the* system of doctrine called platonism.

Sixthly, the *Politics* does not cohere as a thematically coherent whole, but reads like two–books–in–one. The strategic reason for this was outlined in Chapter IV. But, as Aristotle teaches in both this and other works, politics (*politikê*, the subject of his book) is a *practical* species of knowing. The *Nicomachean Ethics* and the *Politics* explicitly say that political doing and learning, as reflective activities, are a practical species of knowledge, a *praktikê*. But the *Politics* which we have, from start to finish appeals to the *theoreticist*, utopian notion of "the ideal state" (as it's called in English). In other words, the book follows two conflicting architectonics. *Two* different *generative strategies* have given birth to it. The more patent key-idea in this two–layered book is that of "the ideal state" (*malíst' eiê kat' euchê*); this perfectionist idea emerges as uneasily striving to be the top stratum in the work. It contrasts with the traditional Athenian moderate idea of "the ancestral constitution (*hê patrios politeia*)," which there is ample reason to believe was the originary one, both because it was dear to the heart of the majority of classical Athenian citizens, and because it fits so well with Aristotle's habit of *moderation* in all things *and* his explicit operational recommendations about it in the *Nicomachean Ethics*.

Lastly, the *Politics* should not be read in separation from the account of the Ancestral Constitution to be found in the *The Athenian Constitution*, the friendly history compiled in Aristotle's life-time. We have seen for what purpose the idea of "the-most-to-be-desired state" came into existence and be juxaposed to the ancestral constitution; namely, in order to bedim the lustre of the moderate idea. Modern readers do not recognize it as the oligarchist syntagm that it was in mid–fourth century Athenian culture. The text of the *Politics*, as we have it, makes "the most-wished-for state" equivalent to "the best state (*hê aristê politeia*)." Grammatically speaking, both are superlatives, but dianoetically viewed they are only perfective, namely, not achievable in practice only approximateable. What prohibits Aristotle from having been the one to invoke "the ideal, the most-to-be-wished-for state" as standards of comparison, is that he would at once have been marked as an oligarchist and extremist. So, there are two historiographic puzzles here: not just that the readership has not found it strange for the moderate Aristotle to be guided by an extremist idea (as at least half of the *Politics* is), but also that we have not inquired into why Aristotle, the author of the most original book on rhetorical devices, never comments on this most blatant—and, we must admit, most successful—of strategic rhetorical devices.

Is it not an irony of intellectual history that, just as we have failed to note that Postmodernism is more Modernist than it admits, so about the Peripatetics we have not perceived that they are less Aristotelian than they have been claimed to be. And, just as "Postmodernism" unashamedly exploits any insight of "Modernism" that pleases it while, at the same time, contradicting it, so the Peripatetics exploited Aristotle's insights at will while also departing at will from the coherence of his encyclopedic system. The difference between the Peripatetics and the Postmodernists is that the former claimed to be *and have been accepted as* `Aristotelians,' because they were never so *explicit* about rejecting or correcting Aristotle as the Postmodernists believe they have been about Modernism. The Neoplatonists, in contrast, knew and stated that they were either interpreting or correcting Aristotle in accordance with platonist and Neoplatonist truth. We are left to ponder, in all this, how deeply embedded in our intellectual tradition pythagorism, platonism and idealism must be for their operation to have remained so unremarked in the very histories of our tradition.

Now, independently of Plato's dialogues, the problem of essentialist definitions does relate to the problematic nature of the theory of ideas. So, if the former problem, as it occurs in the *Euthyphro* stimulates us to think about the relation of the dialogues-as-a-set to the idealist theories developed by the Academy, then we may perceive that every attempt to define a concept is a test or confirmation of the theory. This is because if there are ideas of everything that is, it follows that there should be essentialist definitions of everything. So, if we run into something (such as 'piety,' 'beauty,' 'courage,' 'sôphrosynê,' 'justice,' 'friendship')[23] that we cannot define, then the theory of ideas is falsified. Or else, there are not ideas of everything that is (as suggested in the *Parmenides* at one point), and the theory of ideas is inadequate to the explanatory purpose it is supposed to meet.

It is clear, then, that the self-focusing devices which we looked at in the previous section are features of the dialogues whose tacit instructions may not be neglected without damage to the dialogue in which they occur. If Socrates says that what he's going to do next is fabulate, then we must take what he goes on to say as a fabulation, not as the model political program which the oligarchists and platonists self-servingly say it is. To understand a work-of-art we must follow the leads into the universe of its meanings which it itself provides. Leads or interpretants that seek to take us into the work from premises alien to its interests and design will necessarily mislead; they are, in fact, evasions of the burden of the work. Thus, as a final example, a sociological interest in the courting habits of eighteenth–and nineteenth–century landed gentry will bypass the wider, more basic interest in the human condition of Jane Austen and George Eliot. Of course, if the historical sociologist who does this also declares that *Emma* and *Middlemarch* are to be treated as *only* sociological tractates, then we would say that s/he has denatured their works and quite missed their point. And so it is with readers who take Plato's works to be doctrinal tractates expounding a system of doctrine, rather than the brilliant dramatizations which they are of deeply interesting intellectual interactions between some Greek intellectuals of reputation and the most intellectually honest and consistently ethical character the West has known, the Socrates of Plato's authentic dialogues.

Notes

1. "I follow Aristotle's practice: the conversation of the others is so put forward as to leave him the principal part" (Winstedt). We can't be sure, however, that Cicero is not himself de–dramatizing Aristotle's practice, given that all of antiquity misread Plato in this way, and that Cicero's own "dialogues" are only nominally dialogues, and read like the expositions which they are.

2. Unless he is taken 'antilogistically,' as refuting and defending both sides of a given claim, and as doing *within* the dialogue something like what Plato is doing in his *oeuvre* as a whole, namely, both refuting and defending doctrines and modes of argumentation by placing them in confrontation with each other, and so putting them on exhibit or under observation for us the readers.

3. Not to repeat myself, I refer the reader to works in which these matters are discussed at greater length than in the present work: "Plato: the Open Mind," *Modes of Greek Thought* (1971); "Methodology of a Misreading," *Intl.Studies in Philosophy* No.X (1978); "Plato, Platonism and the Question of the Laws," *Papers of the Soc. for the Study of the Hist. of Philosophy* (1976);

Plato's Dialogues One by One (1984); *The City–State Foundations of Western Political Thought* (2 rev.ed. 1993); Xenophon's Defense & Plato's Apology," *New Essays on Socrates* ed. E.Kelly (1984); *Nietzsche and Greek Thought* (1987); "On the Form & Authenticity of the 'Lysis'," *Ancient Philosophy* Vol.X, No.2 (1990); "Bakhtin, Dialogism, and Plato's Dialogues," *Ellenikê Philosophikê Epitheorese* t.6, 18 (1989); "Dialogism, Socrates, & Source–Criticism," in *The Philosophy of Socrates*, Proceedings, 2nd Intl.Conf. on Greek Philosophy, Samos, 1990; "The Politics of a Sophistic Rhetorician," *Quaderni Urbinati di Cultura Classica* 41.2 (1992); "Plato's Ironies: Textural, Structural, and Allusional: The Mathematical Humor in Books VIII & IX of the *Republic*," *Intl. Studies in Philos.* (1994); "The Hellenistic Obliteration of Plato's Dialogism," *Plato's Dialogues: New Studies and Intepretations* ed. G. Press (1993); "The Son of Apollo Explicated: Plato's Wit, his Irony, and Dialogism," *Plato's Dialogues the Dialogical Approach* (in press).

4. See E.N.Tigerstedt*The Decline and Fall of the Neoplatonic Interpretation of Plato* (Helsinki: Soc. Scientiarum Fennica 1974)

5. H.R. Jauss *Toward an Aesthetic of Reception* tr. T.Bahti (U. of Minnesota Press 1982); *Question and Answer* Forms of Dialogic Understanding, Ed. & tr. M. Hays (U. of Minnesota 1989); W. Iser *The Implied Reader* (Johns Hopkins U.P. 1974), *The Act of Reading* (J. Hopkins U.P. 1978), *Prospecting From Reader Response to Literary Anthropology* (J. Hopkins 1989); see also R.C. Holub *Reception Theory* A Critical Introduction (Methuen 1984).

6. In *The Limits of Interpretation* (Indiana U.P. 1990).

7. *hopôs dê prôton stasis empese*, as at the beginning of the *Iliad* between Achilles and Agamemnon.

8. *Great Dialogues of Plato* ed. & tr. W.H.D. Rouse (Mentor Books 1956). Following Rouse, and J. Adam's commentary on *The Republic of Plato* 2 vol. Ed. with Notes, Comm. and Appendices (Cambridge U.P. 1902, 1963). I treat the subject at greater length in "Plato's Ironies: Structural, Textural, and Allusional, The Mathematical Humor in *Republic* Bks. VIII and IX," *Intl. Studies in Philosophy* (1994).

9. Just as the mythifications of the Sophistic rhetorican from Elea, in the *Politicus* (269a–275d), are smiled at by the elder Socrates in that dialogue, and by the readers who have understood the myth to be an attempt to out-storify the storifications into which Socrates launches at a moment's notice in so many places in the dialogues.

10. This discourse, as I point out in "The Politics of a Sophistic Rhetorician," *Quaderni Urbinati di Cultura Classica*, is both pythagorist and dynasticist. Its conclusion that, under kingly rule, there is no difference between slave and free might have sounded liberating to an audience of slaves and courtiers, but not to Athenians who treasured the ancestral constitution under which they were already free.

11. *Athenian Democracy in the Age of Demosthenes* (Oxford: Blackwell 1991)

12. Cf. *Plato's Dialogues One By One* for a fuller account of the *Gorgias* as an intellectual drama.

13. The theory of misreading, and of better and worse readings, is worked out in my *Literature, Criticism, and The Theory of Signs* (Amsterdam: Benjamins 1995).

14. Cf. again "The Politics of a Sophistic Rhetorician," *Quaderni Urbinati di Cultura Classica*

15. References with this form are to *The New Elements of Mathematics* 4 vol. in 5, ed. C. Eisele (The Hague: Mouton 1976).

16. *Letters to Lady Welby* ed. I. Lieb (New Haven: Whitlock 1953); p.29. "The essential function of a sign," Peirce adds in another letter (SS 31), "is to render inefficient relations efficient,—not to set them in action, but to establish a habit or general rule whereby they will act on occasion." *Semiotics and Significs* The Correspondence between C.S. Peirce & Lady Welby, ed. C.S. Hardwick (Indiana U.P. 1977).

17. F. Wehrli *Die Schule des Aristoteles. Texte und Kommentar* 10 Parts (Basel–Stuttgart: 1944–1959).

18. (Zeller *The Earlier Peripatetics* II. p.441 and note)

19. Cf. my *Understanding Parmenides The Poem, the Dialogue, the All* (in press). In connection with Aristotle's relation to Speusippos, it will be useful to note that Aristotle the nature-inquirer is certainly not in sympathy with the Pythagoreans. He, in fact, does not allow that they are really nature-inquirers (*Metaph.*I.989b–990a), *even though* "all their discussions and investigations are concerned with physical nature." His reason for this is that "the so-called (*kaloumenoi*) Pythagoreans appeal to starting-points and elements alien (*ektopôterois*) to nature–inquiry (*extranee a physiologis*) gotten from nothing that is perceptible (*ouk ek aisthêtôn*)."To idealists, however, this is exactly what makes Pythagoreans good 'philosophers.'

20. Cf. again, The Peripatos, Ch.6 of "Greek Philosophy from Plato to

Plotinus" in *The Cambridge History of Later Greek & Early Medieval Philosophy*; and his *From Platonism to Neoplatonism*.

21. This possibility is developed hypothetically, as a possibility, in an unpublished essay "Aristoxenus on Plato's Auditors: Did Plato Give a Lecture or a Recital?"

22. Cf. U. Eco *The Limits of Interpretation* (Indiana U.P. 1990), and "Eco, Peirce, and Interpretationism," *American Journal of Semiotics* Vol.8, 1991, where the subject is treated at definitive lengths.

23. As in, respectively, the *Euthyphro, Hippias Major, Laches, Charmides, Republic*, and—waiving doubts as to its authenticity—the *Lysis*. We note that these are terms for just the kind of idea that are supposed, by young Socrates in the *Parmenides*, to be most suited to definition.

24. F. Wehrli *Die Schule des Aristoteles. Texte und Kommentar* 10 Parts (Basel-Stuttgart: 1944–1959).

25. (Zeller *The Earlier Peripatetics* II. p.441 and note)

26. Cf. my *Understanding Parmenides The Poem, and the Poetry of 'Pure Being'* (in press). In connection with Aristotle's relation to Speusippos, it will be useful to note that Aristotle the nature-inquirer is certainly not in sympathy with the Pythagoreans. He, in fact, does not allow that they are really nature–inquirers (*Metaph*.I.989b–990a), *even though* "all their discussions and investigations are concerned with physical nature." His reason for this is that "the so-called (kaloumenoi) Pythagoreans appeal to starting–points and elements alien (*allótrioi*) to nature-inquiry (*extranee a physiologis*) gotten from nothing that is perceptible. See also note 19.

References and Bibliography

Alexander	of Aphrodisias *Commentaria in Aristotelis Metaphysica* 2 vol. ed. M.Hayduck (Berlin: Reimer 1891) *On Aristotle's Metaphysics 1*, tr. W.E. Dooley (Cornell U.P. 1989) *On A's Metaphysics 2 & 3*, tr. Dooley & Madigan (Cornell 1992) *Ethical Problems* tr. R.W. Sharples (London: Duckworth 1990)
H.Alline	*Histoire du Texte de Platon* (Paris: Champion 1915)
J.Andrieu	*Le Dialogue Antique* (Paris: Les Belles Lettres 1954)
J.Annas	ed. *Oxford Studies in Anc.Philosophy Supplementary Vol.* 1991
T.Aquinas	*On Being and Essence (De Ente et Essentia)* Tr. Intro. Notes by A.A. Maurer (Toronto: Pontifical Inst. 1949)
Aristophanes	*Clouds* ed.K.J.Dover (Oxford U.P. 1968) *Aristophanes* 3 vols. ed. & tr. B.B.Rogers (Loeb Libr.)
Aristotle	*Aristotelis Opera I and II* ed. I. Bekker (Berlin: De Gruyter 1960) *The Politics of Aristotle* Bks.1-5, ed. Susemihl & Hicks (London: Macmillan 1894) *The Politics* Text & Comm. W.L.Newman 4 Vol. (Oxford U.P. 1902) *The Politics of Aristotle* ed. R.Congreve Notes, Longmans 1874 *Politics* ed. & tr. H.Rackham (Loeb Libr. 1944) *Política* edición bilingüe, Julián Marías y María Araujo, Madrid 1951 *The Politics of Aristotle* Tr. J.E.C. Welldon (Macmillan 1893) *Aristotle's Ethics & Politics* 2 vol. J.Gillies (London: Cadell 1804) *Constitution of Athens* ed. J.E.Sandys Text, Notes, Intro. (London: Macmillan 1924)

The Athenian Constitution ed. & tr. H.Rackham (Loeb Libr. 1952)
Ethics of Aristotle 2 vol. A.Grant Text, Notes, Essays (Longman's1866)
The Nicomachean Ethics, Commentary H.H.Joachim (Oxford U.P. 1951)
Ethics Text & Tr. H.Rackham (Loeb 1947)
De Anima R.D.Hicks Text, Tr., Intro., Notes (Cambridge U.P. 1907)
De Anima In the Version of Wm.Moerbeke & Comm. of Thom.Aquinas,
Tr.K.Foster & K.S.Humphries (Yale U.P. 1951)
Metafísica de Aristoteles 2 vol. V.García Yerba Ed.Trilingüe: Greek,
Latin, Spanish (Madrid: Gredos 1970)
Metaphysics 2 vol. W.D.Ross Rev.Text, Intro.Comm. (Oxford U.P. 1958)
On Coming-To-Be-&-Passing-Away Rev.Text, Intro.Comm. ed. H.H.
Joachim (Oxford: Clarendon 1922)
Parts of Animals Text & Tr. A.L. Peck (Loeb Libr. 1961)
De Partibus Animalium 1943, Crit. & Lit.Commentaries Ingemar Düring
(N.Y. Garland 1980)
Physics ed. D.Ross Rev.Text, Intro. & Commentary (Oxford U.P.1936)
Physics 2 vol. ed. & tr. P.H.Wickstead & F.M.Cornford (Loeb Libr. 1934)
Poetics ed. D.W.Lucas w. Intro. & Comm. (Oxford U.P. 1968)
Prior Analytics, Categories, On Interpretation Text & Tr. H.P.Cokke &
H.Tredennick (Loeb 1962)
Posterior Analytics, Topics Text & Tr. H.Tredennick & E.S.Forster
(Loeb 1960)
The Rhetoric of Aristotle 3 vol. Text & Commentary E.M.Cope
Selected Fragments, vol.XII of Works ed. tr. D.Ross (Oxford U.P. 1952)
Fragmenta Selecta ed. W.D.Ross (Oxford U.P.1955)
Aristoteles Pseudoepigraphus ed. V.Rose (Leipzig: Teubner 1863)

A.H.Armstrong *The Cambridge History of Later Greek & Early Medieval Philosophy*
(Cambridge U.P. 1967) CHLG

H.von Arnim *Zur Entstehungsgeschichte der aristotelischen Politik* (Vienna 1924)

C.Arpe *Philologus 94* (1941)
Das tí ên einai bei Aristotelis 1938 (N.Y. Arno 1936)

F.Ast *Lexicon Platonicum* 3 vols. (Leipzig: Weidmann 1836)
Platon's Leben und Schriften 1816 (repr. Minerva 1976)

Athenaeus *The Deipnosophists* 7 vol. ed. & tr. C.B. Gulick (Loeb Libr. 1961)

E.Barker *The Politics of Aristotle Translated* with Intro. Notes and Appendixes
(Oxford U.P. 1948)

From Alexander to Constantine Passages & Documents, 336 B.C. to A.D. 337 (Oxford U.P. 1956)

J.Barnes, M.   *Articles on Aristotle 2 Ethics and Politics* (N.Y. St. Martin's 1977)
Schofield, R.
Sorabji

H.Bazin   *La République des Lacédémoniens de Xenophon* (Paris: Leroux 1885)

J.Bernays   *Die Dialoge des Aristoteles* (Darmstadt: Wiss.Buchgesellschaft 1968)

E.Berti   *La Filosofia del Primo Aristotele* (Padua: A.Milani 1962)

A.Melero Be-   *Atenas y el Pitagorismo* (Universidad de Salamanca 1972)AP
llido
W.T.Bluhm   *Theories of the Political System* (N.Y. Prentice-Hall 1965)

A.Bloom   *Giants and Dwarfs* (N.Y. Simon & Schuster 1990)

A.Boeckh   *In Platonis ... Minoem eiudsdemque Libros Priores de Legibus*
                 (Halle: Hemmerde 1806)

Boethius   *De Consolatione Philosophiae* & *Tractates* ed. & tr. Stewart, Rand,
                 Tester (Loeb Libr. 1973)
                 De Institutione Arithmetica, De Inst. Musica ed. G.Friedlein, 1867
                 (Frankfurt: Minerva G.M.B.H. 1966)
                 De Topicis Differentis tr., notes, essays E. Stump (Cornell U.P. 1978)
                 In Ciceronis Topica tr., notes, intro. E.Stump (Cornell U.P. 1988)
                 Porphyrii Introductio in Aristotelis Categorias a Boethio Translata, in
                 Porphyry: Isagoge et in Aristotelis Categorias Commentarium; vid.inf.

E.Boisacq   *Dictionnaire Étymologique de la Langue Grecque* (Heidelberg, 1923)

H.Bonitz   *Index Aristotelicus* 2 ed., Vol.V of Aristotelis Opera (Graz: Akademi-
                 sche Druck, repr. 1955)

R.J.Bonner   *Aspects of Athenian Democracy* 1933, (N.Y. Russell & Russell)

E.N.Borza   *In the Shadow of Olympus* The Emergence of Macedon (Princeton 1990)

G.Boter   *The Textual Tradition of Plato's Republic* (Brill 1989)

K.Boudouris   ed. *The Philosophy of Socrates*, Proceedings, 2nd Intl.Conf. on Greek
                 Philosophy, Samos, 1990.

A.C.Bradley   "Aristotle's Conception of the State," *Hellenica* Ed. E. Abbott (London:
                 Rivingtons 1880)

S.Brandt   "Entstehungszeit und zeitliche Folge der Werke von Boethius," *Philo-
                 logus* 62 (1903)
                 ed. Boethius *In Isagogen Commenta* (editio prima, ed. secunda) Corpus
                 Scriptorum Ecclesiasticorum Latinorum (Vienna 1906)

L.Brandwood   *A Word–Index to Plato* (London: Maney 1976)

E.Bréhier   *Historia de la Filosofía* 3 ed. 1948, 2 vol. tr. D. Nañez (Buenos Aires:
                 Editorial Sudamericana 1948)

E.Buchanan   *Aristotle's Theory of Being* (Ann Arbor: Univ. Microfilm 1960) ATB

W.Burkert   "Platon oder Pythagoras? Zum Ursprung des Wortes `Philosophie',"
                 Hermes 88, No.2 (1960)
                 "Review-Article of Thesleff's The Pythagorean Texts of the Hellen-
                 istic Period," in *Pseudoepigrapha I* (Geneva: Fondation Hardt 1972)
                 Lore & Science in Ancient Pythagorism 1962, transl. E.L.Minar
                 (Harvard U.P. 1972)

E.L.Bulwer   *Athens; Its Rise and Fall* (Paris: Baudry's 1837)

G.M.Calhoun   *Athenian Clubs in Politics & Litigation* (Rome: Bretschneider 1964)

A.Cameron   *The Pythagorean Backround of the Theory of Recollection*
                 (Menasha: Banta 1938)

J.Cargill   *The Second Athenian League* Empire or Free Alliance (U.Cal. 1981)

H.Chadwick   *Boethius*. The Consolation of Music, Logic, Theology, and Philosophy
                 (Oxford U.P. 1981)

P.Chantraine   *Dictionnaire Étymologique de la Langue Grecque* (Paris:
                 Klincksieck 1968)

H.Cherniss   *Aristotle's Criticism of Plato & the Academy* (J.Hopkins U.P. 1944)

A.-H.Chroust   *Aristotle New Light on his Life & Work* 2 v. (Notre Dame U.P.1973).

M.T.Cicero   *Academica, De Natura Deorum* ed. & tr. H.Rackham (Loeb Libr. 1951)
De Re Publica, De Legibus ed. & tr. C.W.Keyes (Loeb Libr. 1952)
Letters to Atticus 3 vol. ed. & tr. E.O Winstedt (Loeb Libr. 1956)
De Finibus ed. & tr. H. Rackham (Loeb Libr. 1951)

P.Courcelle   *Late Latin Writers & their Greek Sources* (Cambridge, Mass 1969)

J.K.Davis   *Democracy and Classical Greece* 2 ed. (Harvard U.P. 1993)

A.Delatte   *Études sur la Littérature Pythagoricienne* (Paris: Champion 1915)

Demosthenes   *Orations* 6 vols. ed. & tr. J.Vine & A.Murray (Loeb Libr. 1956)

É.Des Place   *Platon Lexique* 2 vols. (Paris: Les Belles Lettres 1970)

E.Dijksterhuis   *The Mechanization of the World-Picture* tr. Dickshoorn (Oxford U.P. 1961)

A.Dreizehnter   *Untersuchungen zur Textgeschichte der Aristotelischen Politik* (Leiden: Brill 1962)

E.Dupréel   *La Légende Socratique et les Sources de Platon* (Brussels: Sand 1922)

I.Düring   *Aristotle in the Ancient Biographical Tradition* (Göteborg: Acta Universitatis 1957)
& G.E.L.Owen eds. *Aristotle and Plato in the Mid-Fourth Century* (Göteborg: Studia Graeca et Latina 1960)

A.Edel   *Aristotle* (U. of N.Carolina 1982)

L.Edelstein   *Plato's Seventh Letter* (Leiden: Brill 1966)

V.Ehrenberg   *The Greek State* (N.Y. Barnes & Noble 1960)

G.Else   *Aristotle's Poetics: The Argument* (Harvard U.P. 1957)

C.Eucken   *ISocrates Seine Positionen in der Auseinandersetzung mit den zeit-genössischen Philosophen* (Berlin: de Gruyter 1983)
über den Sprachgebrauch des Aristoteles 1868 (Ann Arbor: University Microfilm 1967)

C.Evangeliou   *Aristotle's Categories & Porphyry* (Leiden: Brill 1988)

G.C.Field   *Plato and His Contemporaries* 2 ed. (London: Methuen 1948)

W.Fortenbaugh Editor, *On Stoic and Peripatetic* Ethics The Work of Arius Didymus
                   (New Brunswick: Transaction Books 1983)

W.Fowler   "Polybius' Concept of *Tychê*," *Classical Review* 17 (1903), p.446ff.

E.Frank   *Plato und die sogenannten Pythagoreer* (Halle: Niemeyer 1923)

M.Frede   *Essays in Ancient Philosophy* (U. of Minnesota Press 1987)

E.A.Freeman   "The Athenian Democracy," *Historical Essays* 2nd Series (London:
                   Macmillan 1880)

P.Friedländer   *Plato 3* Tr. H. Meyerhoff (Princeton U.P.1969)

H.Frisch   *The Constitutition of the Athenians* 1942 (Arno repr. 1976)

K.T.Frost   "The Critias and Minoan Crete," *Jour.of Hellenic Studies XXXIII*
                   (1913), p.189–206

A.Fuks   *The Ancestral Constitution* (London: Routledge 1953)

H.G.Gadamer   *Platos Dialektische Ethik* (Hamburg: Meiner 1968)
                   Dialogue and Dialectic tr. P.C. Smith (Yale U.P. 1980)
                   Griechische Philosophie 2 vol., vol.5-6 of *Gesammelte Werke*
                   (Tübingen: Mohr-Siebeck 1985)

L.Gautier   *La Langue de Xenophon* (Geneva: Georg & Cie. 1911)

A.Gellius   *Attic Nights* 3 vol. ed. & tr. J.C.Rolfe (Loeb Libr. 1927)

S.Gersh   *Middle Platonism & Neoplatonism. The Latin Tradition* 2 vol. (Notre
                   Dame U.P. 1986); esp. Ch.9.

M.Gibson   Editor: *Boethius. His Life, Thought, and Influence* (Oxford U.P. 1981)

G.Gilbert   *The Constitutional Antiquities of Sparta & Athens* 2 ed. 1893, transl.
                   Brooks & Nicklin (London: Sonnenschein 1895)

J.Gillies   *Aristotle's Ethics and Politics* 2 Vol. (London: Cadell &Davis 1804)
                   The History of Ancient Greece (Philadelphia: Wardle 1835)

M.Golden   *Children and Childhood in Classical Athens* (J.Hopkins U.P. 1990)

D.W.Graham   *Aristotle's Two Systems* (Oxford U.P. 1987)

F.Grayeff   *Aristotle and his School* (N.Y. Barnes & Noble 1974)

H.Gomperz   "ISocrates und die Socratik," Separatum *Wiener Studien* XXVII.2 (1905)

P.Green   *Alexander to Actium* The Historical Evolution of the Hellenistic Age
                (Berkeley: University of California Press 1990)

A.Greenidge   *Handbook of Greek Constitutional History* (London: MacMillan 1896)

G.Grote   *Plato and the Other Companions of Socrates Vol.IV*, 1888
                (N.Y. B.Franklin 1973)
                Aristotle 2 vol. (London: J.Murray 1872)
                History of Greece A New Edition 12 vol. (London: Murray 1869)

W.K.C.Guthrie   *A History of Greek Philosophy* 6 vol. (Cambridge U.P. 1962-1978)

I.Hadot   "The Role of the Commentaries on Aristotle in the Teaching of Philo-
                sophy Acc. to the Prefaces of the Neoplatonic Commentaries on the
                Categories," *Oxf.Studies in Anc.Philos.* Suppl.Vol. (1991); p.176-189.

E.Hambruch   *Logische Regeln der Platonischen Schule in der Aristotelischen Topik*
                1904 (N.Y. Arno 1976)

B.E.Hammond   *Political Institutions of the Ancient Greeks* 1895 (repr. Argonaut 1970)

N.G.L.Hammond   *History of Greece* to 322 B.C. (Oxford U.P. 1959)

M.H.Hansen   *The Athenian Democracy in the Age of Demosthenes* (Oxford: Blackwell 1991)

C.S.Hardwick   *Semiotics and Significs* The Correspondence between C.S.Peirce & V. Welby
                (Indiana U.P. 1977)

E.Havelock   *The Literate Revolution in Greece* (Princeton U.P. 1982)
                & Hersbell eds. Communication Arts in the Ancient World (Hastings
                House 1978)
                Preface to Plato (Harvard U.P. 1963)
                The Muse Learns to Write (Yale U.P. 1986)

K.F.Hermann   *Lehrbuch der Griechischen Staatsalterthümer* (Heidelberg: Mohr 1855)

L.Hicks   *Manual of Greek Historical Inscriptions* (Oxford U.P.1882)

G.F.Hill   *Sources for Greek History* Between the Persian & Peloponnesian War
                (Oxford U.P. 1907)

R.C. Holub   *Reception Theory* A Critical Introduction (Methuen 1984).

W.Iser   *The Implied Reader* (Johns Hopkins U.P. 1974)
                The Act of Reading (J. Hopkins U.P. 1978)
                Prospecting From Reader Response to Literary Anthropology (J. Hopkins
                1989)

Isocrates   *Works* 3 vols. ed. & tr. L.van Hook (Loeb Libr. 1954)

W.Jaeger   *Aristotle* 1923 Tr. R.Robinson (Oxford U.P.1948)

H.R.Jauss   *Toward an Aesthetic of Reception* tr. T.Bahti (U. of Minnesota Press 1982)
                Question and Answer Forms of Dialogic Understanding, Ed. & tr. M.
                Hays (U. of Minnesota 1989)

E.Johnson   *The Argument of Aristotle's Metaphysics* 1906, (Ann Arbor: University
                Microfilms 1979)

A.Jourdain   *Recherches...sur...L'Origine des Traduccion Latines D'Aristote* 1843,
                (N.Y. B.Franklin, repr. 1960)   ROT

D.Kagan   *The Great Dialogue* Greek Political Thought from Homer to Polybius
                (N.Y. Free Press 1965)
                Pericles of Athens and the Birth of Democracy (N.Y. Touchstone 1991)

E.Kelly   *New Essays on Socrates* (Lanham: U.P.A. 1984)   **NES**

Keyt & Miller   Ed. *A Companion to Aristotle's Politics* (Oxford: Blckwell 1991)

P.Krentz   *The Thirty at Athens* (Cornell U.P. 1982)

D.Laertius   *Lives of the Philosophers* 2 vols. ed.& tr. R.D.Hicks (Loeb 1950)
M.L.Laistner   *A History of the Greek World* 479-323 B.C. 3 ed. (London: Methuen 1957)

B.Levitt   *Supreme Political Power* In Greek Literature in the Fourth Century
                B.C. (U. of Pennsylvania Diss. 1943)

I.Levy　　　　　*Recherches sur les Sources de la Légende de Pythagore* (Paris: Leroux 1926)

Lidell & Scott　*Greek-English Lexicon* New Ed. by H.S. Jones (Oxford U.P. 1948)

I.Lieb　　　　　ed. *Letters to Lady Welby* (New Haven: Whitlock 1953)

A.C.Lloyd　　　*Cambridge History of Later Greek & Early Medieval Philosophy* (1967)

J.O.Lofberg　　*Sycophancy in Athens* (Menasha: Banta n.d.)

P.MacKendrick *Athenian Aristocracy* (Harvard U.P. 1969)
　　　　　　　The Philosophical Books of Cicero (London: Duckworth 1989)

J.Marenbon　　*Early Medieval Philosophy* 480-1150 (London: Routledge, 2 ed. 1988)

A.Marignac　　*Imagination et Dialectique* (Paris: Les Belles Lettres 1951)

H.Martin　　　*Études sur le 'Timée' de Platon* 1841, 2 vol. (Frankfurt: Minerva 1975)

G.Méautis　　　*Recherches sur le Pythagorisme* (Neuchâtel 1922)

S.Mekler　　　　*Academicorum Philosophorum Index Herculanensis* (Berlin 1902)

P.Merlan　　　　*From Platonism to Neoplatonism* (Nijhoff 1953)

H.Micheli　　　*La Révolutions Oligarchique des Quatre-Cents a Athènes* (Geneva: Georg & Cie. 1893)

L.Minio-　　　　*Opuscula: The Latin Aristotle* (Amsterdam;1972)
Paluello　　　　"Boethius als Übersetzer u. Kommentator Aristotelischer Schriften," *Studia Patristica* 2.2, Berlin (1957); pp.358-365.

W.Mitford　　　*History of Greece* 10 vol. (London: Caddell 1822)

J.Moreau　　　*Aristote et Son École* (Paris: Presse Universitaire de France 1962)

P.Moraux　　　*D'Aristote a Bessarion* (Quebec: Université Laval 1970)AB
　　　　　　　A la Récherche de l'Aristote Pérdu Le Dialogue 'Sur la Justice' (Louvain: Publications Universitaires 1957)
　　　　　　　Der Aristotelismus bei den Griechen 2 vol. (N.Y. De Gruyter 1973)

G.Morpurgo-　　*Linguistica e Stilistica di Aristotele* (Roma: Ateneo 1967)
Tagliabue

C.Morris　　　　*Western Political Thought* Vol.I (N.Y. Basic Books 1967)

G.Müller　　　　*Studien zu den Platonischen Nomoi* (Munich: Beck 1951)

G.A.Mullach　　*Fragmenta Philosophorum Graecorum* 1879, 3 vol. (Paris: Firmin-Didot 1928)

J.Ober　　　　　*Mass & Elite in Democratic Athens* (Princeton U.P. 1989)

F.Ollier　　　　　*Le Mirage Spartiate* (Paris: Boccard 1933; Arno Press 1973))

W.Oncken　　　　*Die Staatslehre des Aristoteles* 1870, (Scientia Verlag Aalen 1964)
　　　　　　　　Athen u.Hellas Perikles Kleon Thukydides (Leipzig: Engelmann 1866)

J.Owens　　　　*The Doctrine of Being in the Aristotelian Metaphysics* (Toronto: Pontifical Inst. 1951)
　　　　　　　　Aristotle Coll. Papers of J. Owens, ed. J.R. Catan (SUNY Press 1981)

C.S.Peirce　　　*Collected Papers* 8 vol. ed. Hartshorne, Weiss, and Burks (Harvard U.P. 1938–58)
　　　　　　　　New Elements of Mathematics 5 vol. ed. C. Eisele (The Hague: Mouton 1976)

J.A.Philip　　　*Pythagoras and Early Pythagorism* (Toronto U.P. 1966)

E. des Places　　*Lexique de Platon* 2 vol. (Les Belles Lettres 1964)

Plato & Pseu-　*Opera* 4 vols. Baiter, Orelli, & Winckelmann (Turin: Meyer 1846)
do-Plato　　　　*Laws* 2 vols. ed. E.B.England, Text, Notes, Intro. 1921 (N.Y. Arno 1976)
　　　　　　　　Laws tr. & notes G.Burges (London: Bell 1902)
　　　　　　　　Opera IV: Clitopho Respublica Timaeus Critias, Ed. J. Burnet (Oxford U.P. 1905)
　　　　　　　　Dialogi IV Politeia Timaios ... Kritias Ed. C.F.Hermann, 1883 (Chicago: Ares n.d.)
　　　　　　　　The Timaeus of Plato, 1888 Ed. & Tr. Intro. & Notes R. Archer-Hind (N.Y. Arno 1973)
　　　　　　　　Timaeus Critias Cleitophon Menexenus Epistles Ed. & Tr. R.G. Bury (Loeb Libr. 1929)
　　　　　　　　Works Vol.II Republic Timaeus Critias Tr. H.Davis (London: Bell 1883); and *Plato's Dialogues* Tr. B. Jowett (N.Y. Random 1937)

Plutarch　　　　*Lives* 11 vol. tr. & ed. B. Perrin (Loeb Library 1918)
　　　　　　　　Moralia 17 vol. Cherniss et. al. (Loeb Library)

Polybius   *The Histories* 6 vols. ed. & tr. W.R.Paton (Loeb Libr.1954)
                Selections from Polybius Ed. & Annotated by J.Strachan-Davidson
                (Oxford U.P. 1888)

Porphyry   *Porphyrii Philosophi Platonici Opuscula Selecta* ed. A.Nauck, 1860
                (repr. Hildesheim 1963)
                Isagoge et in Aristotelis Categorias Commentarium, Commentaria in
                Aristotelem Graeca IV.1; ed. A.Busse (Berlin: Reimer 1887)
                Textual Remarks on Ptolemy's Harmonica & Porphyry's Commentary
                (Götheborg: Studia Graeca et Latina 27, 1969)
                Isagoge Tr. Intro. Notes E.W. Warren (Toronto: Pontifical Inst. 1975)

Poseidonius   *The Fragments* vol.I ed. L.Edelstein & I.G.Kidd (Cambridge U.P. 1972)

J.H.Randall   *Aristotle* (Columbia U.P. 1960)
                "The Functionalism & Dynamics of Aristotle," Papers of the Society for
                Ancient Greek Philosophy (SAGP), Burlington 1958.
                "Substance as Process," The Review of Metaphysics X.4 (1957): 580–601.
                The School of Padua and the Emergence of Modern Science (Padua:
                Editrice Antenore: 1961)
                The Career of Philosophy 3 vol. (Columbia U.P. 1962–1977)
                How Philosophy Uses Its Past (Columbia U.P. 1963)
                Plato: Dramatist of the Life of Reason (Columbia U.P. 1970)
                Hellenistic Ways of Deliverance and the...Christian Synthesis
                (Columbia U.P. 1970)

M.Reesor   *The Political Theory of the Old and Middle Stoa* (N.Y. Augustin 1951;
                & Bryn Mawr Dissertation)

H.Ritter   *Histoire de la Philosophie Ancienne* 4.vol. tr. C. Tissot (Paris: Ladrange
                1835)

A.S.Riginos   *Platonica* The Anecdotes Concerning the Life and Writings & Plato
                (Leiden:Brill 1976)

A.Rivaud   *Timée Critias* (Paris: Les Belles-Lettres 1925, 3 ed. 1956)

K.Robb   *Language and Thought in Early Greek Philosophy* (Monist Libr.1983)

J.T.Roberts   *Athens on Trial* The Antidemocratic Tradition in Western Thought
                (Princeton U.P. 1994)

D.Roloff   *Platonische Ironie* Das Beispiel Theaitetos (Heidelberg: Winter 1975)

W.D.Ross   *Aristotle* (N.Y. Barnes & Noble 1949)

E.Sagan   *The Honey and the Hemlock* (N.Y. Basic Books 1991)

E.Salin   *Die Griechische Utopie* (Munich: Duncker 1921)

W.Schadewaldt *Monolog und Selbsgepräch* (Berlin: Weidmann 1926)

M.Schanz   *Studien zur Geschichte des Platonischen Textes* (Wurzburg: Stahel 1874)

P.M.Schuhl   *La Fabulation Platonicienne* (Paris: P.U.F. 1947)

R.Sealey   *A History of the Greek City-States 700–338 B.C.* (U.Cal. Press 1976)
                The Athenian Republic (Penn State U.P. 1987)

J.Shiel   "Boethius' Commentaries on Aristotle," Medieval & Renaissance Studies
                4 (1958); pp.217–244.

P.Shorey   *What Plato Said* (Chicago U.P. 1937)
                "Tychê in Polybius," Classical Philology 16 (1921), p.281ff.

H.Shute   *History of the Process by which the Aristotelian Writings Arrived at their
                Present Form*, 1888 (N.Y. Arno 1976)

G.R.Sievers   *Geschichte Griechenlands vom Ende des Peloponnesischen Krieges* bis
                zur Schlacht bei Mantinea (Kiel: Universität 1840)

Simplicius   *In Aristotelis de Caelo de Caelo Commentaria* ed. I.L.Heiberg
                (Berlin: Reimer 1894)
                *In Aristotelis Physicorum Libros Quattuor Priores et Libros quattuor
                Posteriores Commentaria* 2 v. ed. H.Diels (Berlin:Reimer 1882, 1895)

R.K.Sinclair   *Democracy & Participation in Athens* (Cambridge U.P. 1988)

R.Sorabji   ed. *Aristotle Transformed* The Ancient Commentators & Their
                Influence(Cornell U.P. 1990)

C.Starr   *The Aristocratic Temper of Greek Civilization* (Oxford U.P. 1992)

F. van Steen-   *Aristotle in the West* The Origins of Latin Aristotelianism in the West
berghen   (Louvain: Nauwelaerts 1955)

L.Strauss   *On Tyranny: An Interpretation of Xenophon's Hiero* (Free Press 1950)

Thoughts on Machiavelli (Glencoe Free Press 1958)
What is Political Philosophy? (Glencoe: Free Press 1959)
Socrates and Aristophanes (Chicago U.P. 1966; Midway 1980)
Xenophon's Socratic Discourse: An Interpretation of the 'Oeconomicus' (Cornell U.P. 1970)
Xenophon's Socrates (Cornell U.P. 1972)
The City and Man (Rand McNally 1962)
The Argument & the Action of Plato's Laws (Chicago U.P.1975)
Political Philosophy ed. H.Gildin (Bobbos-Merrill 1975)
Studies in Platonic Political Philosophy (Chicago U.P. 1983)

A.Szegedy-   *The Nomoi of Theophrastus* (N.Y. Arno Press 1981)
Maszak

L.Tarán   *Academica: Plato, Philip of Opus, & the Pseudo-Platonic Epinomis* (Philadelphia: Amer. Philological Society 1975)
                Speussippus of Athens Critical Study, Related Texts, Commentary (Leiden: Brill 1981)
                Review of P. Moraux's *Der Aristotelismus bei den Griechen* von Andronikos bis Alexander von Aphrodisias, Gnomon Band 53 (1981); 721–750.

W.W.Tarn   *Hellenistic Civilization* (London: Arnold 1927)

V.Tejera   *Modes of Greek Thought* (N.Y. Appleton-Century 1971)
                "Methodology of a Misreading," *Intl.Studies in Philosophy* No.X (1978).
                "Plato, Platonism and the Question of the Laws," *Papers of the Soc. for the Study of the Hist. of Philosophy* 1976
                Plato's Dialogues One By One (N.Y. Irvington 1984)   PDOBO
                The City–State Foundations of Western Political Thought (Lanham: U.P.A. 2 rev.ed. 1993)
                History as a Human Science (Lanham: U.P.A. 1984)
                "Xenophon's Defense & Plato's Apology," New Essays on Socrates ed. E. Kelly (Lanham U.P.A 1984)
                Nietzsche & Greek Thought (Dordrecht: Nijhoff 1987)   NGT
                "On the Form & Authenticity of the `Lysis'," *Ancient Philosophy* Vol.X, No.2 (1990)
                "Bakhtin, Dialogism, and Plato's Dialogues," *Ellenikê Philosophikê Epitheorêsê* t.6, 18 (1989); p.280–295.
                History and Anti-History in Philosophy, with T.Z. Lavine (Dordrecht: Kluwer 1989)
                "Eco, Peirce, & Interpretationism," *Amer.Jour. of Semiotics 8* (1991)
                "Dialogism, Socrates, & Source-Criticism," in *The Philosophy of Socrates*, Proceedings, 2nd Intl.Conf. on Greek Philosophy, Samos, 1990.

"The Politics of a Rhetorical Sophist," *Quaderni Urbinati di Cultura Classica* (1991–92)
"The Son of Apollo Explicated: Plato's Wit, his Irony, and Dialogism," *Plato's Dialogues: the Dialogical Approach* (in press)
"Plato's Ironies: Textural, Structural, and Allusional. On the Mathematical Humor in Books VIII & IX of the *Republic*," (*Int.Studies in Philos.*)
"The Intellectual Content of Hellenistic Alienation," *Proceedings, IV Intl.Conference of Greek Philosophy*, Rhodes 1992.
Art and Human Intelligence (N.Y. Appleton-Century 1965)
Semiotics From Peirce to Barthes (Leiden: Brill 1988)
Literature, Criticism, and the Theory of Signs (Amsterdam: Benjamins 1994)
Aristotle's Organon The Poetics, The Rhetoric, The Analytics (Mellen U.P. 1996)
American Modern: The Path Not Taken Aesthetics, Metahysics, and Intellectual History in Classic American Philosophy (Rowman, Littlefield1996)
Understanding Parmenides: the Poem, the Dialogue, the All (in press)

Themistius   *Paraphrases Aristotelis Librorum* . . . 2 vol. [I: tôn Analyt.Hyster. tês physik.akroaseôs; II: peri psychês, peri mnêmês k.anamnêseôs, peri hypnou k.egrêgoreôs, peri enupniôn, peri tês kat'hypnon mantikês] ed. L. Spengel (Leipzig: Teubner 1866)

Themistii   *Orationes* ed. W. Dindorf (1832); repr. G.Olms 1961.

H.Thesleff   *Introduction to the Pythagorean Writings of the Hellenistic Period* (Abo Akademi 1961)
The Pythagorean Texts of the Hellenistic Period (Abo Akademi 1965)
"On the Problem of the Doric Pseudo-Pythagorica," *Pseudoepigrapha I* (Geneva: Fondation Hardt 1972)
Studies in the Styles of Plato (Abo Akademi 1967)
Studies in Platonic Chronology (Helsinki: Soc. Scientarum Fennica 1982)

I.Thomas   *Greek Mathematical Works* 2 vol. ed. & tr. (Loeb Libr. 1939–41)

Thucydides   *History of the Peloponnesian War* 3 vols. ed. T.Arnold, Notes (Oxf.1830)
Thucydides 2 vols. Transl. B.Jowett (Oxford U.P. 1900)

E.N.Tigerstedt   *The Decline and Fall of the Neoplatonic Interpretation of Plato* (Helsinki: Soc. Scientiarum Fennica 1974)
Plato's Idea of Poetical Inspiration (Soc.Scient.Fennica 1969)

M.Timparano-   *Pitagorici Testimonianze e Frammenti* 3 vols. (Nuova Italia 1957–1964)
Cardini

H.T.Tobin   *Timaios Locri On the Nature of the World and the Soul* (Chico, Calif.:
                 Scholars Press 1985)

M.N.Tod   *Greek Historical Inscriptions 600–323 B.C.*, 2 vols. (Oxford 1933 & 1948)

F.Überweg   *History of Philosophy* 2 vol. Tr. G.S. Morris (N.Y. Scribner's 1871)
                 HPU
C.J. de Vogel   *Pythagoras and Early Pythagoreanism* (Assen: Van Gorcum 1966)

K.von Fritz   *The Theory of the Mixed Constitutions* (Columbia U.P.1954)
                 Pythagorean Politics in Southern Italy (Columbia 1940)

L.Weber   "Platons' 'Atlantikos' und sein Urbild," *Klio XXI* (1927), p.245–87.

T.B.L.Webster   *Art & Literature in Fourth Century Athens* (London: Athlone 1956)

W.Welliver   *Character, Plot and Thought in Plato's Timaeus-Critias*
                 (Leiden: Brill 1977)

U.Wilamowitz-Moellendorff *Platon Leben und Werke* 5 ed. (Berlin: Weidmann 1959)

F.Wehrli   *Die Schule des Aristoteles*. 10 vol. (Basel: Schwabe 1944–1959)

L.Whibley   *Political Parties in Athens during the Peloponnesian War* (Cambridge
                 U.P. 1889)
                 Greek Oligarchies (N.Y. Putnam 1896)

A.D.Winspear   *The Genesis of Plato's Thought* 1940 (Russell & Russell 1956)
                 & T.Silverberg*Who Was Socrates?* 1939 (N.Y. Russell & Russell 1960)
                 Wood & Wood *Class Ideology & Ancient Political Theory* (Oxford U.P.
                 1978)

F.J.Woodbridge   *The Son of Apollo* Themes of Plato (Boston: Houghton 1929)
                 Aristotle's Vision of Nature ed. J.H.Randall Jr. (Columbia U.P.1965)

Xenophon   *Memorabilia* & *Oeconomicus, Symposium* & *Apology* ed. & tr. E.C.
                 Marchant, and O.J.Todd (Loeb Libr. 1953)
                 Hellenica Text & Notes ed. Marchant and Underhill (Arno repr. 1979)
                 Hellenica ed. & tr. C.Brownson (Loeb Libr. 1961)
                 Cyropaedia abridged ed. C.W.Gleason (American Book Co. 1897)
                 Scripta Minora Hiero, Agesilaus, Constitution of the Lacedaemonians ...
                 Constitution of the Athenians ed.& tr. Marchant & Bowersock (Loeb 1968)

E.Zeller   "Über den Ursprung der Schrift von den Gesetzen," Part I of Platonische
               Studien 1839 (Amsterdam: Rodopi 1969)
               Platonische Studien, 1839 (Rodopi 1969)
               Plato and the Older Academy Tr. Alleyne & Goodwin (Longmans 1876)
               Aristotle and the Earlier Peripatetics 2 Vol. Tr. Costello & Muirhead
               (London: Longmans 1897)

Abbreviations

AAL	= The Argument and the Action of the Laws L. Strauss, 1975
ACA	= Aristotle's Constitution of Athens ed. Sandys, 1893
AC	= The Athenian Constitution ed. & tr. H. Rackham, 1952
AD	= Athenian Democracy A.H.M. Jones, 1964
AT	= Aristotle Transformed ed. R. Sorabji, 1990
CA	= The Constitution of the Athenians ed.–tr. H. Frisch, 1942
CAAW	= Communication Arts in the Ancient WorldHershbell Havelock, 1986
CM	= The City and Man L. Strauss, 1962
CPT	= Character, Thought & Plot in Plato's Timaeus–Critias W. Welliver, 1977
CHLG	= Cambridge History of Later Greek . . . Philosophyed. A.C. Lloyd, 1967
CSEL	= Corpus Scriptorum Ecclesiasticorum Latinorumed. S. Brandt, 1906
CSFWPT	= The City–State Foundations of Western Political Thought V. Tejera, 1993
DCA	= Democracy in Classical Athens J.K.Davies, 1993 2 ed.
EAP	= Essays in Ancient Philosophy M. Frede, 1987
FAL	= "On the Form and Authenticity of the *Lysis*"V. Tejera, 1990
GO	= Greek Oligarchies L. Whibley, 1896
HAW	= A History of the Ancient World N.G.L. Hammond, 1986
HPAW	= History of the Process by which the Aristotelian Writings Arrived at their Present Form H. Shute, 1880
HPU	= History of Philosophy F. Ueberweg, 1871
IPQM	= In Platonis qui vulgo fertur Minoem eiusdemque Libros . . . de Legibus A. Boeckh, 1806
LFVJ	= Literarische Fehden im Vierten Jahrhundert Teichmüller; Breslau: 1884
LSAP	= Lore and Science in Ancient PythagoreanismW. Burkert, 1962
MGT	= Modes of Greek Thought V. Tejera, 1971
NES	= New Essays on Socrates ed. E. Kelly, 1984
NGT	= Nietzsche and Greek Thought V. Tejera, 1987

PDOBO	= Plato's Dialogues One By One V. Tejera, 1984
PEP	= Pythagoras & Early Pythagoreanism J. de Vogel, 1966
PHC	= Plato and His Contemporaries G.C. Field, 1930
PLS	= Platons Leben und Schriften F. Ast, 1839
POP	= "Platon oder Pythagoras? Zum Ursprung des Wortes 'Philosophie' W. W. Burkert, 1960
PS	= Platonische Studien E. Zeller, 1839
PP	= Political Philosophy L. Strauss, 1975
PTHP	= The Pythagorean Texts of the Hellenistic Period H. Thesleff, 1965
RA	= Aristotle J.H. Randall, 1960
SA	= Socrates and Aristophanes L. Strauss, 1980
SPN	= Studien zu den Platonischen Nomoi G. Müller, 1951
SPPP	= Studies in Platonic Political Philosophy L. Strauss, 1983
TAA	= The Thirty at Athens P. Krentz, 1982
TAPA	= Transactions of the American Philological Association
XSD	= Xenophon's Socratic Discourse L. Strauss, 1970
XS	= Xenophon's Socrates L. Strauss, 1972
WPP	= What is Political Philosophy? L. Strauss, 1959